The Voice of My Beloved

University of Pennsylvania Press

MIDDLE AGES SERIES

Edited by Edward Peters
Henry Charles Lea Professor
of Medieval History
University of Pennsylvania

A complete listing of the books in this series appears at the back of this volume

The Voice of My Beloved

The Song of Songs in Western Medieval Christianity

E. Ann Matter

upp

University of Pennsylvania Press
Philadelphia

Printed in the United States of America

Library of Congress Cataloging-in-Publication Data
Matter, E. Ann.
The voice of my beloved : the Song of songs in western medieval Christianity / E. Ann Matter.
p. cm. — (University of Pennsylvania Press Middle Ages series)
Includes bibliographical references.
ISBN 0-8122-8231-0
1. Bible. O.T. Song of Solomon—Criticism, interpretation, etc. —History—Middle Ages, 600-1500. I. Title. II. Series.
BS1485.2.M38 1990
223'.906'0902—dc20

89-28621
CIP

In Memory of Cora Elizabeth Lutz

Contents

Acknowledgments

Because I have been interested in commentaries on the Song of Songs since I first began to study the Middle Ages, the completion of this book gives me the opportunity to thank a long list of organizations, friends, teachers, and students who have helped me to understand and articulate the subject.

I am grateful to the American Philosophical Society and the National Endowment for the Humanities for grants which supported research and travel to European manuscript libraries. The Research Foundation of the University of Pennsylvania funded the preparation of the manuscript for publication.

The University of Pennsylvania Press was encouraging and supportive in moving the book toward publication. I am especially grateful to my colleague Edward Peters, editor of the Middle Ages Series, and to Alison Anderson, whose insightful editing produced a far more smooth and consistent manuscript than she had been given. Of course, any inaccuracies which remain are my sole responsibility.

Much of the research for this book was done in libraries in Europe. I am especially glad to have worked in the Salle des manuscrits of the Bibliothèque Nationale of Paris, and the Sala di consultazione of the Università Cattolica del Sacro Cuore in Milano. The staff of the Van Pelt Library of the University of Pennsylvania were unfailingly courteous and prompt with assistance in tracking down far-flung references.

Among the many friends who have had a hand in this project, I thank especially Grover Zinn, who showed me my first medieval commentary on the Song of Songs; and Marvin Pope, who shared his vast knowledge of and fascination with the Song of Songs while he was working on his own translation and commentary. Others who encouraged me to continue study of this difficult but entrancing subject include Seth Brody, Caroline Bynum, Elizabeth Clark, Marcia Colish, Arthur Green, Robert Kraft, Roland Murphy, Jaroslav Pelikan, Christa Rakich, Phyllis Trible, and students in a number of seminars on medieval exegesis at the University of Pennsylvania. Other colleagues, to whom I am endebted for specific ideas, are thanked in the footnotes of this book.

I owe a special debt to those who read all or part of the work in progress: Mary Rose D'Angelo, Anne McGuire, Paul Meyvaert, Judith Neaman, James O'Donnell, and especially Angela Locatelli and Carla Locatelli, who read the entire manuscript more than once, and without whom this book would not have taken the shape it did.

Finally, I would like to remember two great scholars who died as I was working on this book, but who have left indelible marks on it: Beryl Smalley, whose *The Study of the Bible in the Middle Ages* first introduced me to the complex workings of medieval biblical exegesis, gave kind advice and encouragement about this project on a number of occasions. Like all studies in this field, my book owes much to her imagination and erudition.

Cora Lutz, whom I met over a manuscript in the Beinecke Library in my first month of graduate school, was always an inspiration. We became friends in the years in which I was one of a number of young scholars who assisted her with articles ranging from her beloved tenth-century schoolmasters to the birds and folklore of Connecticut. All who knew her remember her wisdom, charm, and kindness. I will never forget the example she set of scholarship as a generous exchange rather than a competitive venture. With profound gratitude, I dedicate this book to her memory.

Abbreviations

ASOC	*Analecta sacri ordinis cisterciensis* (Rome, 1945–1964)
AC	*Analecta cisterciensa* (Rome, 1964 ff.)
AHDLMA	*Archives d'histoire doctrinale et littéraire du moyen âge* (Paris, 1926 ff.)
BLE	*Bulletin de littérature ecclésiastique* (Toulouse, 1899 ff.)
CC	*Corpus Christianorum* (Turnholt, 1952 ff.)
CCCM	*Corpus Christianorum, Continuatio Medievalis*
CCSL	*Corpus Christianorum, Series Latina*
CH	*Church History* (Chicago, 1932 ff.)
Clark	Elizabeth A. Clark, "The Uses of the Song of Songs: Origen and the Later Latin Fathers," in *Ascetic Piety and Women's Faith: Essays on Late Ancient Christianity* (Lewiston, N.Y.: Edwin Mellen Press, 1986) pp. 386–427
CPL	*Clavis Patrum Latinorum*, ed. E. Dekkers (Steenbrugge: in Abbatia Sancti Petri, 1961)
CSEL	*Corpus scriptorum Ecclesiasticorum Latinorum* (Vienna, 1866 ff.)
DA	*Deutsches Archiv für [Geschichte* (Weimar, 1937–43)] *Erforschung des Mittelalters* (Cologne and Graz, 1950 ff.)
GCS	*Die Griechischen Christlichen Schriftsteller der ersten drei Jahrhunderte* (Leipzig, 1901 ff.)

Herde	Rosemarie Herde, *Das Hohelied in der lateinischen Literature des Mittelalters bis zum 12. Jahrhundert* Studi Medievali 3 Ser., 8 (1967) = Münchener Beiträge zur Mediävistik und Renaissance-Forschung 3, 1968
HTR	*Harvard Theological Review* (Cambridge, Mass., 1908 ff.)
JAAR	*Journal of the American Academy of Religion* (1967 ff.)
JEH	*Journal of Ecclesiastical History* (Cambridge, 1950 ff.)
JTS	*Journal of Theological Studies* (London, 1899 ff.)
LCC	*Library of Christian Classics* (Philadelphia: Westminster Press)
de Lubac	Henri de Lubac, *Exégèse médiévale: Les quatre sens de l'Écriture* 4 vol (Paris, 1959–64)
MGH	*Monumenta Germaniae Historica inde ab a.c. 500 usque ad a.c. 1500*, ed. G. H. Pertz et al. (Berlin, Hanover, etc., 1826 ff.)
MGH, PLAC	*Poetae Latini Aevi Carolini*, 2 vol, ed. E. Dümmler (1881,84)
MGH *Scriptorum*	14 vol., ed. H. G. Pertz et al. (1826–1833)
MSt	*Medieval Studies* (Toronto, 1939 ff.)
OB	Bernard of Clairvaux, *Sancti Bernardi opera*, ed. J. Leclercq, C. H. Talbot, and H. M. Rochais (Rome: Editiones Cistercienses, 1957 ff.)
Ohly	Friedrich Ohly, *Hohelied-Studien: Grundzüge einer Geschichte der Hoheliedauslegung des Abendlandes bis um 1200* (Wiesbaden: Franz Steiner Verlag, 1958)
PL	*Patrologia Latina*, ed. J. P. Migne, 217 + 4 index vols. (Paris, 1841–61)

PLSupp	*Patrologia Latina, Supplementa*, ed. A. Hamman (Paris, 1958 ff.)
Pope	Marvin H. Pope, *Song of Songs: A New Translation and Commentary*. The Anchor Bible 7C (New York: Doubleday and Company, 1977)
RAug	*Recherches augustiniennes* (Paris, 1958 ff.)
RB	*Revue bénédictine* (Maredsous, 1884 ff.)
RHE	*Revue d'histoire ecclésiastique* (Louvain, 1900 ff.)
Riedlinger	Helmut Riedlinger, *Die Makellosigkeit der Kirche in den Lateinischen Hoheliedkommentaren des Mittelalters*, Beiträge zur Geschichte der Philosophie und Theologie des Mittelalters 38,3 (Münster: West. Aschendorff, 1958)
RSPT	*Revue des sciences philosophiques et théologiques* (Paris, 1907 ff.)
RTAM	*Recherches de théologie ancienne et médiévale* (Louvain, 1929 ff.)
Sabatier	*Bibliorum Sacrorum. Latinae versiones antiquae, seu vetus Italica, et caeterae quaecunque in codibus mss. & antiquorum libris reperii paruerent*, ed. P. Sabatier (Reims, 1743; Paris, 1751)
SC	*Sources chrétiennes*, ed. H. de Lubac and J. Danielou (Paris, 1941 ff.)
Smalley	Beryl Smalley, *The Study of the Bible in the Middle Ages*, second edition (Oxford: Oxford University Press, 1952/Notre Dame, Ind.: Notre Dame University Press, 1964)
SpF	*Spicilegium Friburgense. Texte zur Geschichte des kirchlichen Lebens*, ed. G. G. Meersseman et al. (Frieiburg, Switzerland, 1963 ff.)
ST	*Studi e testi* (Palermo, 1979 ff.)

StMon	*Studia Monastica* (Barcelona, 1959 ff.)
Stegmüller	Fr. Stegmüller, *Repertorium Biblicum medii aevi*, 11 vols (Madrid: Consejo Superior de Investigaciones Cientificas, 1950–80)
TT	*Temi e testi* (Rome, 1952 ff.)
TU	*Texte und Untersuchungen zur Geschichte der altchristlichen Literatur* (Leipzig/Berlin, 1882 ff.)
Vaccari	Albertus Vaccari, *Cantici Canticorum: Vetus Latina, translatio a S. Hieronymo ad graecum textum Hexaplarem emendata* (Rome: Edizioni di Storia e Letteratura, 1959)
ZiDA	*Zeitschrift für deutsches Altertum und deutsches Literatur* (Wiesbaden, 1841 ff.)
ZKG	*Zeitschrift für Kirchengeschichte* (Gotha/Stuttgart, 1878 ff.)

The Vulgate Text of the Song of Songs

INCIPIT LIBER
CANTICA CANTICORUM

1:1 Osculetur me osculo oris sui
  quia meliora sunt ubera tua vino
2 fraglantia unguentis optimis
  oleum effusum nomen tuum
ideo adulescentiæ dilexerunt te
3 trahe me post te curremus
introduxit me rex in cellaria sua
exultabimus et lætabimur in te
memores uberum tuorum super vinum recti diligunt te
4 nigra sum sed formosa filæ Hierusalem
sicut tabernacula Cedar
  sicut pelles Solomonis
5 nolite me considerare quod fusca sim
  quia decoloravit me sol
filii matris meæ pugnaverunt contra me
posuerunt me custodem in vineis
  vineam meam non custodivi
6 indica mihi quem diligit anima mea
ubi pascas ubi cubes in meridie
ne vagari incipiam per greges sodalium tuorum
7 si ignoras te o pulchra inter mulieres
egredere et abi post vestigia gregum
et pasce hedos tuos iuxta tabernacula pastorum
8 equitatui meo in curribus Pharaonis assimilavi te
  amica mea
9 pulchrae sunt genæ tuae sicut turturis
  collum tuum sicut monilie
10 murenulas aureas faciemus tibi vermiculatas argento
11 dum esset rex in accubitu suo nardus meus dedit odorem suum

THE BOOK BEGINS
THE SONG OF SONGS

1:1 Let him kiss me with the kiss of his mouth
for your breasts are better than wine
2 fragrant with the best ointments
your name oil poured out
therefore the young girls have loved you
3 draw me we will run after you
the king led me into his storerooms
we will rejoice and be glad in you
mindful of your breasts better than wine the upright love you
4 I am black but beautiful daughters of Jerusalem
like the tents of Cedar
like the skins of Solomon
5 do not look at me because I am dark
for the sun has discolored me
the sons of my mother fought against me
they have placed me as a guard in the vineyards
my vineyard I have not kept
6 show me you whom my soul loves
where you pasture where you lie at midday
lest I begin to wander after the flocks of your companions
7 if you do not know yourself o fairest of women
go out and follow the tracks of the flocks
and pasture your kids beside the tents of the shepherds
8 to my cavalry in the Pharoah's chariots I have likened you
my friend
9 your cheeks are fair like the turtle dove's
your neck like necklaces
10 we will make you chains of gold inlaid with silver
11 while the king was on his couch my nard gave out its fragrance

12 fasciculus murræ dilectus meus mihi
inter ubera commorabitur
13 botrus cypri dilectus meus mihi
in vineis Engaddi
14 ecce tu pulchra es amica mea
ecce tu pulchra oculi tui columbarum
15 ecce tu pulcher es dilecte mi et decorus
lectulus noster floridus
16 tigna domorum nostrum cedrina
laquearia nostra cypressina

2:1 ego flos campi
et lilium convallium
2 sicut lilium inter spinas
sic amica mea inter filias
3 sicut malum inter ligna silvarum
sic dilectus meus inter filios
sub umbra illius quam desideraveram sedi
et fructus eius dulcis gutturi meo
4 introduxit me in cellam vinariam
ordinavit in me charitatem
5 fulcite me floribus stipate me malis
quia amore langueo
6 leva eius sub capite meo
et dextera illius amplexabitur me
7 adiuro vos filiæ Hierusalem
per capreas cervosque camporum
ne suscietis neque evigilare faciatis dilectam quoadusque
ipsa velit
8 vox dilecti mei
ecce iste venit saliens in montibus
transiliens colles
9 similis est dilectus meus capræ hinuloque cervorum
en ipse stat post parietem nostram
despiciens per fenestras
prospiciens per cancellos
10 et dilectus meus loquitur mihi
surge propera amica mea formosa mea et veni
11 iam enim hiems transiit
imber abiit et recessit
12 flores apparuerunt in terra
tempus putationis advenit

12 a little bundle of myrrh is my beloved to me
 between the breasts he shall linger
13 a cluster of cypress is my love to me
 in the vineyards of Engaddi
14 behold you are fair my friend
 behold you are fair your eyes of doves
15 behold you are fair my beloved and beautiful
our bed is flowery
16 the beams of our house are of cedar
 our rafters are of cypress

2:1 I am the flower of the field
 and the lily of the valley
2 like a lily among thorns
 so my friend among daughters
3 like the apple tree among trees of the woods
 so my beloved among sons
under the shadow of the one I had loved I sat
and his fruit sweet to my throat
4 he brought me into the wine cellar
 he has disposed charity in me
5 support me with flowers, surround me with apples
 for I languish with love
6 his left arm under my head and
 his right arm will embrace me
7 I adjure you, daughters of Jerusalem
 by the goats and the stags of the field
neither arouse nor cause to awaken my beloved until
 she wishes
8 the voice of my beloved
behold, he comes leaping on the mountains
 springing across the hills
9 my beloved is like a goat and a young of stags
behold, he stands behind our wall
looking in through the windows
 watching through the lattices
10 and my beloved speaks to me
arise swiftly my friend my beautiful, and come
11 for now the winter has passed
 the rain has gone and departed
12 flowers appear on the earth
 the time of pruning has come

vox turturis audita est in terra nostra
13 ficus protulit grossos suos
vinae florent dederunt odorem
surge amica mea speciosa mea et veni
14 columba mea in foraminibus petrae
in caverna maceriæ
ostende mihi faciem tuam
sonet vox tua in auribus meis
vox enim tua dulcis
et facies tua decora
15 capite nobis vulpes vulpes parvulas
quæ demoliuntur vineas
nam vinea nostra floruit
16 dilectus meus mihi et ego illi
qui pascitur inter lilia
17 donec aspiret dies et inclinentur umbræ
revertere similis esto dilecte mi caprae aut hinulo cervorum
super montes Bether

3:1 in lectulo meo per noctes
quæsivi quem diligit anima mea
quæsivi illum et non inveni
2 surgam et circuibo civitatem
per vicos et plateas
quæram quem diligit anima mea
quæsivi illum et non inveni
3 invenerunt me vigiles qui custodiunt civitatem
num quem dilexit anima mea vidistis
4 paululum cum pertransissem eos
inveni quem diligit anima mea
tenui eum nec dimittam
donec introducam illum in domum matris meae
et in cubiculum genetricis meae
5 adjuro vos filiæ Hierusalem
per capreas cervosque camporum
ne suscitetis neque evigilare faciatis dilectam donec ipsa velit
6 quae est ista quae ascendit per desertum sicut
virgula fumi
ex aromatibus murræ et turris
et universi pulveris pigmentarii
7 en lectulum Salomonis
sexaginta fortes ambiunt ex fortissimis Israhel

the voice of the turtle dove is heard in our land
13 the fig tree has put out its thick shoots
the flowering vines have given off a smell
arise my friend my lovely one and come
14 my dove in the clefts of the rock
in the hollow of the wall
show me your face
let your voice sound in my ears
for your voice is sweet
and your face is beautiful
15 catch for us the foxes, the little foxes
who destroy the vineyards
for our vineyard is flowering
16 my beloved is mine and I am his
who pastures among the lilies
17 until the day breathes and the shadows lean
return my beloved, be like the goat or a young of stags
on the mountains of Bether

3:1 on my bed through the nights
I sought him whom my soul loves
I sought him and I did not find
2 I will arise and go around the city
through the streets and the courtyards
I will seek him whom my soul loves
I sought him and I did not find
3 the watchmen found me who guard the city
have you seen him whom my soul has loved?
4 when I had hardly passed by them
I found him whom my soul loves
I held him nor will I let go
until I lead him into the house of my mother
and into the chamber of her who bore me
5 I adjure you, daughters of Jerusalem
by the goats and the stags of the field
neither arouse nor cause to awaken the beloved until she wishes
6 who is this who comes up through the desert like a column
of smoke
from the spices of myrrh and frankincense
and all the powders of the perfumer?
7 behold, the bed of Solomon
sixty strong men surrounding it of the strongest of Israel

8 omnes tenentes gladios et ad bella doctissimi
uniuscuiusque ensis super femur suum propter
timores nocturnos
9 ferculum fecit sibi rex Salomon
de lignis Libani
10 columnas eius fecit argenteas
reclinatorium aureum
ascensum purpuream
media caritate constravit
propter filias Hierusalem
11 egredimini et videte filiae Sion
regem Salomonem in diademate
quo coronavit eum mater sua
in die disponsionis illius
et in die lætitiæ cordis eius

4:1 quam pulchra es amica mea
quam pulchra es
oculi tui columbarum
absque eo quod intrinsecus est
capilli tui sicut greges caprarum
quae ascenderunt de monte Galaad
2 dentes tui sicut greges tonsarum
quae ascenderunt de lavacro
omnes gemellis fetibus
et sterilis non est inter eas
3 sicut vitta coccinea labia tua
et eloquium tuum dulce
sicut fragmen mali punici ita genae tuae
absque eo quod intrinsecus latet
4 sicut turris David collum tuum
quæ aedificata est cum propugnaculis
mille clypei pendant ex ea
omnis armatura fortium
5 duo ubera tua sicut duo hinuli
gemelli qui pascuntur in liliis
6 donec aspiret dies et inclinentur umbrae
vadam ad montem murrae et ad
collem turris
7 tota pulchra es amica mea
et macula non est in te
8 veni de Libano sponsa veni de Libano

8 all holding swords and most learned in warfare
each one's sword on his thigh because of
nocturnal fears
9 King Solomon made a litter for himself
from the wood of Lebanon
10 its columns he made of silver
the pillow of gold
the ascent of purple
the middle he has piled up with charity
for the daughters of Jerusalem
11 go forth and see, daughters of Sion
King Solomon in the diadem
with which his mother crowned him
on the day of his betrothal
and on the day of his heart's rejoicing

4:1 how fair you are, my friend
how fair you are
your eyes of doves
besides that which lies within
your hair like a flock of goats
which have come up from Mount Galaad
2 your teeth like a flock of shearlings
that have come up from a washing
all pregnant with twins
and no barren one among them
3 your lips like a band of scarlet
and your speech is sweet
like grains of pomegranates so your cheeks
besides that which lies within
4 like a tower of David your neck
which is built with bulwarks
a thousand shields hang from it
all the armor of strong men
5 your two breasts like two kids
twins who pasture among the lilies
6 until the day breathes and the shadows lean
I will go to the mountain of myrrh and to the hill
of frankincense
7 you are all fair, my friend
and there is no spot in you
8 come from Lebanon, bride come from Lebanon

veni coronaberis
de capite Amana
de vertice Sanir et Hermon
de cubilibus leonum
de montibus pardorum
9 vulnerasti cor meum soror mea
sponsa vulnerasti cor meum
in uno oculorum tuorum
et in uno crine colli tui
10 quam pulchræ sunt mammae tuae
soror mea sponsa
pulchiora ubera tua vino
et odor unguentorum tuorum super omnia aromata
11 favus distillans labia tua sponsa
mel et lac sub lingua tua
et odor vestimentorum tuorum sicut
odor turis
12 hortus conclusus soror mea sponsa
hortus conclusus fons signatus
13 emissiones tuae paradisus malorum punicorum
cum pomorum fructibus
cypri cum nardo
14 nardus et crocus
fistula et cinnamomum
cum universus lignis Libano
15 fons hortorum
puteus aqua viventium
quæ fluunt impetu de Libano
16 surge aquilo et veni auster
perfla hortum meum et fluant aromata illius

5:1 veniat dilectus meus in hortum suum
et comedat fructum pomorum suorum
veni in hortum meum soror mea sponsa
messui murram meam cum aromatibus meis
comedi favum cum melle meo
bibi vinum meum cum lacte meo
comedite amici bibite
et inebriamini carissimi
2 ego dormio et cor meum vigilat
vox dilecti mei pulsantis
aperi mihi sor mea amica mea

come, you will be crowned
from the peak of Amana
from the top of Sanir and Hermon
from the lions' dens
from the leopards' mountains
9 you have wounded my heart, my sister
bride, you have wounded my heart
by one of your eyes
and in one hair of your neck
10 how fair are your breasts
sister my bride
your breasts fairer than wine
and the fragrance of your unguents above all spices
11 your lips drip honeycomb, bride
honey and milk under your tongue
and the fragrance of your garments like the fragrance
of frankincense
12 a garden enclosed, sister my bride
a garden enclosed, a fountain sealed
13 your emissions a paradise of pomegranates
with the fruits of the fruit trees
cyprus with nard
14 nard and saffron
cane and cinnamon
with all the trees of Lebanon
15 the fountain of the gardens
a well of living waters
which flow rushing from Lebanon
16 arise, north wind and come, south wind
blow through my garden that its spices may flow

5:1 let my beloved come into his garden
and eat the fruit of his apples
come into my garden, my sister bride
I gathered my myrrh with my spices
I ate honeycomb with my honey
I drank my wine with my milk
eat friends, drink
and be drunk, dearest ones
2 I sleep and my soul keeps watch
the voice of my beloved knocking
open to me, my sister my friend

columba mea immaculata mea
quia caput meum plenum est rore
et cinicinni mei guttis noctium
3 expolavi me tunica mea quomodo induar illa
lavi pedes meos quomodo iniquinabo illos
4 dilectus meus misit manum suam per foramen
et venter meus intremuit ad tactum eius
5 surrexi ut aprerirem dilecto meo
manus meae stillaverunt murra
digiti mei pleni murra probatissima
6 pessulum ostii aperui dilecto meo
at ille declinaverat atque transierat
anima mea liquifacta est ut locutus est
quaesivi et non inveni illum
vocavi et non respondit mihi
7 invenerunt me custodes qui circumeunt civitatem
percusserunt me vulneraverunt me
tulerunt pallium meum mihi custodes murorum
8 adiuro vos filiæ Hierualem
si inveneritis dilectum meum
ut nuntietis ei quia amore langueo
9 qualis est dilectus tuus ex dilecto o pulcherrima mulierum
qualis est dilectus tuus ex dilecto quia sic adiurasti nos
10 dilectus meus candidus et rubicundus
electus ex milibus
11 caput eius aurum optimum
comæ eius sicut elatae palmarum
nigræ quasi corvus
12 oculi eius sicut columbae super rivulos aquarum
quæ lacte sunt lotae et resident iuxta fluenta
plenissima
13 genae illius sicut areolae aromatum consitae a pigmentariis
labia eius lilia distillantia murram primam
14 manus illius tornatiles aureae plenæ hyacinthis
venter eius eburneus distinctus sapphyris
15 crura illius columnæ marmorae quae fundatae sunt super bases
aureas
species eius ut Libani electus et cedri
16 guttur eius suavissimum
et totus desiderabilis
talis est dilectus meus
et iste est amicus meus filiae Hierusalem

my dove, my spotless one
for my head is full of dew
and my hair of the drops of the nights
3 I have taken off my garment how should I put it on again?
I have washed my feet how should I soil them?
4 my beloved put forth his hand through the hole
and my belly trembled at his touch
5 I rose to open to my beloved
my hands dripped myrrh
my fingers full of the finest myrrh
6 I opened the bolt of the door to my love
but he had turned away and gone over
my soul melted as he spoke
I sought him and I did not find him
I called and he did not answer me
7 the watchmen found me who go around the city
they beat me, they wounded me
they took my cloak from me the guardians of the walls
8 I adjure you, daughters of Jerusalem
if you find my beloved
tell him that I languish of love
9 of what sort is your beloved of beloved o fairest of women
of what sort is your beloved of beloved that you so adjure us?
10 my beloved is white and ruddy
chosen from thousands
11 his head finest gold
his hair exalted like of palms
black as the raven
12 his eyes like doves on streams of waters
which are washed with milk and sit down beside the
brimming streams
13 his cheeks like gardens of spices planted by the perfumers
his lips lilies dripping finest myrrh
14 his hands crafted of gold full of hyacinths
his belly ivory garnished with sapphires
15 his legs columns of marble which are set upon
golden bases
his appearance as Lebanon chosen as the cedar
16 his throat very soft
and all desirable
such is my beloved
and he is my friend, daughters of Jerusalem

17 quo abiit dilectus tuus o pulcherrima mulierum
quo declinavit dilectus tuus et quaeremus
eum tecum

6:1 dilectus meus descendit in hortum suum
ad areolam aromatis
ut pascitur in hortis
et lilia colligat
2 ego dilecto meo et dilectus meus mihi
qui pascitur inter lilias
3 pulchra es amica mea suavis
et decora sicut Hierusalem
terribilis ut castrorum acies ordinat
4 averte oculos tuos a me
quia ipsi me avolare fecerunt
5 dentes tui sicut grex ovium quae ascenderunt
de lavacro
omnes gemellis fetibus et sterilis non est in eis
6 sicut cortex mali punici genae tuae
absque occultis tuis
7 sexaginta sunt reginae et octoginta concubinae
et adulescentularum non est numerus
8 una est columba mea perfecta mea
una est matris suae electa genetrici suae
viderunt illam filiae et beatissimam praedicaverunt
reginae et concubinae et laudaverunt eam
9 quae est ista quae progreditur quasi aurora consurgens
pulchra ut luna electa ut sol
terribilis ut acies ordinata
10 descendi ad hortum nucum ut viderem poma convallis
ut inspecerem si floruisset vinea
et germinassent mala punica
11 nescivi anima mea conturbavit me
propter quadrigas Aminadab
12 revertere revertere Sulamitis
revertere revertere ut intueamur te

7:1 quid videbis in Sulamiten
nisi choros castrorum
quam pulchri sunt gressus tui in calciamentis filia principis
iunctura feminum tuorum sicut monilia
quae fabricata sunt manu artificis

17 where is your beloved gone o fairest of women?
where has your beloved turned aside and we will seek him with you

6:1 my beloved went down into his garden
to the garden of spices
to graze in the gardens
and gather lilies
2 I am my beloved's and my beloved is mine
who grazes among the lilies
3 you are fair my friend, sweet
and beautiful like Jerusalem
terrible as a battle line drawn up from camps
4 turn away your eyes from me
for they make me flee
5 your teeth like a flock of sheep that have come up from a washing
all pregnant with twins and no barren one among them
6 like the skin of a pomegranate your cheeks
besides your hidden things
7 sixty are the queens and eighty the concubines
and of the young girls there is no number
8 one is my dove, my perfect one
she is one of her mother the elect of her who bore her
the daughters saw her and they proclaimed her most blessed
the queens and concubines praised her
9 who is this who comes forth like the rising dawn
beautiful as the moon, chosen as the sun
terrible as the battle line drawn up?:
10 I went down to the nut grove to see the apples of the valley
to see whether the vineyards had flowered
and the pomegranates had budded
11 I did not know my soul disturbed me
because of the four-wheeled cart of Aminadab
12 return return, Sulamite
return return, that we may behold you

7:1 what will you see in the Sulamite
but companies from the camps?
how fair are your steps in sandals, daughter of princes
the joints of your thighs like jewels
which are made by the hand of a craftsman

2 umbilicus tuus crater tornatilis numquam indigens poculis
venter tuus sicut acervus tritici vallatus liliis
3 duo ubera tua sicut duo hinuli gemelli caprae
4 collum tuum sicut turris eburnea
oculi tui sicut piscinae in Esebron
quae sunt in porta filiae multitudinis
nasus tuus sicut turris Libani quae respicit contra Damascum
5 caput tuum ut Carmelus
et comæ capitis tui sicut purpura regis
vincta canalibus
6 quam pulchra es et quam decora carissima in deliciis
7 statura tua adsimilata est palmae
et ubera tua botris
8 dixi ascendam in palmam
aprehendam fructus eius
et erunt ubera tua sicut botri vinae
et odor oris tui sicut malorum
9 guttur tuum sicut vinum optimum
dignum dilectum meum ad potandum
labiisque et dentibus illius ruminandum
10 ego dilecto meo et ad me conversio eius
11 veni dilecte mi egrediamur in agrum
commoremur in villis
12 mane surgamus ad vineas
videamus si floruit vinae
si flores fructus parturiunt
si floruerunt mala punica
ibi dabo tibi ubera mea
13 mandragorae dederunt odorem in portis nostris
omnia poma nova et vetera dilecte mi servavi tibi

8:1 quis mihi det te fratrem meum
sugentem ubera matris meae
ut inveniam te foris et deosculetur
et iam me nemo despiciat
2 aprehendam te et ducam
in domum matris meae
ibi me docebis
et dabo tibi poculum ex vino condito
et mustum malorum granatorum meorum

2 your navel is a finely wrought bowl never lacking drink
your belly like a heap of wheat fortified with lilies
3 your two breasts like two kids twins of a goat
4 your neck like a tower of ivory
your eyes like pools in Hesbon
which are in the gate of the daughter of multitudes
your nose like a tower of Lebanon which looks toward
Damascus
5 your head as Carmel
and the hair of your head like purple of a king
bound in canals
6 how fair you are and how beautiful, dearest in delights
7 your stature is likened to a palm
and your breasts to clusters of grapes
8 I said I will go up into the palm
I will gather its fruit
and your breasts will be like clusters of grapes of the vine
and the fragrance of your mouth like apples
9 your throat like the best wine
worthy for my beloved to drink
and for his lips and teeth to chew
10 I am my beloved's and to me his turning
11 come my beloved, let us go out into the field
let us linger in the villages
12 early let us go up to the vineyards
let us see if the vineyards flower
if the flowers bear fruit
if the pomegranates flower
there I will give you my breasts
13 the mandrakes give out fragrance in our gates
all fruits new and old, my beloved, I have saved for you

8:1 who will give you to me for my brother
sucking the breasts of my mother
that I may find you outside and kiss you
and yet no one will despise me?
2 I will seize you and lead you
into the house of my mother
there you will teach me
and I will give you a cup of spiced wine
and the new wine of my pomegranates

3 leva eius sub capite meo
et dextera eius amplexabitur me
4 adiuro vos filiae Hierusalem
ne suscitetis et evigilare faciatis dilectam donec ipsa vellet
5 quae est ista quae ascendit de deserto
deliciis affluens et nixa super dilectum suum
sub arbore malo suscitavi te
ibi corrupta est mater tua
ibi violata est genetrix tua
6 pone me ut signaculum super cor tuum
ut signaculum super brachium tuum
quia fortis est ut mors dilectio
dura sicut inferus æmulatio
lampades eius lampades ignis
atque flammarum
7 aquae multae non poterunt extinguere caritatem
nec flumina obruent illam
si dederit homo omnem substantiam domus suae pro dilectione
quasi nihil despicient eum
8 soror nostra parva et ubera non habet
quid faciemus sorori nostrae in die quando alloquenda est
9 si murus est aedificamus super eum propugnacula argentea
si ostium est conpingamus illud tabulis cedrinis
10 ego murus et ubera mea sicut turris
ex quo facta sunt coram eo quasi pacem reperiens
11 vinea fuit Pacifico
in ea quae habet populos
tradidit eam custodibus
vir adfert pro fructu eius mille argenteos
12 vinea mea coram me est
mille tui Pacifice
et ducenti his qui custodiunt fructus eius
13 quae habitas in hortis
amici ascultant
fac me audire vocem tuam
14 fuge dilecte mi et assimilare caprae
hinuloque cervorum
super montes aromatum

3 his left arm under my head
   and his right arm will embrace me
4 I adjure you, daughters of Jerusalem
neither arouse nor cause to awaken the beloved until she wishes
5 who is this who comes up from the desert
   flowing with delights and leaning on her beloved?
under the apple tree I aroused you
there your mother was corrupted
   there she who bore you was violated
6 place me as a seal upon your heart
   as a seal upon your arm
because love is as strong as death
   jealousy hard like hell
its lamps, lamps of fire
   and of flames
7 many waters cannot extinguish charity
   nor rivers drown it
if a man were to give all the fortune of his house for love
   they would disdain him as nothing
8 our sister is small and she has no breasts
what shall we do with our sister on the day she is spoken for?
9 if she is a wall, let us build on it bulwarks of silver
   if she is a door, let us seal it with boards of cedar
10 I am a wall and my breasts like towers
since I am made in his presence as if finding peace
11 The vineyard of the Peaceful One
   in it there are people
   he gave it over to the watchmen
a man brings for its fruit a thousand silver pieces
12 my vineyard is before me
a thousand to you, Peaceful One
   and two hundred to those who guard its fruit
13 you who live in the gardens
   the friends listen
   make me hear your voice
14 flee, my beloved, and be like a goat
   and a young of stags
on the mountains of spices

Commentary on the Text

The Latin is adapted from the critical Vulgate edition of R. Weber,[1] with some changes of spelling to reflect medieval forms more closely, and some changes of phrasing to emphasize parallelisms. As anyone who has used this Stuttgart text is aware, one of its great strengths is the critical apparatus, which shows so clearly that there never was just one Vulgate version of the Bible. The Stuttgart edition is a composite, not a medieval copy of the Song of Songs; the many variant readings it preserves testify to a number of textual traditions, some regional, which may have presented commentators with some different words or phrasings. In my discussions of individual commentaries, I have quoted the Song of Songs text presented by each author, making no effort to bring them into agreement with this version.

The parallel English translation is my own. It attempts to be be somewhat literal in order to capture the vocabulary and syntax of the Latin. In deference to medieval orthographic customs, punctuation is minimal and limited to those spots at which it is necessary for sense.

It is important to realize, however, that not all medieval Latin Song of Songs texts were Vulgate versions. Recognition and identification of other Bible versions is a necessary challenge, for several of the commentaries I have examined are based on such texts. In the Middle Ages, non-Vulgate biblical quotations come mostly from the liturgy, a very conservative form of textual transmission. Some authors, while using an essentially Vulgate version of the Song of Songs, will cite an occasional verse from "another version" to make or strengthen a point. Unfortunately, these pre- (or extra-) Vulgate versions of the Song of Songs are as elusive as they are common.

There is as yet no critical edition of the Song of Songs in the Beuron *Vetus Latina* series,[2] but a few non-Vulgate versions of the Song of Songs can be traced through a number of important studies, showing a variety of critical methodologies. The oldest, the "Vetus Italica" of Sabatier, is a collection of non-Vulgate readings taken from one manuscript and numerous citations in early Christian authors and liturgies.[3] In 1926, de Bruyne identified two non-Vulgate versions, which he called the pre-Jerominian version (=VET) and Jerome's revision of Origen's *Hexapla* (=REV).[4] Vaccari's edition of 1959 makes use of all of these versions, but is based on a sixth-century Vatican manuscript, a copy of Jerome's hexaplaric revision.[5] More recently, the complex question of this welter of ancient versions has been studied by Sagot, who demonstrates that Ambrose of Milan used a variety of Song of Songs texts, depending on his sources, the date of composition of each treatise, and the use to which he wished to put a given verse.[6] This formula holds generally for the medieval authors with which this book is concerned, but it is compounded by the reverence for Jerome which gave both the Vulgate and his hexaplaric revision special authority. Although nowhere in this book have I attempted a detailed analysis of these other Latin Song of Songs versions, I have tried try to identify the source and to suggest the function of each non-Vulgate passage cited.

Notes

1. *Biblia sacra iuxta Vulgatam versionem*, ed. R. Weber (Stuttgart: Deutsche Bibelgesellschaft 1969, 1983) vol. 2, pp. 997–1002.

2. The *Vetus Latina* Institute is based at the Archabbey of Beuron, Germany. Its mission is a complete critical edition of the old Latin versions of each book of the Bible. In print to date are Genesis, a number of the Pauline epistles, and Wisdom.

3. Sabatier, vol. 2, pp. 374–388. Part of this text was redone by André Wilmart, "L' Ancienne version latine du Cantique I–III.4," RB 28 (1911) 11–36. Sabatier's preface describes a double-columned manuscript of the Song of Songs headed "Vulgatus" and "LXX." Wilmart has identified this as the twelfth-century manuscript Saint-Thierry 24, today Reims, B. M. 142 (E.225); a contemporary copy is Paris, B. N. lat. 2647, ff. 31v–37.

4. D. de Bruyne, "Les Anciennes versions latines du Cantique des Cantiques," RB 38 (1926) 97–122. VET is based on two manuscripts: Salzburg, Sankt Peter IX.16 (c. 8–9), and Graz, University fol. 167 (c. 12). REV is found in Sankt Gallen 11 (c. 8), and in works by Jerome, Cassian, Eucherius of Lyons, Bede, and Augustine.

5. The base text is Vatican lat. 5704, a manuscript from the library of Cassiodorus. See also J. W. Halporn, "Cassiodorus' Citations from the Canticum Canticorum and the Composition of the *Expositio Psalmorum*," RB 95 (1985) 169–184.

6. Solange Sagot, "Le 'Cantique des Cantiques' dans le 'De Isaac' d'Ambroise de Milan. Étude textuelle et recherche sur les anciennes versions latines," RAug 16 (1981) 3–57.

The Voice of My Beloved

Chapter One

Introduction to the Genre

The complexities of the commentary on and use of the Song of Songs in medieval Europe may seem on first consideration to be of limited interest, addressing only specialists in Christian literature. Actually, the subject is relevant to many aspects of the study of medieval religious culture, for this biblical book asserted a far-reaching impact. Conventional medieval readings of the Song of Songs, for example, influenced the symbolic understanding of the Church and the theological concepts of the relationship between the life of the body and of the soul, and thus between human and divine love. These conventional readings flourished as part of the monastic tradition of biblical commentary, which, I will argue, developed into a genre of medieval Latin literature. The extraordinary literary self-awareness of this tradition is evident in the nearly one hundred extant commentaries and homilies on the Song of Songs written between the sixth and the fifteenth centuries, texts which show great complexity and virtuosity of allegorical interpretation.[1]

Before turning to the definition of this genre, I would like to make a few comments about the difficulties a modern reader may find in approaching medieval exegesis. The exegetical tradition in general, although essential to medieval culture, is only beginning to be studied by modern scholars. An enormous amount of medieval Christian writing, perhaps the greatest single part, was commentary on the Bible; yet these texts have attracted only a small portion of the scholarly attention of medievalists. Not until the landmark work of Beryl Smalley in the middle of this century was medieval exegesis recognized as a legitimate field of study. Writing after Smalley's death, R. W. Southern made specific reference to the debt contemporary medievalists owe to her perception of medieval, rather than modern, literary forms:

> In 1927, when Beryl Smalley began to study the Bible in the Middle Ages, I think it would be true to say that the Bible had almost no place in the minds

> of medieval historians. . . . It was generally understood of course that the Bible became important as a moving force in politics in the sixteenth and seventeenth centuries; but it could be left out of the account, so it seemed, of the preceding thousand years. . . . Beryl Smalley did more than anyone to bring about [a] change by making all medievalists aware of the Bible in their midst.[2]

The reasons for this long scholarly neglect are many. As Smalley herself has noted, the intricate source analysis necessary at the first level of study is "complicated and ungrateful work."[3] Because of this difficulty, relatively few Latin biblical commentaries have appeared in critical editions, and even fewer in modern translations. This paucity has contributed to the problem, for the hazards of working from manuscripts or the erratic *Patrologia Latina* editions are well known.

Another difficulty is also at once a result and a condition of the situation: the perception, in the eyes of modern biblical scholarship, that medieval exegesis is "wrong." Medieval Bible scholars worked from poor texts, with little or no knowledge of Hebrew and Greek, and, what is especially problematic for many, they simply *assumed* allegory as the best interpretative tool, and the best way to expose the true nature of the text. This perspective on biblical interpretation needs some elaboration for modern readers, but very few Christian exegetes of the Song of Songs before the modern age seem to have questioned the premise of allegorical interpretation of the text. The great Antiochene scholar Theodore of Mopsuestia probably thought the Song of Songs a secular love poem unworthy of the canon, but he did so only in passing, not in a complete treatise; in any case, his judgment carried little weight for subsequent Latin exegetes.[4] There is no "non-allegorical" Latin tradition of Song of Songs commentary. In the early Church, only the Pelagian theologian Julian of Eclanum is known to have written a non-allegorical interpretation; this is preserved only in the fragments which Bede refuted. At the other end of the Middle Ages, even Nicholas of Lyra, champion of the historical sense of the Bible, argued that the Song of Songs has no literal sense.[5] The Song of Songs commentaries tell a story of the triumph of the allegorical. The ambiguities of the Latin text of the Song of Songs (especially when received as a canonical book of the Bible) can be said to have inspired a traditional of medieval commentary of great allegorical complexity.

For various reasons, however, allegorical interpretation of the Song of Songs did not flourish in the same way apart from the cloister tradition. One of the theological imperatives of the Reformation was the firm establishment of a tradition of literal biblical study which had grown out of the late medieval schools and contrasted sharply to prior monastic practice. Reformation scholars insisted that the Bible speaks plainly, on the literal level. Further, they insisted that it should speak in the vernacular. Thus, the boom in biblical studies of the sixteenth century brought with it disdain for what was increasingly seen as the artifice of medieval allegory. Later in the modern period, the growth of the form-critical analysis of Scripture, seeking to reconstruct the original form and function of each biblical book, shifted the emphasis even farther away from medieval exegetical norms. Twentieth-century biblical scholars are mostly concerned either with the original form of a book, or with its theological potential. In the case of the Song of Songs, the usual result is interpretation of the text as a celebration of human love.[6] Some aspects of the concerns of modern biblical study were not totally foreign to medieval scholarship (for Origen, Jerome, Theodulf, and others had done their best to establish an authoritative biblical text), but these concerns were certainly not at the heart of the medieval interpretive process, which accepted the Latin text and allegorical interpretation as normative. Allegorical commentaries on the Song of Songs can be found after the Middle Ages in some specialized Christian contexts (among the New England Puritans, for example), usually for specific rhetorical purposes.[7] In general, however, the allegorical tradition passed into the modern period mostly as a series of tropes used as rhetorical or symbolic figures, an evolution which will be discussed in the final chapter of this book. Thus, the long tradition of allegorical commentary on the Song of Songs lost its internal coherence along with its place in the company of scholars.

Lack of originality is another issue modern scholars have raised about medieval biblical interpretation; this accusation is a further example of the application of modern critical standards to the medieval literary process. It is certainly true that most medieval commentaries work within a well-defined tradition, each treatise incorporating specific parts of earlier ones. The result is usually a composite, one too often characterized by modern scholars as "pastiche" or "mere catena." As Judson Allen has described this gap between medieval and modern understandings: "Some twentieth-century poetic theorists have spoken of the heresy of paraphrase—medieval commentary exists as an assertion of the very orthodoxy of paraphrase."[8] The "heresy of paraphrase" attitude tends to misunderstand, and simply to miss, the way creativity functioned in the medieval literary tradition. Originality in medieval biblical commentary should not be judged by what "new" interpretations remain when all of the sources have been bracketed; indeed, the resulting texts would sometimes be limited to conjunctions and prepositions! Rather, originality is here the *process* of borrowing, re-working, using old material in new ways to show the imagination and talents of a given author. Medieval authors cited others as a subtle, but understood, form of respect. They did not distinguish between borrowing and the creation of new ideas. True creativity was often seen in the *way* disparate sources were conceived to fit together.

It is a modern misunderstanding of medieval literary practice in general to dismiss these efforts as plagiarism or ignorance, and medieval exegesis as too complicated, unoriginal, or just "wrong." But this modern judgment, linked to the condemnation of allegorical interpretation, undermined the authority of the medieval tradition. Gradually, the great tomes of medieval Bible commentary, no longer appreciated, understood, or even read, began to gather dust.

Medieval Latin commentary on the Song of Songs is especially victim to this misunderstanding and neglect since it was always allegorical (in fact, it included some of the most elaborate and fanciful examples of medieval allegory). The tradition is, furthermore, heavily dependent on a few important commentaries which set lines of interpretation basically incompatible with the approach of modern biblical scholars to the Song of Songs. In fact, the Song of Songs is a book of the Bible that does not particularly appeal to modern theological exegesis, since it offers no divine law, moral precepts, or sacred history. This last observation makes it all the more intriguing that the Song of Songs was the most frequently interpreted book of medieval Christianity.

This profusion of medieval commentaries on the Song of Songs attracted the attention of German medievalists in the 1950s, and resulted in the publication of important studies by Friedrich Ohly and Helmut Riedlinger. Ohly's book summarizes the major Greek and Latin Song of Songs commentaries from 200 to 1200, and ends with consideration of twelfth-century vernacular versions from northern France. Riedlinger concentrates on the image of the spotless Church in Song of Songs interpretation; his study is more detailed, including many manuscript sources, and also covers the thirteenth to fifteenth centuries. Both books proceed chronologically, and organize authors by their religious orders, for example, as Benedictines, Dominicans, Augustinian Canons. Both Ohly and Riedlinger cover a vast amount of material, some from unpublished sources. No study of the Song of Songs in medieval Europe, including mine, could be undertaken without their help; yet I hope to accomplish something very different.

This book sketches the broad outline of Song of Songs interpretation in the Latin Middle Ages by approaching the Latin commentaries generated by this biblical book as a genre of medieval literature. I contend that medieval biblical commentary in general should be understood as a broad genre because the treatises display a clear consciousness of belonging to a type, a method, a mode of literature. To medieval scholars, the Bible represented an untouchable category of literary expression, set apart from all other texts: it was the map of divine reality and therefore the means through which that reality was revealed to human consciousness. That this revelation was more cryptic than straightforward would not be surprising to western medieval thinkers, since, following Augustine, they understood divine reality to be perceived only through the imperfections and distortions of human nature.[9] That *veritas* is found hidden *sub umbra et figura* is an essential concept of medieval hermeneutics in general; it is prominent, for example, in medieval eucharistic theology, which draws heavily on the exegetical tradition.[10] In this tradition the Word of God, as an artifact of ever-present revelation preserved in time, needs clarification and elaboration. This is the fundamental task of medieval exegesis, a form of literature developed to interpret the Bible (book by book, verse by verse, sometimes word by word) by making explicit the visions of eternal truth shimmering behind the veil of the words of the text.

In the medieval perception, therefore, the Bible itself could be seen as an example of what M. M. Bakhtin calls a "primary" or "simple" genre formed "in unmediated speech communication," while biblical exegesis, especially in the form of discrete commentaries on individual books, is a "secondary" or "complex" genre, absorbing, elaborating, and transforming the primary genre.[11] Within this broad definition, I would argue that Song of Songs commentaries make up a special category, constituting a sub-genre of their own, an example of what Maria Corti has described as the "internal transformation" of one genre into another; the second participates and shares with the first but eventually develops characteristics of its own.[12]

The broad genre of medieval biblical commentary spawned a number of other sub-genres, traditions of interpretation of particular biblical books or pericopes which had extensive lives of their own. One such sub-genre is illustrated by the commentaries on the Hexameron (the six days of creation); another by the exegesis of the Sermon on the Mount. These texts were commented on in a self-conscious literary tradition from the time of Ambrose and Augustine through the scholastic period, both as part of commentaries on Genesis and Matthew, and as independent texts.[13] Such a diverse and subtle literary tradition should be distinguished, it seems to me, from the often polemical use of isolated verses (the two swords in Luke 22:38 or the power of binding and loosing conferred upon Peter in Matthew 16:19 and 18:18) which serve as widespread proof-texts.

The particular sub-genre of Song of Songs exegesis owes much to the especially immediate verbal nature of the text, enunciated throughout in the first person and generally construed as a dialogue, as well as to the book's seemingly secular (even bawdy) subject-matter, which provides an inexhaustible source for discernment of the divine truth *sub umbra et figura*. The significance of these elements becomes clearer if the exegetical tradition of the Song of Songs is compared to that of the book of Job. Job was interpreted by Gregory the Great as essentially a revelation about human moral life. Gregory's magisterial commentary was much admired by later medieval authors: it remained such a standard that it was often excerpted for *florilegia*, while the book of Job itself never inspired any variant exegesis, nor any prolific tradition of commentaries.[14] In contrast, medieval exegetes were drawn to the Song of Songs over and over, their commentaries, concatenations of the borrowed and the new, moving from one level of interpretation to another, developed in a coherent tradition of its own with continual, and very sophisticated, reference to itself.[15]

This approach to genre largely circumvents the categories by which, ever since Aristotle, literary critics have tended to type literary forms according to a combination of their inherent characteristics and the effect they produce upon the reader. Aristotle's categories: epic, comedy, tragedy, and "dithyrambic" (a long lyric), set the broad lines of what is considered "literature as art" in every period of modern western thought that has been exposed to the *Poetics*. That these categories are still strong in this century can be seen in the work of Northrop Frye, who complains about the limits of traditional theories of genre ("an underdeveloped subject in criticism"), and yet essentially offers refinements of Aristotle's categories, of which he retains the basic vocabulary.[16] As Corti has pointed out, there are basically two ways of defining genre: by the Aristotelian categories, "abstract, atemporal, deductive"; or by features of a more "historic, diachronic and inductive" nature.[17] My use of the term operates from the second, historical/cultural point of view. Describing Song of Songs commentaries as a genre thus requires an expansion of the Aristotelian, categorical, understanding of genre; in this expansion, I am following the suggestions of a number of modern critics.

Gerard Genette, for example, shows that it was common in late antique and medieval rhetoric, and even in criticism at the turn of the nineteenth century, to pack all the known forms of literature into the classically received categories. Genette reproduces a circular diagram by means of which Goethe placed over forty types of literature in concentric circles in relation to the three spokes of drama, lyric, and epic. That diagram serves to illustrate how these deductive categories of genre cannot satisfactorily represent the subject of the present book, for it includes, in the outermost circle between lyric and epic and alongside fable, the category "allegorical interpretation."[18] Genette, in contrast, denies any fundamental, or "natural," definition of genre, and allows only the most relative trans-historical basis to the concept. He claims instead that genres are determined empirically, because they show an existential attitude, "an anthropological structure," "mental disposition," "imaginative scheme," or perhaps even a "*sentiment*." Genres are thus firmly rooted in history, at least in the modes of enunciation by which means they are perceived.[19]

Russian critics, from a different point of view, have developed the ground upon which this argument can stand. B. V. Tomashevskii, for example, constrained genre "within its historical limits," claiming that "only the consciousness of contemporaries can testify infallibly which genre a particular work belongs to," for "genre is not an abstract scientific category, but a living, historical formation, a real category, against which may be set the real features that determine the genre of a particular work."[20] This emphasis on cultural/historical *reality* is also important in the genre theory of Bakhtin, who, in a joint work with P. N. Medvedev, approached the subject by beginning:

> If we approach genre from the point of view of its intrinsic thematic relationship to reality and the generation of reality, we may say that every genre has its methods and means of seeing and conceptualizing reality, which are accessible to it alone.[21]

The literary system of medieval Christian culture did not show any concern for the genre of the Song of Songs in its original context, as Hebrew love poetry. The "reality of the text" was that it was received as part of the Bible, one of the books of Solomon. Yet neither Proverbs nor Ecclesiastes, the other books in this category, nor indeed, as we have seen, even the popular book of Job, inspired the profusion of texts which were generated in order to explain the Song of Songs. We must look instead at the more complex place of the Song of Songs in medieval Latin culture in order to explain its attraction to medieval exegetes. I submit that the Song of Songs was so popular partly because it provided an extraordinarily rich ground for the elaboration of allegory, and therefore provided an unparalleled opportunity for finding the truth hidden beneath the figures of the text. As chapter three will argue, the Song of Songs was consistently interpreted by medieval exegetes along the lines of a series of assumed meanings placed in the text by the Holy Spirit, meanings which could only be made clear through the process of allegorical interpretation.

This form of literature, with its own assumptions and strategies, grew out of a set of attitudes about the Song of Songs which had been inherited from Jewish interpretation, and which were first set into a new, Christianized, form by Origen of Alexandria. The Song of Songs tradition as it developed in medieval Europe can be seen as an example of a genre which functioned in a far wider context than its original purpose, that is, the explication of one biblical book. The very nature of the Song of Songs, its intense sensual imagery and rhetorical immediacy, provided many compelling texts, highlighted by the tradition of interpretation, which were used in other theological tasks, for example, in mariology, eschatology, and the late medieval wave of piety *in imitatio Christi*. It is important to note that these uses cannot be fully understood apart from the exegetical tradition of the Song of Songs, in which the basic understandings of the texts were developed. The full context of the medieval Song of Songs genre thus expands even beyond Bakhtin's "secondary genre" to the role of a "metacritical genre," one that provides an important key to other literary forms.

For example, the understanding of the Song of Songs as the heavenly epithalamium between Christ and the Church or Christ and the human soul, the interpretations in circulation since the time of Origen, encouraged the adaptation of selected verses for liturgies of the Virgin Mary; this use in turn led to commentaries on a consistent mariological level of interpretation for the entire Song of Songs. Once the complete text had been interpreted in a mariological mode, many more passages became influential in the development of marian piety, and ultimately, marian dogma. This process is a classic example of Corti's "internal transformation" of the genre. The function of Song of Songs commentaries can therefore only be perceived within the broad context of medieval Christian literary expression. Thus it should not be surprising that from the perspective of modern biblical criticism, that is, torn out of context, the form has now lost the richness of its original function.

But in the original context, both the form and function were well recognized and considered quite viable. The Song of Songs commentary genre was an assumed and important part of medieval poetics, guide to what Tzvetan Todorov, following Jauss, has called the "expectations" of the literary process:

> In every period, a certain number of literary types become so familiar to the public that the public uses them as keys (in the musical sense) for the interpretation of works; here the genre becomes, according to the expression of Hans Robert Jauss, a "horizon of expectation." The writer in his turn internalizes this expectation; the genre becomes for him "a model of writing."[22]

In other words, the many Latin commentaries on the Song of Songs became an easily-recognized model for medieval authors. The ultimate proof of its power as a genre, what Ohly has characterized in "topic and definition," as the "most constantly fixed form (*Gattung*)" of the [medieval Christian] age,[23] can be seen in its expansion into many forms of medieval literature, not only into the discipline of biblical exegesis. An investigation of how the genre influenced other forms of medieval literature is the subject of the last chapter of this book.

Beginning from this literary argument about the Song of Songs commentaries as genre, the discussion moves out to the impact of the genre on Latin Christian culture, including ecclesiology, apocalyptic, sexuality, and literary creativity. This exploration will require a multidisciplinary approach, which will, I hope, tell a very complicated story. I am only too aware that I cannot tell the entire story, for the subject is too vast. But I propose to introduce the genre according to its thematic features, and to demonstrate how the prevailing aspects of Song of Songs interpretation functioned in its medieval context. Commentaries will be introduced and discussed according to subject, rather than in a chronological, geographical, or institutional order. By "subject" I mean the variety of recognized, and to some extent standardized, *readings* of the text of the Song of Songs. Since I will concentrate on the thematic (and in the sense of standard, "classical") features of the genre, most of the interpretations considered are from the pre-scholastic period, almost all before 1200, although the final chapter will extend the range somewhat to suggest some of the far-reaching ways this genre was felt and used in the "secular" literature of the Middle Ages, especially in the vernacular.

I begin historically, therefore, with the role in western Europe of the Song of Songs interpretation of Origen of Alexandria. This is not a simple story, for Origen was a figure of doubtful orthodoxy and an intellect of the most recondite platonic assumptions, and therefore not the easiest model for medieval exegetes. Origen's interpretation is in fact such a *tour-de-force* of allegory that even modern critics, as I will show, are sometimes still at pains to repudiate it together with the supposed legacy of Christian sexual repression in which it participates. Parts of Origen's works on the Song of Songs were translated into Latin, although in an emended form, by Jerome and Rufinus; these were widely circulated in the Middle Ages. In the second chapter, I will show that they were directly available to, and suggest that they were directly consulted by, a number of key exegetes of the Latin tradition throughout the Middle Ages.

Origen's works were only the beginning of the elaborate system of allegory from which this genre developed. Chapter three addresses the nature of allegorical exegesis, approaching it through examples of various ancient and medieval systems intended primarily for the interpretation of sacred Scripture. Modern theory of allegory, especially as employed by critics who begin their analysis of medieval texts with the questions, assumptions, and vocabulary of the medieval scholars, will be used to clarify the method that is so esentially linked to the Song of Songs. The chapter ends with an analysis of the particularly interesting allegorical method set out and employed by one important commentary on the Song of Songs, that of the twelfth-century author Honorius Augustodunensis.

This example breaks the chronological flow of my narrative about the genre of Song of Songs interpretation, but it does so for a particular reason. I wish to show, by means of an unusually elaborate but undeniably elegant example, how complicated medieval allegory of the Song of Songs actually became. The themes seen in Honorius's commentary touch every subsequent chapter of this book. His virtuosic work thus shows the danger of categorizing Song of Songs commentaries according to any one level or mode of interpretation. An analysis of Honorius's long commentary on the Song of Songs thus serves at once to awaken the reader's critical perceptions of how medieval allegory functions, and to alert the reader that it is the very nature of this allegorical tradition to transgress categories.

Each of the next two chapters takes as its basis one of these categories, the two central modes of interpretation, or "modes of reading" made famous by John Cassian: "allegory," here used as a specific technical term which relates the Song of Songs to Christ and the Church; and "tropology," a moral level of interpretation, which understands the text as dealing with the love between Christ and the human soul. Most medieval Latin treatments of the Song of Songs take one of these approaches as their starting point, even though they may touch on a number of other levels of interpretation. I will not attempt to list every known treatise which proceeds according to these categories, for these can be found in the works of Ohly and Riedlinger. Instead, I will organize each chapter around a specific development or issue of western medieval culture which is highlighted by allegorical and tropological interpretations of the Song of Songs.

Chapter four will focus on the commentaries that expand the idea of the Church as the chosen spouse. This was the most common form of medieval interpretation of the Song of Songs; it developed an idea inherited from Jewish exegesis, but contested the inheritance by strong opposition to Judaism, often represented in the commentaries as "the Synagogue." These commentaries in the allegorical mode also decry forms of Christianity which the authors found unacceptable: heretical groups outside the Church or corruption within it. The Song of Songs was invoked by these authors in response to the particular situation of the Church in each age. Chapter four illustrates development in this response. The fourth-/fifth-century commentaries of Apponius and Gregory of Elvira will be briefly treated to show two contrasting ideas of the relationship between Judaism and Christianity at a period of crucial Christian self-definition. Notions of belonging and abandonment in the lively debates about Christian institutions provide a basis for the use of the Song of Songs to express the "insider/outsider" mentality of medieval Christianity. The expansion of the monastic ideal in western Europe is reflected in the extremely influential Song of Songs commentaries of Gregory the Great and the Venerable Bede. A capstone to this latter vision of the Song of Songs is the influential Carolingian commentary of Haimo of Auxerre, a compendium in the allegorical mode which became a standard for Song of Songs exegesis in the period of struggle over the relative powers of Church and state. Over the course of centuries, related concerns about the institutional Church brought Song of Songs exegesis into thematic convergence with commentary on the Apocalypse. Monastic stress on individual devotion, and an increased concern about the *purity* of the Church, reached a logical conclusion in the Song of Songs commentary of the eleventh-century author Robert of Tombelaine. This concern for purity, perhaps in reaction to the increasing institutionalization of medieval Christianity, was inspired by and reflected in the Song of Songs tradition, and is evident in pictorial representations of the Song of Songs. The allegorical tradition is especially rich as a model of how the genre "evolves" through the Middle Ages, becoming increasingly more moral, and therefore more personal, in its approach.

The shift of vision from allegorical to tropological, characterized by Judson Allen as the shift from "beliefs" to "behavior,"[24] was accompanied by an emphasis on the human soul, and resulted in a type of interpretation paramount in the Song of Songs commentaries of the twelfth century. In chapter five, I will describe two related but separate trends of tropological exegesis which reached a peak in twelfth-century exegesis. The first, the Cistercian tradition emanating from the famous series of homilies written by Bernard of Clairvaux, was a high point of a tradition of mystical contemplation particularly adapted to the cloister. The other, the spirituality of the Augustinian Canons, reflected a moral teaching attuned to the stresses of life in the world. The spirituality of the canons, especially those associated with the school of Saint Victor in Paris, paved the way for an important burst of venacular piety in the later Middle Ages, another transformation of the genre. Both types of moral interpretation of the Song of Songs reflected, and perhaps helped to shape, prevalent late medieval ideas about human nature and about the relationships among love, eroticism, and the body. Tropological interpretation of the Song of Songs in general, therefore, emphasized the type of spiritually erotic (or perhaps erotically spiritual) love language that is found already in Origen. It was an important part of both monastic and lay piety of the mystical marriage with Christ, a phenomenon that has raised a certain amount of controversy among modern historians and theologians, especially those working from the point of view of feminist theory.

By a particular development, a complication of the genre, these two levels of interpretation, the allegorical and the tropological, were combined in a series of readings which portray the Song of Songs as the portrait of the love between God and the Virgin Mary. The mariological expositions examined in chapter six derive from ancient Christian liturgies for feasts of the Virgin, which make ample use of the Song of Songs; what began as homily or liturgical commentary gradually developed into an independent tradition of allegorical interpretation. Again, this reading is enthusiastically embraced by some of the most famous authors of the twelfth century: Honorius Augustodunensis, Rupert of Deutz, Hugh of Saint-Victor, Alan of Lille. The understanding of the Virgin Mary as the exalted spouse of the Song of Songs emphasizes her flexible nature in medieval Christian piety: she is the bride of God, and the mother of God; she represents the Church, and each individual Christian. The double transformation of mariological exegesis of the Song of Songs (inward, from liturgical use to commentary; outward, in concert with the developing cult of the Virgin Mary) shows the extreme complexity of twelfth-century readings of the Song of Songs.

The final chapter continues the discussion of broader questions, describing some of the many ways in which interpretations of the Song of Songs were integrated into the so-called secular literature of the Middle Ages. Starting in the eleventh century, the Song of Songs and selected traditional interpretations were translated into the vernacular languages of western Europe, beginning with German. Late medieval devotional treatises in vernacular languages also made use of the common allegorical readings of the Song of Songs. Also notable is the appearance of standard motifs from Song of Songs interpretation in a variety of poetic forms. The influence of Song of Songs commentary on medieval Latin poetry is clear from the many recurrent phrases and stock images which presuppose traditional understandings. By the end of the thirteenth century, the allusions evident in Latin poetry had found their way as well into Spanish, English, French, and German love songs, ballads, and courtly poetry.

Much of the use of the genre in vernacular literature is widely separated in tone and purpose from the Latin commentary tradition. The common understanding of the Song of Songs as a literary text, and of the commentary on the Song of Songs as "metagenre," produced a variety of literary tropes, common rhetorical devices based on the widely known allegories. These tropes could range very far from the world of biblical exegesis, but they were nevertheless meant to evoke a common world of allegorical meaning, one not immediately evident to us.

In this final chapter, I make suggestions which I hope will be pursued by others more expert in the study of medieval vernacular traditions. My purpose in venturing out of the realm of ecclesiastical Latin literature is to show some ways in which Song of Songs commentary itself overlaps with new and developing medieval literary genres, proving the remarkable impact of the tradition on medieval culture. This process shows, in fact, to what extent the Song of Songs commentary genre was, as all genres are, a model of reality.

Notes

1. See the Appendix for a list of the major medieval interpretations of the Song of Songs.

2. R. W. Southern, "Beryl Smalley and the Place of the Bible in Medieval Studies, 1927–84," in *The Bible in the Medieval World: Essays in Honor of Beryl Smalley*, ed. Katherine Walsh and Diana Wood, Studies in Church History Subsidia 4 (Oxford: Basil Blackwell, 1985) p. 1.

3. Smalley, p. 38.

4. Ohly says of Theodore: "Zwar hat er vielleicht keinen ganzen Hohelied-kommentar verfasst, aber doch zumindest in einem ausführlichen Brief, der einer knappen Paraphrase gleichkam, seine Auffassung des von ihm als unkanonisch betrachteten biblischen Buches ausgesprochen," p. 55; but see note 5, where he indicates that Theodore's ideas about the canonicity of the text are not altogether clear.

5. "Postillae venerabilis Patris, Fratris Nicholai de Lyra super Canticum

Canticorum," in *Biblia Sacra cum glossa interlineari, ordinaria et Nicholai Lyrani Postilla* . . . , six volumes (Venice, 1588), vol. III, ff. 355r–368v. Pope's commentary, pp. 124–125, discusses Nicholas of Lyra's ties to the Jewish exegetical tradition, especially to the Targums. For a note about the contrast of this position to Lyra's overall approach to exegesis, see Judson Boyce Allen, *The Friar as Critic: Literary Attitudes in the Later Middle Ages* (Nashville, Tenn.: Vanderbilt University Press, 1971) p. 10. For Bede and Julian of Eclanum, see chapter four below.

6. Scholars who are basically interested in the original context of the Song of Songs include Marvin Pope and also Michael V. Fox, *The Song of Songs and the Ancient Egyptian Love Songs* (Madison: University of Wisconsin Press, 1985). Examples of modern theological interpretation based on this philogical knowledge include Robert Gordis, *The Song of Songs: A Study, Modern Translation, and Commentary* (New York: Jewish Theological Seminary Press, 1954), second edition: *The Song of Songs and Lamentations: A Study, Modern Translation, and Commentary* (New York: Jewish Theological Seminary Press, 1974), Roland E. Murphy, "Canticle of Canticles," in *The Jerome Biblical Commentary*, ed. R. E. Brown et al. (Englewood Cliffs, N.J.: Prentice-Hall, 1968) pp. 506–510. See the beginning of chapter three for further discussion of these and other modern commentaries.

7. Prudence L. Steiner, "A Garden of Spices in New England: John Cotton's and Edward Taylor's Use of the Song of Songs," in *Allegory, Myth, and Symbol*, ed. Morton W. Bloomfield, Harvard English Studies 9 (Cambridge, Mass.: Harvard University Press, 1981) pp. 227–243. Steiner compares these allegorical expositions to the tradition of Jewish interpretation, but seems oddly unaware of the Christian tradition of Song of Songs exegesis.

8. Judson Boyce Allen, *The Ethical Poetic of the Later Middle Ages: A Decorum of Convenient Distinction* (Toronto: University of Toronto Press, 1982) p. 211.

9. Important expression of this relationship between the divine ideal and its human (temporal) manifestation is found in the writings of Augustine: it is a major theme of *De civitate Dei*, and is also found in *Confessiones*, Book X in general, and XIII, v.6–vii8.

10. For example, the famous debate between the ninth-century monks of Corbie, Paschasius Radbertus and Ratramnus, which revolved around the proper definition of *figura* and *veritas* with regard to the historical body of Christ in the eucharist. Both authors argue from the interpretation of biblical passages, especially the miraculous feedings of the Hebrews in the wilderness of Sinai; see *Paschasii Radberti, De corpore et sanguine Domini*, ed. B. Paulus, CCCM 16 (Turnhout, 1969) pp. 25–28, and *Ratramnus, De corpore et sanguine Domini*, ed. J. N. Bakhuizen Van den Brink (Amsterdam, 1954, second edition, 1974) p. 44.

11. M. M. Bakhtin, "The Problem of Speech Genres," translated by Vern W.

McGee, in *Speech Genres and Other Late Essays*, ed. Carly Emerson and Michael Holquist (Austin: University of Texas Press, 1986) pp. 61–62, 98; see chapter six, note 67 below.

12. Maria Corti, *Principi della communicazione letteraria* (Milano: Bompani, 1976); English translation by Margherita Bogat and Allen Mandelbaum: *An Introduction to Literary Semiotics* (Bloomington and London: Indiana University Press, 1978) pp. 124–131.

13. Latin commentaries on the six days of creation begin with important texts from the fourth/fifth centuries, the *Hexameron* of Ambrose of Milan, and four interpretations of Augustine: *De Genesi contra Manichaeos, De Genesi ad litteram, De Genesi ad litteram, imperfectus liber*, and book XIII of the *Confessiones*. There are medieval treatments of the same pericope by Claudius of Turin, Hrabanus Maurus, Remigius of Auxerre, Gibert of Nogent, Hugh of Saint-Victor (several versions), Denis the Carthusian, Bonaventure (a *Hexameron* text), and Eckhart. Augustine's *De sermone Domini in monte secundum Matthaeum* and the popular sermons of John Chrysostom on Matthew inspire a similar set of commentaries.

14. Gregory the Great, *Moralia in Iob*, ed. M. Adriaen, CCSL 143, 143A, 143B (1979–1985). This text was widely circulated in the Middle Ages through three important collections: the *Liber de expositione veteris et novi testamenti* of Gregory's chancellor Paterius, PL 79:685–916 (see also A. Wilmart, "Le Recueil Grégorien de Paterius et les fragments wisigothiques de Paris," RB 39 (1927) 81–101); the *Sententiarum* of Taio of Saragosa, PL 80:727–990; and the *Egloga de moralibus Iob* of the Irish monk Lathcen, ed. M. Adriaen, CCSL 145 (1969). None of these claims to be anything but a composite of Gregory's exegesis. See chapter four, note 35 and chapter three, note 25.

15. Bakhtin says that a distinctive feature of all "speech-genres" which constitute the first level of generic definition is the existence of each enunciation as a link of a chain, tied both to precedent and to reception, organized with great complexity, and to a large extent determinative of possible originality, pp. 69, 94–96; 78, 80–81.

16. Aristotle, *Poetics* I; the four genres are introduced immediately. Much of the surviving work consists of analysis of what is proper especially to tragedy; as readers or viewers of Umberto Eco's *The Name of the Rose* are well aware, the loss of Aristotle's discussion of other genres, especially comedy, has led to fanciful speculation. Plato, for his part, groups the four as three, linking comedy and tragedy as equally imitative, while characterizing dithyramb as the poet's own voice, and epic as a combination of the two, *The Republic*, Book III (394 C). Northrop Frye, *Anatomy of Criticism: Four Essays* (Princeton, N.J.: Princeton University Press, 1957) pp. 247–248, describes two levels of literary categorization: by mode (the relationship of the actions of the characters and the attitude of the author to the readers) and by genre (analogies of literary form); see also pp. 95–99 for a discussion of genre, p. 366 for a short definition of mode.

17. Corti, pp. 115–119. Corti argues that the second approach allows for

study of "the transformation of literary genres" by way of "synchronic cuts in the diachronic development of genres [which] allow for confrontations that tend to shed light on the dynamics of history," pp. 117, 116.

18. Gérard Genette, *Introduction à l'architexte* (Paris: Éditions du Seuil, 1979) p. 58. Earlier, Genette commented on one result of this process of seeking a fit of genres: "Les tentatives ultérieures de systématisation, à la fin de l'Antiquité et au Moyen Âge, s'efforcent d'intégrer la poésie lyrique aux systèmes de Platon ou d'Aristote sans modifier leurs catégories." p. 30

19. Genette, p. 72 (quoting Durand, Jolles, Mauron). See also p. 81.

20. Quoted from L. M. O'Toole and Ann Sullivan, translators and editors, *Russian Poetics in Translation*, Formalist Theory vol. 4 (Oxford: Holden Books Ltd., 1977) p. 18. These ideas, originally published in 1927–28, have become so pervasive in the literature of genre that Heather Dubrow begins her introductory text on the subject with the observation that "genre, as many students of the subject have observed, functions much like a *code of behavior* established between the author and his reader." *Genre*, The Critical Idiom 42 (London and New York: Methuen, 1982) p. 2. (Emphasis mine.)

21. M. M. Bakhtin and P. N. Medvedev, *The Formal Method in Literary Scholarship: A Critical Introduction to Sociological Poetics*, trans. Albert J. Wehrle (Cambridge, Mass.: Harvard University Press, 1985) p. 133.

22. Tzvetan Todorov, *Introduction to Poetics*, trans. Richard Howard, Theory and History of Literature 1 (Minneapolis: University of Minnesota Press, 1981) p. 62. Jauss defines this term in the essay "Genres and Medieval Literature," in *Toward an Aesthetic of Reception*, trans. Timothy Bahti (Minneapolis: University of Minnesota Press, 1982), especially pp. 88, 102. See also the introduction to the latter volume by Paul de Man, p. xii.

23. "Kaum eine andere literarische Gattung ist in ihrem Gegenstand und ihrer Bestimmung durch Epochen hin so gleichbleibend festgelegt wie der Schriftkommentar." Ohly, p. 303.

24. Allen, *The Ethical Poetics*, pp. 213–214.

Chapter Two

Hidden Origins: The Legacy of Alexandria

The essential framework of medieval Latin commentary on the Song of Songs developed in the rarified intellectual atmosphere of Alexandria, far from the cloisters and schoolrooms of medieval Europe. To understand the basic premises on which the genre developed we need to consider first, and in some detail, the elusive but fascinating figure of Origen of Alexandria. In fact, few figures in Christian history present as complicated a picture as Origen, nor does his role become simpler for all that he is universally acknowledged as the founder of Christian allegorical interpretation of the Song of Songs. The purpose of this chapter is to explain how Origen set the stylistics of the allegory and the basic themes of medieval Song of Songs interpretation.

Origen's Life and Thought

Origen was born in Egypt ca. 185, and died in Palestine ca. 254. His career is thus prior to the great ecumenical councils, beginning with Nicaea in 325, at which Christian doctrine was formally defined. Nevertheless, the scope and influence of Origen's theological and exegetical works are perhaps unique in Christianity. He is known as the first great Christian theologian, and the one who made the most successful bridge between the revealed religion of the Bible, complete with traditional modes of Jewish interpretation, and Greek philosophy.[1] It is precisely this bridge that made possible the Christian tradition of Song of Songs commentary.

Origen's contact with the rabbis of Palestine has only begun to be studied in depth; as Elizabeth Clark has written, "Recent scholarly interest has shifted from Origen the mystic to Origen the preacher and exegete, and in doing so has transported us from Alexandria to Caesarea."[2] While essentially polemical in his attitude towards Judaism, Origen showed a marked respect for Jewish knowledge of the Bible. He attempted to learn the languages and techniques of early rabbinic interpretation to provide Christians with better tools for refutation. Scholars with an interest in the development of Christian typological exegesis have pointed out that essential elements of Origen's allegorical method, including puns and paronymic detours, have their roots in Judaic interpretation.[3] And Clark goes beyond this theoretical concern to remind us that an important *theme* of Origen on the Song of Songs is the relationship of Judaism to Christianity, insofar as the biblical text is presented as the triumph of the Church in "her" relationship of love with Christ. This important connection will be considered later in this chapter, where Origen's treatments of the Song of Songs will be considered in some detail.

Origen's Platonism, on the other hand, has been widely studied. Like his younger pagan contemporary Plotinus, Origen is thought to have been intellectually shaped in the classroom of the great Alexandrian teacher, Ammonius Saccas. Like Plotinus (who is generally credited as the founder of the Neoplatonic tradition), Origen understood reality as hierarchical; he used a concept similar to the "great chain of being" to explain the relationship between an uncreated, eternal God and the created world. In his defense of Christianity against the philosopher Celsus, Origen claims that the Christian idea of faith, moderated through this Platonic system, is entirely reasonable, no less rigorous than the accepted study of secular literature:

> For in Christianity, if I make no vulgar boasting, there will be found to be no less profound study of the writings that are believed; we explain the obscure utterances of the prophets, and the parables in the gospels, and innumerable other events or laws which have a symbolical meaning.[4]

Contra Celsum (after 245) is Origen's classic encounter with Hellenistic philosophy; an earlier work *De prinicipiis* (*Peri archon*—before 230) also makes important connections between the Christian revealed God of creation and the Platonic conception of a First Principle. Origen's Platonic framework led to three important theological formulations about salvation and the body of the resurrection. These concepts, which became increasingly controversial within the Christian community, explain in part Origen's increasingly shady reputation in medieval Europe.

The first, paralleling a Neoplatonic concept of divinity expressed in three *hypostases*, led to an understanding of the Trinity as "three distinct and graded beings."[5] This approach became especially problematic after the trinitarian definition of the Council of Nicaea (325), although, since Origen also argued that all three persons of the Trinity were divine, there was a certain amount of controversy among Nicene and Arian Christians of the fourth century as to which side understood Origen properly.

The second formulation, from the philosophical doctrine known as *apokatastasis*, began with conception of the return of the soul to the divinity from which it comes, and resulted in a doctrine of universal salvation. However optimistic, there was nothing simple about this system, for Origen envisioned a cycle of worlds, of which ours is but one, through which the soul must progress. Against the Gnostics, Origen insisted that both the imperfections of creation and human free will are, as Trigg puts it, "the means whereby God, as a loving Father, coaxes children home."[6]

The third concept, also developed in a polemical context, ran counter to later orthodox theories of a continuity between corporeality and eternity. Like many Christians in the first centuries of the common era, Origen believed that the body of the resurrection was of a different quality than the human body on earth. Quoting Paul's distinction between "spiritual" and "earthly" bodies in 1 Corinthians 15:24, Origen said to Celsus:

> Therefore our hope is not one of worms, nor does our soul desire a body that has rotted. . . . For since the nature of this body is to be entirely corruptible, this mortal tabernacle must put on incorruption.[7]

Thus, the distinction between earthly and heavenly corporeality is an important factor in Origen's approach to Scripture in general, one which had a necessary influence on his complex understanding of the Song of Songs. This element was not always fully understood by medieval exegetes who worked from a different theological stance; as chapter five will show, the idea of a direct relationship between the mortal and the incorruptible body is central to later readings of the Song of Songs as the love between God and the soul.

Origen's Reputation in Early Christianity

Origen's influence on the Christian tradition, and especially on the developing themes of Song of Songs exegesis, is thus especially remarkable since his doctrinal formulations did not always end up in the theological mainstream. Origen was, in fact, condemned by the Second Council of Constantinople, called by the Emperor Justinian, in 553. A posthumous declaration of heresy is not otherwise unknown in the Christian tradition, although perhaps three hundred years is the record chronological lapse. At the very least, in Origen's case, such controversy may even be taken as evidence of his theological legacy, and of the wide currency of his ideas long after his death. Origen also created some storms during his lifetime, especially over his ordination in Caesaria in 230, which Bishop Demetrius took as an affront to the Alexandrian Church, and which contributed to Origen's long exile in Palestine. But, whatever the contemporary or posthumous doubts about Origen's orthodoxy, his commitment to Christianity was life-long, leading to his imprisonment during the Persecutions of Decius, ca. 250. Origen's last writings are accounts of this experience, and he died in obscurity.

Origen's importance was, paradoxically, first felt in Alexandria, the city from which he had been exiled.[8] Dionysius, a former student, and bishop until his death in 264, did much to popularize this particular version of Christian Platonism. Several Alexandrian authors of the next generation drew extensively on Origen; one of these, Pamphilius, who had studied in Alexandria, carried his theological and exegetical methods back to Palestine. Pamphilius also wrote the first biography of Origen. In the early fourth century, Methodius of Olympus (Asia Minor) also was influenced by Origen, but objected to certain aspects of his theology, especially his ideas about the resurrection of the flesh. Pamphilius and Eusebius, later Bishop of Caesarea, wrote an *Apology for Origen* against such attacks, affirming Origen's salvation theology. The sixth book of Eusebius's *Ecclesiastical History* gives a life of Origen from which comes most of our biographical information, for example, the famous (or, rather, infamous) account that he made himself a eunuch for the sake of the kingdom of God. As Peter Brown has noted, this action may not have been motivated, as we tend to think, so much by a simple hatred of the body as by a desire to "shift the massive boundary between the sexes," so that the body could be free to "act as a blazon of the freedom of the spirit."[9]

A separate tradition of the influence of Origen comes from two fourth-century Alexandrians, Evagrius Ponticus and Didymus the Blind, who championed Origen's exegetical and speculative works respectively. Evagrius, an important figure in early monasticism, transmitted the works of Origen to his pupil, John Cassian. Origen's allegorical methods were preserved by Cassian in the *Collationes*, a miscellany of the lives of the desert fathers which were later prescribed by the *Regula* of Benedict of Nursia as required reading in monasteries.[10] Didymus, in turn, influenced a series of texts important in the transmission of Origen's biblical interpretation, including the *Philocalia* of Gregory of Nazianzus and Basil the Great, a *catena* through which parts of Origen's writings were preserved in Greek. Another Cappadocian author, Gregory of Nyssa, was closely connected to Basil and Nazianzus, and strongly dependent on Origen for his mystical interpretation of the Song of Songs.[11] Even more directly related to the Song of Songs tradition is another student of Didymus, Rufinus of Aquileia, who translated into Latin parts of Origen's *De principiis*, and his commentaries on Romans and the Song of Songs. But the most complex and important student of Didymus, and one whose relationship to Origen over time ran the gamut from plagiarism to condemnation, was Jerome.

Jerome made great use of Origen's biblical studies, especially the *Hexapla*, a six-column comparison of Hebrew and Greek versions of the Bible, in his important Latin Bible translation which we know as the *Vulgata*. Jerome also translated many of Origen's homilies, including those on the Song of Songs, and made a new translation of *De principiis*, claiming that Rufinus had subjected the text to excessive laundering to preserve Origen's reputation. Jerome wanted instead to translate Origen into Latin as accurately as possible, warts and all. To contemporaries, this aroused the suspicion that Jerome was somehow defending Origen rather than purifying him; a charge to which Jerome indignantly replied that he had never been, or at least had ceased to be, an "Origenist."[12] Significantly, by this time (ca. 398), Jerome had been influenced by the most vocal of the anti-Origen party, Epiphanius, and had developed severe reservations about Origen's theology.

The scathing and untiring attacks on Origen by Epiphanius can be understood as one by-product of the sharpening of the boundaries of Christian doctrine after the Council of Nicaea. Here, both Arius, whom the council declared anathema, and his chief opponent, Athanasius, appealed to Origen's theology in arguing their positions. Epiphanius, a bishop from Cyprus who had been present at Nicaea, went so far as to claim that Origen was the primary cause of Arius's heretical trinitarian teachings. After Epiphanius, Origen's reputation was somewhat dubious, especially in the Greek-speaking world of Eastern Christianity. But the monks of the Egyptian and Syrian deserts continued an enthusiastic "Origenist" tradition which provoked a wave of criticism. The controversy was not easily settled, in fact, disputes over "Origenist" monks were direct causes of both the banishment of John Chrysostom in the fifth century, and the condemnation of Origen by Justinian in the sixth century.

Further discussion of the tortured path of Origen's reputation in the world of Greek-speaking Christians falls outside the focus of this book. This influence must nevertheless be acknowledged. For one thing, it illustrates Origen's legacy of a complex and rich mode of discourse to a world just beginning to take on doctrinal and hierarchical definition. For another, it provides an intriguing contrast to the history of Origen's writings in the Latin west, to which I now turn.

The role of Origen in the shaping of the Vulgate Bible is obvious testimony to his importance in Latin Christianity. This role is also immediately instructive of how he was most influential. It is, in fact, Origen's approach to the interpretation of the Bible, not his sweeping systematic theology, that had the most impact in the west. This is due in part to language barriers, but also simply to the differing concerns of eastern and western Christianity. Origen's biblical exegesis had the advantage of an enormously influential Latin patron, Ambrose, Bishop of Milan.[13] Ambrose was the most important expositor of the mystical senses of Scripture in the early Latin Church; and of course, it was Ambrose who taught Augustine how to penetrate the seemingly ungainly literal sense of the text to reveal its true and salvific meaning.[14] The acceptance of this allegorical mode of discourse is one of the most important steps in the development of the genre of medieval biblical commentary. The story of Origen in Latin Christianity, then, can be told by tracing the influence of his exegesis of a number of important biblical books from Ambrose to the High Middle Ages. The role of Origen in shaping the medieval Latin understanding of the Song of Songs is crucial. In many ways, the symbolic and allegorical flowering with which this book is concerned has its discursive roots in the soil of Alexandria.

Origen on the Song of Songs

I have already made the point that Origen's vision of the Song of Songs was crucial for all subsequent Christian interpretation, East and West. This is partly because his was the first important Christian commentary on the Song of Songs. Only that of Hippolytus of Rome is earlier, but this text was known to the western Middle Ages in mere fragments, and under the name of Ambrose.[15] Origen's interpretations, in contrast, were fully attributed to their author, although they also survive only in part and in Latin translation.

There are two extant works by Origen on the Song of Songs: a commentary, written between 240–244, originally in ten books of which survive a prologue and commentary to 2:15; and two homilies, written ca. 244, which cover exactly one verse less. Later sources also attest to a two-book treatise from Origen's youth no longer extant. The two extant texts are almost exclusively known in the Latin translations of Rufinus (the *Commentary*) and Jerome (the *Homilies*).[16] Although the Greek texts of these works are no longer extant, some original passages from the *Commentary* were preserved in various important works: the *Philocalia* of Nazianzus and Basil, the *catena* on the Song of Songs by Procopius, and other, anonymous, *catenae*.[17] The commentary on the Song of Songs by Gregory of Nyssa gives further evidence for the importance of Origen's interpretation in Greek-speaking Christian lands, at least to the fifth century. But it is, paradoxically, in the Latin west, and most especially through the translations of Rufinus and Jerome, that Origen's interpretation of the Song of Songs had the greatest influence. The fact that these are translations should be stressed, since we are essentially left with interpretations that have in themselves been through a process of interpretation. Therefore, the differing natures of these Latin versions of Origen need further attention.

Although Jerome and Rufinus differed considerably in their estimation of Origen, it is nevertheless clear that their translations of Origen manifest the same theological agenda.[18] Indeed, both approached the task of translations with a desire to rescue Origen from what they (in common, perhaps, with most Latin Christians) saw as heterodoxy, perhaps deriving from excessive Platonism.[19] Rufinus, apparently stung by Jerome's criticism of his translations, defended himself in several treatises dedicated to demonstrating that Origen's theology of the Trinity and the resurrection of the flesh were out of step with the prevailing notions of orthodoxy.[20] Rufinus pointed out that many early Christian authors (for example, Clement of Alexandria and Tertullian) were guilty of the same lapses, although they in turn raged against the Gnostics and Marcionites. Rufinus praised Origen's wisdom, and dedicated himself to the task of producing translations suitable for the spiritual advancement of his post-Nicene audience.[21] The willed modifications of these translations show the beginnings of the shaping of the genre of Song of Songs commentary as a theological tool; winning credence was added to the original goal of explication of the text.

As Jerome became aware of Epiphanius's critique of Origen, and as he came to fear that Rufinus's revised translations would gain acceptance, he grew more critical. In one place, in anticipation of Justinian, he calls Origen an out-and-out heretic.[22] This condemmnation however, always tinged with respect for Origen's zealous Christian life and profound knowledge of the Scriptures.[23] In fact, on the subject of the interpretation of the Song of Songs, Jerome has nothing but admiration for Origen. In Jerome's dedicatory epistle to Pope Damasus, Origen is praised as having, literally, outdone himself:

> Origenes, cum in ceteris libris omnes vicerit,
> in cantico canticorum ipse se vicit.
>
> Although in other books Origen conquered everyone,
> on the Song of Songs he conquered himself.[24]

This praise may have embarrassed Jerome later on, when he became an outspoken critic of Origen's theology. But, in spite of its perceived theological lapses, Jerome continued to admire Origen's exegesis, especially that of the Song of Songs. Even Jerome, then, played a role in presenting Origen to the Latin Christian world as the standard for further interpretation, that is, both as a model of exegesis and as a persuasive (if somewhat dangerous) example of exegetical art.

Origen's two great works on the Song of Songs thus were preserved in fragmentary translations by rival ecclesiastical figures, both striving to re-express the insights of the texts according to a dominant ideology quite unlike Origen's theological context. The extant Latin versions of the *Homilies* and *Commentary* differ in some respects, but they complement rather than contradict one another, and offer a coherent interpretation of the Song of Songs, one which supports the suggestion that the *Homilies* are dependent on, indeed, a simplified version of, the *Commentary*. Direct parallels are evident at many points of the interpretation. Both works, for example, interpret the title as an indication that this is the greatest of all biblical songs: just as the "holy of holies" means the most sacred place, so the Song of Songs is the most sacred song. The sacrality is, furthermore, complex and seemingly contradictory from the start; for this sacred song is an epithalamium, a wedding hymn, written as a spiritual drama between the bride and the bridegroom.[25] Of course, this is not meant physically. Origen is at pains to stress the spiritual nature of the book, through which lens the bridegroom would be seen as God and the bride as either (and the flexibility must be stressed) the Church or the Christian soul. The *Commentary* begins:

> This little book is an epithalamium, that is a nuptial song, which it seems to me that Solomon wrote in a dramatic form, and sang after the fashion of a bride to her bridegroom, who is the word of God, burning with celestial love. Indeed, he loves her deeply, whether she is the soul, made in his own image, or the Church.[26]

On the face of it, this flexibility may seem to be begging the question of true interpretation. Yet the insistence here on multivocality of the biblical text follows Origen's discussion of the multiple meanings of Scripture which he saw as generally divided into body, soul (*psyche*), and spirit. In Book IV of his great theoretical work, *De principiis*, Origen explains in detail how the historical sense gives rise at once to christological, spiritual, and/or mystical meanings.[27] This follows from Origen's theology, which, as we have seen, was philosophically hierarchical and very concerned with the possibility of a physicality expressed in both earthly and heavenly terms. It must also be noted that this passage from *De principiis* is in itself an allegorical interpretation of the Wedding at Cana (John 2:1–11) in which the three *or* four measures of water are miraculously turned into wine, just as the words of Scripture reveal three or four levels of meaning. It seems that the theoretical principles of interpretation Origen sets out elsewhere are put into practice in both the *Commentary* and the *Homilies* on the Song of Songs.

As the more detailed work, the *Commentary* is far more elaborate about the theme of spiritual love. In the lengthy prologue, Origen sets forth a theory of allegorical interpretation of Scripture with sources in many places, perhaps most significantly in rabbinic exegesis. First, he repeats the teaching of Jewish scholars that the Song of Songs is one of the few passages of the Bible which must be kept from the spiritually immature, as it is "strong" rather than "milky" food.[28] Many of the points of interpretation of the prologue echo themes of Jewish interpretation: besides this esoteric warning, the importance of the superlative title and the history of salvation through the progressive revelation of divine songs are all closely related to themes developed by the rabbis of Palestine in relation to the Song of Songs. Urbach even describes Origen's exegetical technique as an elaboration in full rhetorical style of short *dicta* and pithy statements of the Jewish sages of third-century Palestine.[29]

The *Commentary* and the *Homilies* of Origen on the Song of Songs are very closely associated with one another, yet each work has its individual character, having been written for a manifestly different purpose. Origen speaks in the prologue of the *Commentary* about the difficulty of the text he interprets, while Jerome borrows his metaphor of meat and milk to describe the *Homilies* as the suckling's version of this interpretation.[30] A further irony is that, even though these works were translated into Latin with different (if equally suspicious) attitudes towards Origen, a comparison of the two translations shows remarkably consistent exegesis of specific passages. In spite of the added interpretative filter of translation, and the disagreements, competition, and even animosity between Jerome and Rufinus, it is possible to grasp some outline of what Origen's own reading of the Song of Songs must have been. And, after all, the common themes presented by these Latin fragments are Origen's legacy to the Latin tradition of Song of Songs exegesis.

Besides the themes noted above, the prologue to the *Commentary* includes a long discussion of spiritual love with reference to Greek dialogues, and an analysis of the Song of Songs in relation to the other "Solomonic" books, Proverbs and Ecclesiastes. None of these elements is found in the *Homilies*. Where the *Commentary* explains at length, digresses, and spins theories, the *Homilies* are relatively succinct, as befitting exegesis for those still young in the faith. Perhaps because of this intended audience of "Christian sucklings," the *Homilies* give a more ordered interpretation of the Song of Songs, proceeding line by line, while the *Commentary* often takes an entire verse at a time, and moves back and forth in its exposition, more in the narrative style we would rather expect from a sermon. Yet, while many differences are stylistic and may be attributed to Rufinus and Jerome, the interpretations of specific verses remain the same.

For example, both texts see Verse 1:3, "Your name is oil poured out," as a reference to Christ, the anointed one. As *Homily* I puts it:

> Christ is named in the entire earth, (*in universa terra*) in the whole world (*in omni mundo*) my Lord is preached; for "oil poured out" is his "name."[31]

Part of the much fuller interpretation of the *Commentary* makes the same point:

> One might well see in the same [words] a prophecy pronounced by the Bride about Christ, that it would come to pass at the advent of our Lord and Savior that his name would thus be spread about through the orb of the earth (*per orbem terrae*), and through the entire world (*per universum mundum*), that there would be "an odor of sweetness in every place," as the Apostle says: "We are the good odor of Christ in every place; to the one indeed the odor of death unto death, but to others the odor of life unto life." (cf. 2 Corinthians 2:15, 16)[32]

As further support for the contention that this is indeed Origen speaking it should be noted that the same idea, that is, that this verse refers to the name of Christ poured out on the world, is found in the Greek *catena* of Procopius.[33] In a similar fashion, verse 1:12, "my spikenard gave out its fragrance," is interpreted by both texts in relation to the woman who anointed the feet of Jesus (John 12:3), again stressing the ecclesiological interpretation.[34]

Verse 2:6, "his left hand is under my head, his right hand embraces me," is, rather, interpreted in a spiritual sense, developing a verse borrowed from Proverbs to emphasize a distinction between the life of the world and heavenly glory:

> Homily II, 9: The Word of God has both a "left" [hand] and a "right [hand]"; although Wisdom is multiple according to the variety of understanding, down deep it is one. This Solomon teaches about the "left" and "right" [hands] of Wisdom saying: "the length and the years of life are in her [Wisdom's] right [hand], in her left [hand], however, are riches and glory." (Proverbs 3:16)

> Commentary, Book III: For these are the "right" and the "left" [hands] of the Bridegroom, as Proverbs speaks about Wisdom saying: "the length of life is in her right [hand], in her left [hand] is, however, riches and glory." (Proverbs 3:16)[35]

These examples show to what extent Origen's *Homilies* and *Commentary* on the Song of Songs were received in the Latin tradition as a coherent interpretation; in fact, as these passages show, it is not always possible to tell the specific source of a quotation. There emerges instead from an analysis of these interpretations an overall sense of Origen's approach to the text: allegorical, multivocal, awash in references to other passages in Scripture, deeply attuned to the Jewish tradition of interpretation from which he adopted the basic model of approach to the Song of Songs. The model operates basically and simultaneously on two levels of interpretation, reading the Song of Songs as the love between either Christ and the Church or Christ and the soul. The first level of interpretation was and continued to be the more important; it shows Origen's involvement in the complex developing theological framework of ecclesiology. "The Church" in Origen's interpretation of the Song of Songs appears as multifaceted as Scripture itself: the Church is pre-existent, visible in the Old Testament and among the Gentiles, on earth, and, in its mystical fulness, in the body of Christ.[36]

This spiritual rhetoric of the Song of Songs is Origen's legacy to medieval interpretation, a legacy which deserves to be carefully traced through medieval Christian exegesis. I will take up this task at the end of this chapter. First, though, I would like to point to some of the difficulties modern scholars have had with Origen's allegorical method, as these are indicative of some of the problems modern scholarship has had in recognizing what I call the genre of Song of Songs interpretation.

Modern Readings of the Allegorical Method

Patricia Cox Miller has pointed out that the prologue to Origen's *Commentary* on the Song of Songs is framed by a banquet metaphor drawn ultimately from Plato's *Symposium*. Miller writes: "This association of food, words, and bliss is characteristic of Origen's understanding of language in his Commentary on the Song of Songs; indeed, it is one of that work's major themes."[37] *Food*, after all, is an essential part of the text of the Song of Songs, and no explication can avoid confrontation with referents, with the milk, apples, dates, honey, and other delicacies the lovers offer to each other. Furthermore, the force of *words* is represented by the rhetoric of personification: the Word is personified, while Christ becomes the lover, the Bridegroom who presides at his own wedding feast. Finally, *bliss* is the word Miller uses to translate *eros*, the passionate love with which the Song of Songs is concerned:

> "*eros* holds the highest place at this banquet" (*Comm. in Cant.* 2.8, 165/159). *Eros*, the name of God as well as the name of the Word of God, as Origen

argues at length, presides over this feast of words (*Comm. in Cant.*, pro. 2, 68–71/31–35. The delights of this banquet are words, and the place of honor is held by *the word*, language itself. Speaker and lover have been fused, and the reality over which the speaker-lover presides is linguistic.[38]

The curiously blatant eroticism of the Song of Songs is one of the most obvious features of the text, a feature that has aroused in some twentieth-century scholars a basic mistrust of the medieval tradition of allegorical interpretation. William E. Phipps has offered this description of the way in which this passionate narrative became the vehicle of what he calls the repressed sexuality championed by the Church.

> Allegory was brought to the rescue. Having noticed the effective way in which the philosophers had recast the sensuous gods of Homer and Hesiod into ethereal ideals, Christian theologians were quick to interpret the sensuous celebration by a couple in Song of Songs as a non-physical prayer communion between a pious Christian and his ever-loving God. Thus the passionate paean which the church had inherited from the authoritative books of the synagogue was converted into what was thought to be a harmless mysticism.[39]

Given the tone of this analysis, it is perhaps not surprising that Phipps stresses the story of Origen's self-castration as a means for understanding of what he sees as a perverse hermeneutic. Part of Phipps's vexation with the allegorical commentary on the Song of Songs lies in the self-revealing nature of many early Christian and medieval commentaries. On Bernard of Clairvaux, he observes:

> As with other allegorists, Bernard's alleged exposition tells us nothing about the scriptural text, but rather exposes the turmoil of the mystic composer. ... "If you drive nature out with a pitchfork," Horace sagiously [sic.] observed, "she will find a way back."[40]

And yet, nowhere in Origen's interpretations of the Song of Songs has eroticism been driven out. In fact, as Miller shows, Origen is insistent about using the word *eros*, rather than the more "respectable" *agape* to describe the love of which the text speaks. For Origen, the Song of Songs celebrates the erotic desiring, seduction, and wounding—the "deep lacerations"—which Roland Barthes has characterized as the *jouissance* (the *eros*) in the relationship of the reader with a text.[41] As Miller puts it: "In Origen's writing, the Song of Songs is a text that desires the reader and not the other way around. . . . For Origen, as for Barthes, the text is an erotic body where word and reader, Bridegroom and Bride, are joined."[42]

Miller's appropriation of Barthes's hermeneutics has added a deeper understanding of the function of eroticism in Origen's treatment of the Song of Songs. It suggests part of an answer to the accusation that "allegory was brought to the rescue," for it shows that allegory here serves to emphasize, rather than diminish, the erotic tension of the text. Yet it is discomforting to note that Miller's interpretation of Origen also ignores the tension between the eroticism of the body and the eroticism of words and concepts inherent in the Song of Songs, for her reading dismisses reference altogether and makes the erotic body the *text* itself, and the banquet of lovers a banquet of *words*. While Phipps objects to the conversion of a "passionate paean" into "harmless mysticism," Miller ignores the specter of corporeal bliss altogether by focusing entirely on "the pleasure of the text."

Neither critic, then, takes to heart the fact that Origen's interpretation of the Song of Songs highlights the ambivalence of what Barbara Johnson has called "the rhetoric of sexual difference." Johnson stresses the power of the inextricability between sexuality and literature:

> Somehow, however, it is not simply a question of literature's ability to say or not to say the truth of sexuality. For from the moment literature begins to try to set things straight on that score, *literature itself becomes inextricable from the sexuality it seeks to comprehend.* It is literature that inhabits the very heart of what makes sexuality problematic for us speaking animals. *Literature is not only a thwarted investigator but also an incorrigible perpetrator of the problem of sexuality.*[43]

"The problem of sexuality" is certainly one of the most compelling aspects of medieval Christian literature on the Song of Songs. Indeed, it is a problem of words and bodies: of bodies *as* words, and of words *about* the body. Deeply encoded in the texts themselves is the mirror of both the ideal and the experiential, reciprocally interacting. To reject or ignore the difference between these aspects of human desire and linguistic self-expression is to turn a deaf ear to the many manifestations of bliss which drew Origen and his followers to this particular biblical text. Yet this has been the pattern of modern hermeneutics of traditional Christian literature.

Perhaps the most uncompromising critique of the bodily language (that is, words *about* the body) of Christian spiritual love as codified for posterity by Origen comes from modern feminist thought, especially the philosophy of Mary Daly. Daly has offered an understanding of the relationship between spiritual and physical passion which operates by a principle of inversion of the traditional Christian categories. In her system, neither "purity" nor "lust" carry their traditional understandings. Instead, she proposes that purity and lust—in her terms, elemental being and elemental longing—literally "be-long" together, and have only been separated through the perversity of patriarchal culture. Daly does not specifically consider Origen, but in her terms his interpretations of the Song of Songs and the literary tradition which it inspired can be described as using the language of lust to describe the attainment of purity. They thus fit into a category which Daly calls "sado-asceticism," illustrating a condition "altogether dependent upon the sadomasochistic obsessions from which it tries to escape. The direction of the 'escape' is further futile fixations."[44] Daly's rather comical examples portray ascetic heroes of early Christianity fleeing into the wilderness, where lust literally *pursues* them with visions of beautiful naked women. This situation is, Daly argues, is a direct result of the insistence of western patriarchy on the separation of body and soul: "Sadospirituality [is] phallic flight from lust into lust-full asceticism."[45]

The irony of this analysis is that it is surprisingly close to that of Phipps, who also worries about the seeming exclusion of sexuality from Christian allegorical narrative. With Miller, Daly shares a perception of the sublimation of sensuality in Christian spiritual rhetoric, although the two authors perceive the consequences of this sublimation in very different ways.

All of this is characteristic of the tendency Michel Foucault has described as typical of Christian discourse since the sixteenth century, in short, of a modern perception of the spiritual and the sexual, but hardly of Origen's own attitude towards the body, the "humble ass" which could become the "resplendent vehicle of the soul," just as the coarse texture of Scripture is the earthly vehicle for God's revelation.[46] To enter instead upon a more complex and nuanced understanding of the hermeneutical subtleties with which *medieval* Latin authors approached the Song of Songs may help to map the contours of the deep, popular, and pervasive genre of Song of Songs exegesis in the Western Middle Ages.

The Matrix of Origen in Medieval Song of Songs Exegesis[47]

Origen certainly set the tone of the medieval genre of Song of Songs exegesis, for all of the commentaries we shall consider accept without comment the erotic relationship of the protagonists of the poems; many are enthusiastic in presenting the involvement of the reader with the text. Rupert of Deutz, for example, begins his mariological commentary with a passionate outburst:

> What is this exclamation, so great, so sudden? O holy Mary, the inundation of joy, the strength of love, the torrent of voluptuousness totally covered you, totally possessed you, inwardly inebriated [you], and you felt "what eyes have not seen and ears have not heard and the heart of man has not reached," (1 Corinthians 2:9) and you said "Let him kiss me with the kiss of his mouth." (Song of Songs 1:1)[48]

Origen's influence here is not directly thematic; rather it is by way of legitimization, allowing this emotional reading of the Song of Songs with very little distance between the text and the interpretation.

Yet most scholars limit Origen's direct influence to the Song of Songs tradition of twelfth-century France, and this with caution.[49] They are willing to grant indirect influence, especially through the incomplete commentary of Gregory the Great, and are quick to credit Origen with the invention of the standard Christian interpretation, but in a most remote manner.[50] There has been a scholarly reluctance to believe that Origen's works were actually read by early medieval exegetes.

And yet, even a cursory consideration of Origen's works on the Song of Songs must begin with the acknowledgement that they are known to us primarily in Latin translation. And this raises the interesting question of how the *Commentary* and the *Homilies* were preserved in the West. Because of their simple nature, or perhaps because of medieval veneration for Jerome, the *Homilies* were more widespread and widely quoted in the Middle Ages. Over forty manuscripts dating from the sixth to the fifteenth centuries are extant; their provenances reflect every region of Europe and every style of religious life, from seventh-century Corbie to fifteenth-century Italy.[51] The *Commentary* is extant in about thirty manuscripts, the earliest of which dates from the eleventh century.[52] Even allowing for the possibility that a book could exist without actually having been read, this evidence suggests that Origen's Song of Songs *Commentary* was anything but scarce in medieval Europe, and that his *Homilies* on the Song of Songs were downright popular.

Still, because so few medieval commentaries quote Origen extensively or by name, modern scholars prefer to think of the many copies of his Song of Songs interpretations as decorative rather than functional items of medieval libraries. I would like to take issue with this theory as both impractical and insensitive to the norms of medieval source citation. Medieval readers did not take books lightly; books were difficult to obtain and carefully consulted. Why, if there were so many copies of Origen's interpretations of the Song of Songs, were they not used more openly?

We have already noted one good reason for Origen's low profile: his known heterodoxy. No medieval author could make many points by citing a heretic. But it is also standard procedure in medieval exegesis to draw on as many references as possible while acknowledging as few as necessary. Especially before the scholastic age, exegetes saw their task to be bringing together many learned opinions into one seamless exposition, not in clearly delimiting received and original ideas. And, even though commentary itself can be seen as an act of misreading, these authors did not feel the necessity to react against "strong writers" that Harold Bloom has described as particularly characteristic of Romantic literature. Medieval commentary on the Song of Songs "belongs to the giant age before the flood, before the anxiety of influence became central to poetic consciousness."[53] Within these expectations, Origen's Song of Songs expositions were alive and well in medieval Latin exegesis. I can by no means claim to give an exhaustive discussion of the ways in which they were put to use, for these are just beginning to be understood by modern medievalists, but a few examples will suffice to show how the hidden beginning was continued.

Two fourth-century exegetes, Apponius and Gregory of Elvira, show the open influence of Origen.[54] Ambrose of Milan was influenced by Origen's approach to the Bible in general, as we have seen. Ambrose actually wrote no commentary on the Song of Songs, but cited the text frequently in his writings, always with a spiritual or (admittedly going beyond Origen) a mariological interpretation. Ambrose's comments on verses of the Song of Songs were widely diffused through a systematic *catena* put together by the twelfth-century Cistercian, William of Saint-Thierry.[55] It is also no surprise that Jerome, the translator of Origen's *Homilies* on the Song of Songs, showed the influence of Origen's interpretations. Origen on the Song of Songs is especially evident in Epistle 22, a letter to Eustochium, in which the Song of Songs is cited twenty-five times in support of the spiritual marriage expected of a virgin dedicated to Christ.[56] This is a clear example of the thematic evolution of the genre in the centuries immediately following Origen.

Of course, Apponius, Gregory of Elvira, Ambrose, and Jerome all wrote before the condemnation of Origen in 553. While they may be argued to reflect a muted sense of Origen, they do not present the problem of his influence in its most drastic form. Let us turn, therefore, to the Middle Ages proper, after Origen had been formally declared a heretic, to see the scope of his influence on Song of Songs interpretation.

The influence of Origen is clearly seen in several important medieval commentaries on the Song of Songs, such as that of Gregory the Great.[57] Many interpretations first wrought by Origen (including those of 1:12 and 2:6) are echoed in the ninth-century treatise of Haimo of Auxerre.[58] These reverberations may come from an important intermediary source, the Song of Songs commentary of the Venerable Bede, but in his short prologue, Haimo departs significantly from Bede's model:

> Solomon, inspired by the Holy Spirit, composed this little book about the marriage of Christ and the Church, and made a sort of epithalamium of Christ and the Church, that is, a marriage song. And therefore this little book is called the Song of Songs, since it excels all songs. For just as one says King of Kings, and Lord of Lords, and solemnity of solemnities, so one says Song of Songs, an account of its excellence and dignity. The book is in this way most obscure, since no person is commemorated there, and it is composed in a rather comic style.[59]

Nearly every element of this introduction can be found in some form in Origen's prologues to either the *Commentary* or the *Homilies* on the Song of Songs. They are not found in Bede's commentary. Haimo never mentions his sources by name, but it seems likely that Origen was among them. It is also interesting to see the ways the genre has changed since Origen: how one of Origen's options for interpretation is presented as the basic theme of the Song of Songs, and how the same thematic ideas are presented with subtle changes. Haimo's conception of the "obscurity" of the book is very limited in comparison to that of Origen, since it relates only to a problem *in* the narrative (who are the characters?) rather than a problem *of* narrative. Haimo is clearly not grappling with the text of the Song of Songs in the depth that Origen did, partly because Origen had already done so.

Haimo's succinct, straightforward interpretation of the Song of Songs was a vastly popular text which survives in over seventy manuscripts dated before 1300, and in printed editions starting in 1508.[60] No other Song of Songs commentary was so widely available in medieval libraries.

Haimo's basically ecclesiological exposition thus made one level of Origen's vision of the Song of Songs widely available in medieval Europe. The other level of meaning which Origen found in the Song of Songs, the love between God and the soul, can be seen in a minor mode from the time of Gregory the Great onward. This interpretation becomes common among the eleventh-century reformers, for example, the commentary on the Song of Songs by John of Mantua (ca. 1081) which begins by stating "Solomon's intention in this book is to teach contemplation."[61] John then restates Origen's discussion of the function of Solomon's three books from the prologue of the *Commentary*, completely uncited.

The spiritualizing of the eleventh-century reformers was a prelude to the most fertile period of Christian commentary on the Song of Songs. In the twelfth century, Origen is finally acknowledged as an important source for the commentary tradition. His name first appears in the *Glossa ordinaria*, that popular running gloss on the Bible. One of two early versions of the gloss to the Song of Songs, a twelfth-century text, quotes extensively from Origen's *Homilies*.[62] Through the *Glossa*, many of Origen's interpretations entered the equally popular *Aurora*, a metrical paraphrase of the Bible written by Peter Riga between 1170 and 1200 in Reims and revised by Aegidius of Paris before 1220.[63] The *Aurora* also shows direct knowledge of Origen's *Homilies*; the prologue to the section on the Song of Songs begins with a metrical paraphrase of Jerome's dedicatory epistle to Damasus:

> Only Origen, although he outdid all wise men
> In other books, on the book of Solomon
> Outdid himself with his Canticles work;
> With miraculous art he mixed the useful and the sweet
> Thus he sweated to fill ten books.[64]

Origen's debut as an open source coincides with the flowering of a remarkable spiritual fervor in medieval Christianity. In the twelfth century, the highpoint of the genre of Song of Songs exegesis, the love songs were turned to with increasing frequency as a guide to the spiritual life. This phenomenon again emphasizes the evolution of the genre: what Origen proposed as a variety of interpretative possibilities gradually became didacticism. There is still a variety of interpretation in the genre, however: some authors, like Honorius Augustodunensis, use the four senses of Cassian (thus following a follower of Origen) as a rhetorical model for a multiple understanding of the poems[65] others, like Rupert of Deutz, read the Song of Songs as a poem of love between God and the Virgin Mary.[66] But it is Origen's sense of the drama of Christ and the soul that predominates in twelfth-century exegesis, and the eighty-six homilies of Bernard of Clairvaux that dominate this spiritual understanding.

Bernard's homilies were inspired by and intended for the devotional life of the Cistercian movement.[67] This was clearly fertile ground, for in the century following, six other Cistercian commentaries on the Song of Songs were written, all inspired by Bernard's text.[68] In turn, Bernard was inspired by Origen. Helmut Riedlinger has shown fourteen instances of thematic dependence.[69] Other parallels can be added: discussion of the books of Solomon, identification of Solomon as the Peaceful One, the place of the Song of Songs in biblical canticles as indicated by its superlative title, the interpretation of the opening verse "let him kiss me with the kiss of his mouth," and the fact that Bernard's eighty-six homilies go only four verses beyond the Latin texts of Origen's interpretations.[70]

Since Bernard and Origen shared a passionate concern for the union of the soul with God, these parallels are not surprising. But here, as in much of the preceding tradition, the debt goes unacknowledged; the only reference to Origen in these sermons is a borrowed rebuke about his christology.[71] Leclercq has consequently suggested that Bernard may have known Origen only through an intermediary source.[72] But it should also be noted that Geoffrey of Auxerre, who was asked to undertake the official Cistercian completion of Bernard's interpretation, names Origen and Bernard as the two great expositors of the text, and quotes unmistakably from the Song of Songs *Homilies* of Origen.[73] It seems less strained to suggest that Bernard, like many medieval exegetes, was unwillingly dependent upon Origen's vision of the Song of Songs. Perhaps, though, it could be argued that Bernard's popular exegesis actually encouraged open reference to Origen in the second half of the twelfth century.

The legacy of Origen in the genre of Song of Songs interpretation thus has two sides, perpetually in tension. On the one hand, Origen is the brilliant exegete who "conquered himself" in expounding the holiest song in Scripture; on the other, he is merely a shadow, the heretic who can be quoted but not acknowledged. But even a shadow tradition can be vigorous. This one flourished among the scores of scribes, librarians, and abbots who saw to it that Origen on the Song of Songs, in particular Jerome's translation of the *Homilies*, was readily available in medieval libraries.

This shadow tradition first entered medieval vernacular literature through the most influential translation of the age, the Middle High German part of the double commentary of Williram of Ebersberg. Williram's treatise is strictly dependent on Haimo, combining a poetic version in Latin hexameters with a German prose paraphrase.[74] This curious text, in various forms, was read throughout the later Middle Ages. Its popularity helps to explain the widespread transmission of Origen's vision of the Song of Songs into the new and vibrant world of medieval vernacular literature.

More will be said in chapter seven about the impact of the Song of Songs genre on vernacular literature. I would like to close this consideration of the explicit role of Origen with a story told by one of the most famous of medieval German visionary women, Elisabeth of Schönau. Elisabeth, a Cistercian who died in 1164, was urged by her brother, Egbert, to inquire of the Virgin Mary as to the state of Origen's soul. Perhaps she knew Origen only from the use of his work on the Song of Songs in marian liturgies, for she claims that he praised the Virgin *honorifice et amabiliter* in many places. Still, Elisabeth worried about the fact that the Church condemned Origen because of "many heretical things found in his writings." The Virgin replied that, although the Lord did not wish to reveal much of this matter to Elisabeth, she should know that Origen's error was not a result of evil, but of his over-zealous immersion in the profundities of Scripture; consequently, his penance was not grave.[75] Origen was beyond any doubt the originator of a Christian literary genre in which the seemingly simple carnal passion of the Song of Songs was changed into a complex, but equally erotic spiritual drama of Christ the heavenly Bridegroom. Far from serving as a warning, he seems to have inspired many other Christian writers to zealous immersion in the profundities of Scripture. But Origen's traces in the tradition are as allusive as the Song of Songs itself. One can look for, and (as I hope I have shown) find, fully conscious borrowing from his *Homilies* and *Commentary* in the exegesis of a number of influential authors. His influence may even have stretched beyond the monastic schools and the world of

Latin commentary on a Latin Bible which he helped to form. The hidden origin of this tradition is in itself an example of the ellipses and puns of the allegorical tradition, a subject which will be taken up in the next chapter. Finally, as for Origen, I cannot help but think that medieval exegetes and biblical expositors of all sorts felt his presence keenly, and gladly believed, as the Virgin Mary revealed to Elisabeth of Schönau, that "his penance was not grave."

Notes

1. Important studies of Origen are J. Danielou, *Origène* (Paris: La Table Ronde, 1948), Henri Crouzel, *Origène et la "Connaissance Mystique"* (Paris: Desclée de Brouwer, 1961), and Joseph Wilson Trigg, *Origen: The Bible and Philosophy in the Third-Century Church* (Atlanta: John Knox Press, 1983). See also the introductions of Henry Chadwick, *Origen: Contra Celsum* (Cambridge: Cambridge University Press, 1965), and Rowan Greer, *Origen: An Exhortation to Martyrdom, Prayer, and Selected Works* (New York: Paulist Press, 1979).

2. Clark, p. 386. For background on Origen's intellectual contact with early rabbinic thought, see the excellent discussion of Judith R. Baskin in "Rabbinic-Patristic Exegetical contacts in Late Antiquity: A Bibliographical Appraisal," in *Approaches to Ancient Judaism* Volume V: *Studies in Judaism and Its Greco-Roman Context*, ed. William Scott Green, Brown Judaic Studies 32 (Atlanta: Scholars Press, 1985) pp. 61–64. Among the important studies of this question are Reuven Kimelman, "Rabbi Yohanan and Origen on the Song of Songs: A Third-Century Jewish-Christian Disputation," HTR 73 (1980) 567–595; E. E. Urbach, "The Homiletical Interpretations of the Sages and the Exposition of Origen on Canticles, and the Jewish Christian Disputation," *Scripta Hierosolynitana* 22 (1971) 248–275; N. Lange, *Origen and the Jews* (Cambridge: Cambridge University Press, 1976). For more recent studies focusing on the Jewish context with which Origen may have had contact, see Roger Brooks, "Straw Dogs and Scholarly Ecumenism: The Appropriate Jewish Background for the Study of Origen," and Paul M. Blowers, "Origen, the Rabbis, and the Bible: Toward a Picture of Judaism and Christianity in Third-Century Caesarea," in *Origen of Alexandria: His World and His Legacy*, ed. Charles Kannengiesser and William L. Petersen (Notre Dame, Ind.: University of Notre Dame Press, 1988) pp. 63–95, 96–116. I would like to thank Martha Himmelfarb for her help with this material.

3. Jon Whitman, "Origen's Descent; Antony's Ascent," in *Allegory: The Dynamics of an Ancient and Medieval Technique* (Cambridge, Mass.: Harvard Uni-

versity Press, 1987) pp. 68–77. See also Tzvetan Todorov, *Symbolism and Interpretation*, trans. Catherine Porter (Ithaca, N.Y.: Cornell University Press, 1982) p. 105; Todorov's understanding of patristic exegesis as a "finalist" interpretation will be discussed in more detail in the next chapter.

4. *Contra Celsum* 1:9, trans. Chadwick, p. 12. The discussion continues through 1:11. For an unusual analysis of Celsus's attitude toward the Bible, see Marcel Borret, "L'Écriture d'après le païen Celse," *Bible de tous les temps, 1. Le Monde grec ancien et la Bible*, ed. Claude Mondésert (Paris, 1984) 171–193.

5. This is especially clear in the *Dialogue with Heracleides*, ed. J. Scherer, *Entretien d'Origène avec Héraclide et les évèques ses collègues sur le Père, le Fils, et l'Âme* (Cairo: Publications de la Société Fouad I de Papyrologie, 1949), English translation by Henry Chadwick in Oulton and Chadwick, *Alexandrian Christianity*, LCC 2, pp. 430–455. The quotation is from W. H. C. Frend, *The Rise of Christianity* (Philadelphia: Fortress Press, 1984) p. 377.

6. Trigg, p. 111. For Origen's Platonism, see also Frend, pp. 373–381.

7. *Contra Celsum* V,19, trans. Chadwick, p. 279; see also VI,29.

8. See Trigg's essay on the aftermath of Origen, pp. 246–256.

9. Peter Brown, *The Body and Society: Men, Women, and Sexual Renunciation in Early Christianity* (New York: Columbia University Press, 1988) p. 169. The reference is to Eusebius, Eccles. Hist. 6.8.2–3.

10. John Cassian, *Collationes* xiv, viii, ed. E. Pictery, SC 54 (1958) 189–93. *Regula Sancti Benedicti*, 42, ed. R. Hanslik, CSEL 75 (1960). On Cassian, see also Owen Chadwick, *John Cassian: A Study in Primitive Monasticism* (Cambridge: Cambridge University Press, 1968).

11. PG 44: 775–1120, and ed. H. Langerbeck, *Gregorii Nysseni Opera*, VI (Leiden: Brill, 1960). See also the new English translation of the complete commentary by Brother McCambley (Brookline, Mass: Hellenic College Press, 1987).

12. Defending his translation of Origen's homilies on the Song of Songs, Jerome wrote to Pammachius and Oceanus, "legi, inquam, legi Origenem et, si in legendo crimen est, fateor—et nostrum marsuppium Alexandrinae chartae euacuarent—:si mihi creditis, Origeniastes numquam fui; si non creditis, nunc esse cessavi." Epistle 84, ed. I. Hilberg, CSEL 55 (1913) p. 124.

13. Ambrose's borrowing from the Song of Songs expositions of Origen in the *De Isaac*, CSEL 32, 1 (1896) pp. 640–700) has been studied by Solange Sagot, "Le 'Cantique des Cantiques' dans le 'De Isaac d'Ambroise de Milan," RAug 16 (1981) 3–57. For more general treatments of this author, see G. Madec, *Saint Ambroise et la philosophie* (Paris: Études Augustiniennes, 1974), and H. Savon, *Saint Ambroise devant l'exégèse de Philon le Juif* (Paris: Études Augustiniennes, 1977). A *catena* of Song of Songs commentary attributed to Ambrose was circulated throughout the Middle Ages; the best-known version is printed in PL 15 (1887):1947–2060.

14. For a study of Ambrose's influence on Augustine, see Peter Brown, *Au-*

gustine of Hippo (Berkeley: University of California Press, 1969) pp. 79–87. The classical understanding of this association is sketched by Pierre Courcelle, *Recherches sur les Confessions de S. Augustin* (Paris: E. de Boccard, 1950). Augustine tells how Ambrose opened for him the mysteries of the Bible in *Confessiones* VI, iv.6:

> Littera occidit, spiritus autem uiuificat (2 Cor. 3:6), cum ea, quae ad litteram peruersitatem docere uidebantur, remoto mystico uelamento spiritaliter aperiret, non dicens quod me offenderet, quamivis ea diceret, quae utrum vera essent adhuc ignorarem.

Ed. L. Verheijen, CCSL 27 (1981) p. 77.

15. Riedlinger, pp. 20–23; Ohly, p. 15.

16. The texts are edited by Baehrens, *Origenes Werke* 8, GCS 33 (1925) pp. xiv–xx and 26–60 for the homilies; xx–xxviii and 61–241 for the commentary. All page references are to these editions. See also the edition of the homilies by O. Rousseau, SC 37bis (1966), and the English translation of R. P. Lawson, *Origen. The Song of Songs. Commentary and Homilies*, Ancient Christian Writers Series 26 (New York: Newman Press, 1957). Jerome refers to "alios tomos II, quos super scripsit in adulescentia" among Origen's treatments of the Song of Songs, Epistle 33 (to Paula), ed. I. Hilberg, CSEL 54, 1 (1910) pp. 256–257.

17. See ed. Baehrens, p. xxviii for a discussion of the Greek fragments.

18. For a comparison of Jerome and Rufinus as translators of Origen, see G. Bardy, *Recherches sur l'histoire du texte et des versions latines du De principiis d'Origène* (Paris: 1923), E. Champion and Friedhelm Winkelmann, "Einige Bemerkungen zu den Aussagen des Rufinus von Aquileia und des Hieronymus über ihre Übersetzungstheorie und Methode," in *Kyriakon: Festschrift Johannes Quasten*, ed. Patrick Granfeld and Josef A. Jungmann (Münster, Westf.: Verlag Aschendorff, 1970) vol. 2, pp. 532–547. In "*Ad Verbum* or *Ad Sensum*? Latin Translation Theory in the Fourth Century," a paper presented at the Philadelphia Seminar on Christian Origins in May, 1989, William Adler suggested that Rufinus invoked a general theory of translation *ad sensum*. Jerome, in contrast, usually claimed to translate *ad sensum*, but invoked translation *ad verbum* in the case of the Bible and in the polemic with Rufinus over Origen's *De principiis*. Adler characterizes Jerome as usually driven more by apologetic and polemical concerns than by a coherent theory of translation.

19. "si philosophorum argutias propiis tractatibus miscuisset et a malo exordio in fabulas quasdam et deliramenta procedens Christianum dogma ludum et iocum faceret nequaquam diuinae doctrinae ueritate utens, sed humanae mentis arbitrio et in tantam se ipso magistro intumescens superbiam" Jerome, Epistle 96.6, ed. I. Hilberg, CSEL 55 (1913) p. 163.

20. Rufinus, "De adulteratione librorum Origenis," "Apologia ad Anastasium," "Apologia contra Hieronymum," ed. M. Simonetti, CCSL 20 (1961) pp. 7–22, 25–28, 37–123.

21. In his preface to *De principiis* I, Rufinus says "cum aliquanta offendicula inueniatur in Graeco, ita elimauit omnia interpretando atque purgauit, ut nihil in illis quod a fide nostra discrepet Latinus lector inueniat." ed. M. Simonetti, CCSL 20, pp. 245–246. Winkelmann, p. 544, characterizes this as a choice for practical and ethical, rather than theological, considerations.

22. "Origenes hereticus: quid ad me, qui illum in plerisque hereticum non nego?" Jerome, Epistle 61.2, ed. I. Hilberg, CSEL 54,1 (1910) p. 577. See also Riedlinger, p. 23, note 3. For Jerome's fear of Rufinus's success, see Brown, *The Body and Society*, p. 380. On the condemnation of Origen, see Bardy, pp. 49–86. For a long passage on the errors of Origen, see Jerome, Epistle 96.5–6, ed. I. Hilberg, CSEL 55 (1913) pp. 162–164.

23. "Vult aliquis laudare Origenem? laudet, et laudo: magnus vir ab infantia voluptates in tantum fugiit, ut zelo dei, sed non secundum scientiam ferro truncaret genitalia; calcauit avaritiam; scripturas memoriter tenuit et in studio explanationis earum diebus sudavit ac noctibus." Jerome, Epistle 84.8, ed. I. Hilberg, CSEL 55 (1913) p. 130.

24. Preface to the *Homilies*, p. 26.

25. *Homily* I,1, p. 27/ *Commentary* prologue, pp. 79–80; *Homily* I,1, p. 29/ *Commentary* prologue, p. 61.

26.

> Epitalamium libellus hic, id est nuptiale carmen, dramatis in modum mihi videtur a Solomone conscriptus, quem cecinit instar nubentis sponsae et erga sponsum suum, qui est sermo Dei, caelesti amore flagrantis. Adamavit enim eum sive anima, quae ad imaginem eius facta est, sive ecclesia.

Commentary prologue p. 61. See also *Homily* I,1 pp. 21. Although the homilies do not state in theory that the Bride represents the soul, the interpretation is nevertheless present: I,6, pp. 35–36; II,4, pp. 47–48.

27. *De principiis* IV, 12, ed. P. Koetschau, *Origenes Werke* 5, GCS 30 (1913) pp. 344–345. See also Frend, p. 378, for Origen's Platonic exegesis.

28. *Commentary* prologue, p. 62.

29. Urbach, pp. 257–258. See Pope, pp. 93–102, for a detailed comparison of Origen's prologue to the Targum of the Song of Songs. Although the written redaction of the Targum probably dates to the seventh century, this represents only the date by which the material, from a much earlier oral tradition of Palestinian sages, was crystallized.

30. In his dedicatory epistle to Pope Damasus, Jerome characterizes the *Homilies* as "hos duos tractatus, quos in morem cotidiani eloquii *paruulis* adhuc lactantibusque composuit," ed. Rousseau, CSEL 37bis (1966) p. 62. Brown suggests this refers to Jerome's circle of female spiritual charges, *The Body and Society*, p. 367.

31. *Homily* I,4, pp. 33–34: "In universa terra Christus nominatur, in omni mundo praedicatur Dominus meus; 'unguentum' enim 'effusum' est 'nomen' eius." p. 33.

32. *Commentary* I, pp. 101–108:

Potest sane in his prophetia quaedam videri ex persona sponsae prolata de Christo, quod futurum esset, ut in adventu Domini et Salvatoris nostri nomen eius ita per orbem terrae et per universum mundum diffunderetur, ut fieret "odor suavitatis in omni loco," sicut et Apostolus dicit: "quia Christi bonus odor sumus in omni loco, aliis quidem odor ex morte in mortem, aliis autem odor de vita in vitam." (p. 101)

33. Congruent text of Procopius given by ed. Baehrens, p. 101.
34. *Homily* II, 1–2, pp. 42–44/ *Commentary* II, pp. 165–168.
35.

Habet et "sinistram" et "dexteram" Sermo Dei; sapientia, cum pro intellectus varietate sit multiplex, in subiacenti una est. Ipse Solomon de "laeva" et "dextera" sapientiae docuit dicens: "longitudo enim et anni vitae in dextera eius, in sinistra autem illius divitiae et gloria." (Proverbs 3:16) (*Homily* II,9, p. 54, developed pp. 54–55)

Ipsa est enim hic sponsi "dextera" et "laeva," quae in proverbiis de "sapientia" dicitur, ubi ait: "longitudo enim vitae in dextera eius, in sinistra vero eius divitiae et gloria. *Commentary* III, p. 195 (developed pp. 195–197).

36. For analysis of this theme, see Jacques Chênevert, *L'Église dans le commentaire d'Origène sur le Cantique des Cantiques* (Paris: Desclée de Brouwer, 1969). Along with what is thought of as the "French school" of Origen studies, Chênevert stresses Origen's mystical and spiritual writings. This view is contested by Franz Heinrich Kettler, *Der ursprüngliche Sinn der Dogmatik des Origenes*, Beiheft zur Zeitschrift für die Neutestamentliche Wissenschaft 31 (Berlin: Töpelmann, 1966), who uses *De principiis* to portray Origen as a systematic theologian. My reading of Origen is basically in agreement with Chênevert.

37. Patricia Cox Miller, " 'Pleasure of the Text, Text of Pleasure' Eros and Language in Origen's commentary on the Song of Songs," JAAR 54 (1986) p. 243.

38. Miller, p. 243, especially note 4, for a discussion of terms. In this choice of terminology, Miller is guided by Roland Barthes, *The Pleasure of the Text*, trans. Richard Miller (New York: Hill and Wang, 1975).

39. William E. Phipps, "The Plight of the Song of Songs," JAAR 42 (1974) pp. 86–87.

40. Phipps, pp. 90–91.

41.

Text of pleasure: the text that contents, fills, grants euphoria; the text that comes from culture and does not break with it, is linked to a *comfortable* practice of reading. Text of bliss: the text that imposes a state of loss, the text that discomforts (perhaps to the extent of a certain boredom), unsettles the reader's

> historical, cultural, psychological assumptions, the consistency of his tastes, values, memories, brings to a crisis his relation with language.

Barthes, p. 14.

42. Miller, pp. 245, 251.

43. Barbara Johnson, *The Critical Difference* (Baltimore: Johns Hopkins University Press, 1980) p. 13. Emphases mine.

44. Mary Daly, *Pure Lust: Elemental Feminist Philosophy* (Boston: Beacon Press, 1984) p. 36.

45. Daly, p. 72.

46. Quoted from Peter Brown, *The Body and Society*, p. 177. This chapter is an excellent summary of Origen's attitude towards the body. I am grateful to Patricia Cox Miller for suggesting the link between "codes" of the body and of Scripture. For the shift to a more modern perspective, see Michel Foucault, *La Volonté de savoir* (Paris: Éditions Gallimard, 1976), translated by Robert Hurley as *The History of Sexuality: An Introduction* (New York: Penguin Press, 1978), especially "The Incitement to Discourse," pp. 17–35.

47. I have developed the argument of the rest of this chapter in "Il *Cantico dei Cantici* nel contesto del cristianesimo medievale: L'eredità di Origene," *Aevum* 61,2 (1987) 303–312.

48.

> Quae est ista exclamatio tam magna, tam repentina? O beata Maria, inundatio gaudii, uis amoris, torrens uoluptatis, totam te operuit totam te obtinuit penitusque inebriauit, et sensisti *quod oculus non uidit et auris non audiuit et in cor hominis non ascendit*, et dixisti: *Osculetur me in osculo oris sui.*

Rupert of Deutz, *In Canticum Canticorum* I,1, ed. H. Haacke, CCCM 26 (1974) p. 10. This text will be discussed in detail in chapter six; see chapter six note 32 in particular.

49. Riedlinger, pp. 24–27, for a summary of opinion. See also Valerie Flint, "The Commentaries of Honorius Augustodunensis on the Song of Songs," RB 84 (1974) 196–211. Henri de Lubac disagrees with the prevailing scholarly opinion, I,1, (1959), pp. 221–238.

50. Riedlinger attributes to Origen the interpretation which became the basic ground of exegesis for centuries, p. 41; and shows Origen on the Song of Songs in patristic authors, pp. 78–79.

51. See ed. Baehrens, pp. xiv–xix, and Stegmüller, vol. 4 (1954) #6199.

52. Ed. Baehrens, pp. xx–xxvi; Stegmüller, vol. 4 (1954) #6200.

53. Harold Bloom, *The Anxiety of Influence: A Theory of Poetry* (Oxford: Oxford University Press, 1971) p. 11, speaking of Shakespeare. Bloom continues: "Shakespeare is the largest instance in the language of a phenomenon that stands outside the concern of this book: the absolute absorption of the precursor."

54. Apponius, *In Canticum Canticorum expositio*, ed. B. de Vregille and L. Neyrand, CCSL 19 (1986); Gregory of Elvira, *Tractatus in epithalamium* (*In*

Cantica Canticorum Libri Quinque), ed. J. Fraipont, CCSL 69 (1967) pp. 169–210. See chapter four below.

55. PL 15:(1887): 1947–2060; Riedlinger, pp. 42, 167.

56. Clark, pp. 402–403, notes that Ep. 22 was probably written when Jerome was working on the translation of Origen's *Homilies* on the Song of Songs. The text is edited by I. Hilberg in CSEL 54,1 (1910) pp. 143–211.

57. Gregory the Great, *Expositio in Canticum Canticorum*, ed. P. Verbraken, CCSL 144 (1963), and R. Bélanger, SC 314 (1984), discussed in chapter four below.

58. PL 117:295–358; Ohly, pp. 73–75; Riedlinger, pp. 94–97, for the colorful history of the text (variously ascribed to Cassiodorus, Haimo of Halberstadt, and Thomas Aquinas). For the text, see chapter four below.

59.

> Solomon, inspiratus divino Spiritu, composuit hunc libellum de nuptiis Christi et Ecclesiae, et quodammodo epithalamium fecit Christi et Ecclesiae, id est canticum super thalamos. Unde et Cantica canticorum vocavit hunc libellum, quia omnia cantica superexcellit. Sicut enim dicitur rex regum, et Dominus dominantium, et solemnitas solemnitatum, sic dicuntur Cantica canticorum ob excellentiam et dignitatem. Est autem in hoc obscurissimus iste liber, quia nullae ibi personae commemorantur, et quasi comico stylo compositus est.

PL 117:295A. Compare to Bede, PL 91:1065–1236. This commentary will be discussed in chapter four.

60. Stegmüller, vol. 3 (1951) #3079, as pseudo-Cassiodorus, #3080. A 1508 edition printed in Pavia by Jacob de Burgofrancho is found in Pavia, Biblioteca Universitaria, Miscellanea Ticinensia XVI, #6.

61. "Intentio Salomonis est docere in hoc libro contemplari," *Iohannis Mantuani in Cantica Canticorum*, ed. B. Bischoff and B. Taeger, SpF 19 (1973) p.26 Compare to Origen's prologue commentary, p. 83.

62. Listed by Riedlinger, p. 126 note 8. His version of the gloss was printed in Venice in 1588; Ohly cites another early printing, Antwerp, 1634, pp. 111–112. The *Glossa ordinaria* printed in PL 113 as Walafrid Strabo is a distinct version, mostly from the commentary of Robert of Tombelaine. For the history of the gloss, see Smalley, pp. 46–66.

63. P. E. Beichner, ed., *Aurora Petri Rigae Biblia Versificata* (Notre Dame, Ind.: Notre Dame University Press, 1965), vol. 2 for the Song of Songs. Riedlinger lists quotations from Origen, p. 144, n.10–12.

64.

> Solus Origenes, cum doctos uicerit omnes, / In libris aliis, tamen in libro Salomonis / Ipse sui uictor fuit eius Cantica tractans; / Qui miro studio permiscens utile dulci / Sic desudauit ut dena uolumina complens.

Ed. Beichner, p. 703. Two revisions of this prologue by Aegidius are given on pp. 760–761. Compare all three to Riedlinger's transcription of the Vatican manuscript, p. 144 n.8. The reference to sweat comes from Jerome, Epistle 84, see note 23 above.

65. PL 172:347–469. The two long prefaces (347–358) owe much to Origen, and the preface to the first part (357C–359) sets forth Cassian's scheme. On the twelfth century, see F. Ohly, "Geist und Formen der Hoheliedauslegung im 12. Jahrhundert," ZfDA 85 (1954) 181–197. Cassian's scheme and Honorius's commentary will be discussed at length in the next chapter.

66. Ed. Haacke, see chapter six for this and other commentaries in the marian mode.

67. Bernard of Clairvaux, *Sermones super Cantica Canticorum*, OB 1–2, (1957–1958). For the history of the text see chapter five below.

68. The treatises of William of Saint-Thierry, PL 180:473–546; Gilbert of Hoyland, PL 184:11–252; Geoffrey of Auxerre, ed. F. Gastaldelli, TT 19, 20 (1974); Thomas the Cistercian, PL 206:17–860; and Rupert of Olmütz, unedited, cf. Riedlinger, pp. 179–180.

69. Riedlinger, p. 156 n.7, based on shared biblical quotations.

70. Bernard, 1, 2 OB 1, pp. 3–4/Origen, *Commentary* prologue, p. 75; Bernard, 1,6 OB 1, p.5/Origen, *Commentary* prologue, p. 84; Bernard, 1, 7 OB 1, pp. 5–6/Origen, *Commentary* prologue, p. 80; Bernard, 1, 8 OB 1, p. 6/Origen, *Homily* I,2, pp. 29–31. Bernard's collection ends with a lengthy treatment of Song of Songs 3:1.

71. *Sermo* 54,3, OB 2, p. 104. Taken from Jerome, Ep. 96, 10, ed. I. Hilberg, CSEL 54, 2 (1912) p.163.

72. J. Leclercq, "Origène au xii siècle," *Irenikon* 24 (1951) 430–439, especially p. 432. See also Leclercq, "Saint Bernard et Origène d'après un manuscrit de Madrid," RB 59 (1949) 183–195.

73. As edited by Gastaldelli, vol. 1, p. 100. Note Geoffrey's use of the Origen/Jerome word "floritionis" (from Homily II) p. 45,3. Geoffrey declined the task of completing Bernard's work, but compiled his own commentary, in a long form for leasure reading, and a gloss for hasty consultation.

74. E. H. Bartelmez, *The "Expositio in Cantica Canticorum" of Williram Abbot of Ebersberg, 1048–1085* (Philadelphia: American Philosophical Society, 1967), discussed in chapter seven below.

75. See the edition of Elisabeth's visions by F. W. E. Roth, *Die Visionen der heiligen. Elisabeth und die Schriften der Äbte Ekbert und Emecho von Schönau* (Brünn, 1884), *Liber visionum* III, c. 5, pp. 62–63.

Chapter Three

The Key to the Code: Allegory and the Song of Songs

The last chapter pointed to allegory as a major factor of medieval Song of Songs commentaries, one not always sympathetically received by modern readers. In part this is due to modern suspicion of traditional Christian language about the body, but the problem also clearly begins with the profoundly erotic nature of the text itself. Especially as a canonical book of Christian Scripture, the Song of Songs presents a number of oddities which invite elaboration on a level "beyond" (or at least "away from") the apparent surface. In eight chapters of love lyrics, the Song of Songs suggests unification by means of repeating images and phrases; these hint at the possibility of an underlying structure, but contain no clear narrative development. The Song of Songs thus has inspired a steady stream of commentary which must always begin with the problem of sense at a basic level of the text. In this, it differs essentially from the narrative accounts of the Hebrew Bible (Pentateuch, Former Prophets, Chronicles) since even allegorical interpretations of books like Genesis or Kings assume a level of story-telling as history, which is not clearly present in the Song of Songs. Nor does the Song of Songs fit easily into other biblical categories, such as prophecy, or even "wisdom literature" (the class in which it is usually placed along with Proverbs, Ecclesiastes, and Job) since, on the surface, it tells no sacred history, makes no theological nor moral points, and does not mention God.

The Twentieth-Century Debate

For twentieth-century commentary, the most compelling question has been what the Song of Songs originally "was," that is, what meaning it carried at or before the stage of redaction in which we find it in the Hebrew Bible. Modern interpreters of the Song of Songs, working from the philological, literary, and archaeological discoveries of the nineteenth and twentieth centuries, have arrived at three basic points of view: 1) that the Song of Songs is a collection of love lyrics included in the biblical canon as a testimony to the goodness of human love; 2) that it is a cultic poem with themes drawn from ancient religious traditions, adapted to represent the sacred marriage of God and Israel; 3) that the love between God and Israel is the true meaning of the poem, which was written as a prophetic allegory in the manner of the Book of Hosea.

The first theory, perhaps the most widely accepted, is expounded by a number of scholars from different traditions. The Jewish interpreter Robert Gordis, while acknowledging that the Song of Songs was included in the canon because of allegorical interpretation, argues nevertheless that the text originally spoke of human love.[1] This position is accepted by the Christian scholars Roland E. Murphy[2] and Phyllis Trible; the latter adds a feminist interpretation by reading the Song of Songs as the redemption of mutual human love, lost in Genesis 2–3.[3]

Interpretation of the Song of Songs as an ancient cultic text began with the early twentieth-century discoveries of parallel material in Egyptian and Canaanite religious literature.[4] Marvin H. Pope has stated the most sophisticated contemporary version of this theory, arguing that the Song of Songs originated in a context involving connected rites of fertility and death which were practiced in the ancient world from the Ganges to the Mediterranean.[5] The cult theory lends itself to continual reformulation in the light of new understandings of ancient Mesopotamian, Egyptian, and Ugaritic texts. But as often as they are restated, cultic theories of the Song of Songs are challenged, both by scholars who see in the same ancient parallels an original context of purely secular poetry,[6] and by those, like Gordis, who assess the possibility of a cult connection as at best "a secular reworking of a no longer extant litany of an assumed Israelite cult which left no record of its existence behind it," and, in any case, an unlikely explanation for a text included in a canon which stresses particularistic, *national* literature.[7]

Recognition that the Song of Songs belongs to a collection of Jewish religious literature is the starting point for the third modern approach, which might be characterized as one of historical allegory. This understanding of the text has been articulated by Christian scholars, who see the original meaning of the Song of Songs as an expression of love between God and the people of Israel, expressed in the context of messianic longing and in the language of Hebrew prophecy.[8] The commentary of A. Robert makes it clear that the Bridegroom of the Song of Songs is God, not to be confounded with the Messiah, but that the very name Solomon, "The Peaceful One," is meant to evoke messianic expectations.[9] Although Robert does not insist on the point, it is easy to move from this perspective to the traditional Christian reading of the Song of Songs as telling the love between Christ and the Church.

The tradition of Song of Songs interpretation developed by traditional Judaism is, however, somewhat different from this argument of modern Christian biblical scholarship. As all modern commentators recognize, the inclusion of the Song of Songs in the canon of Scripture was based on the assumption of a recognized and accepted allegorical reading. The Targum and Midrashim on the Song of Songs show two basic strategies for allegorization: the text is understood either as the song of love between God and Israel celebrating the giving of the Torah on Mount Sinai, or as the song of love revealed at the installation of the Ark of the Covenant in the Temple at Jerusalem. It was on the basis of these interpretations, already ancient in the first century of the common era, that Rabbi Akiba defended the canonicity and sacrality of the Song of Songs with the famous phrase: "the whole world is not worth the day on which the Song of Songs was given to Israel, for all the Scriptures are holy, but the Song of Songs is the Holy of Holies."[10]

This heritage of allegory was passed on to Christian exegetes along with the canon of the Hebrew Bible. The Jewish tradition of allegorizing specific passage of Scripture with reference to salvation history is already present in Paul's epistles; from this there developed a general assumption of Christian exegesis that the "Old Testament" is reflected in the "New Testament."[11] For Christian readings of the Song of Songs, especially as popularized by Origen, this assumption automatically suggested the scope of prior meanings; that is, the poems read by Jews as the love between God and Israel naturally find their "true" sense as the love between Christ and the Church.

But even if the last category of modern interpretation of the Song of Songs can be seen as a method for supporting Christian allegorical interpretation, it is nevertheless clear that the argument proceeds, as in all modern biblical scholarship, from the assumption that the true meaning of the text must be determined through a study of the Hebrew text in its original historical context. To a large extent, the modern debates about the Song of Songs center around variant interpretations of this context:

did it primarily affirm the body, echo non-Hebrew cults, or rhapsodize about the love of God and his promises for the salvation of his people? Although they are based on philology, archaeology, and literary structures, it is evident that the answers to these questions are not always, or not only, "scientific." Still, this modern focus on the original function of the Song of Songs is strikingly different from the medieval agreement that the text had no literal or historical sense. A study of medieval Christian exegesis of the Song of Songs brings us instead deep into the forest of allegory.

Theories of Allegory, Medieval and Modern

We have already seen that Jewish allegorical interpretation of the Song of Songs was an important source for the medieval exegetical tradition. There was as well another, equally influential and more theoretical, stream of thought about allegory from which Christian scholars worked.

Modern critics, theoreticians and historians alike, are very well aware of the special role played by *De doctrina christiana*, the theoretical masterpiece of Augustine of Hippo, in the formalization of a western medieval hermeneutic of allegory.[12] Augustine describes the difficulty of Scripture with delight, claiming that the authors of biblical books:

> have spoken with a useful and healthful obscurity for the purpose of exercising and sharpening, as it were, the minds of the readers and of destroying fastidiousness and stimulating the desire to learn, concealing their intention in such a way that the minds of the impious are either converted to piety or excluded from the mysteries of the faith.[13]

For Augustine, the first step in this mental exercise is the recognition of the epistemological chasm between those things which are to be used ("uti") and those things which are to be enjoyed ("frui"). The only proper object of enjoyment, the only thing to be loved in and for itself is God.[14] The purpose of interpretation is to *use* all of the tools of language to *enjoy* God's manifestation in Scripture.

De doctrina christiana is mostly concerned with the elaboration of rules for the use of language to the enjoyment of God; included are elucidations of tropes and other rhetorical devices, and of the limits of allegorical interpretation. Augustine describes the points at which allegory should be triggered, and the ways of making sure that the meanings uncovered are the ones intended by the Holy Spirit. This process is ultimately circular, depending on the recognized meaning of other passages of the Bible. But this method of interpretation is especially important for medieval allegorical exegesis, since it allows for "true" meaning (or, even better, meanings) to be found in the text even beyond those recognized by the author. The passages ends triumphally:

> For what could God have more generously and abundantly provided in the divine writings than that the same words might be understood in various ways which other no less divine witnesses approve?[15]

Augustine's primary concern here is not to map out the concrete number of meanings which the Holy Spirit may have placed in a passage of Scripture, but to call attention to the depth and complexity of these meanings. *De doctrina christiana* does, however, quote at length from the work *Of Rules* by a fellow North-African (though Donatist) theologian named Tyconius. Tyconius "explained seven rules with which, as if with keys, the obscurities of the Divine Scriptures might be opened." These are: "Of the Lord and His Body," "Of the Bipartite Body of the Lord," "Of Promises and the Law," "Of Species and Genus," "Of Times," "Of Recapitulation," and "Of the Devil and his Body."[16] Although each of these titles is meant to point out a different realm of allegory, the *Rules* are too complicated and subtle to have been widely used, in spite of the exposure they received through *De doctrina christiana*. They were known throughout the Middle Ages, however, and may have been the inspiration for the equally cumbersome seven-fold exegesis of Angelomus of Luxeuil on the book of Kings.[17]

At the beginning of his literary career, in the treatise *De utilitate credendi*, Augustine located four levels of meaning in the biblical text: historical (what has been written or done), etiological (the cause for which a thing is done), analogical (showing that the Old and New Testaments do not conflict), and allegorical (showing some things are to be understood figuratively rather than literally).[18] This system is rather vague for use as a guide to specific allegorical interpretations; Augustine actually put it to work in one of his commentaries on Genesis, but few other Latin Christian authors followed this lead. They seemed to find the principles (for example, the idea that the historical sense might be ultimately a *literary* one) more directly useful than the categories. In general, Augustine's scheme provides support for an *approach* to biblical interpretation, stressing the multi-vocality of Scripture and thus continuing the tradition of Origen and Ambrose.

The widespread exegetical practice of the Middle Ages found a more practical framework in the writings of another fifth-century monk, John Cassian. In his ascetical guide, the *Collationes*, speaking of the many possible meanings of the single word "Jerusalem," Cassian wrote:

> Jerusalem may be understood in four ways: according to history (*secundum historiam*) the city of the Jews, according to allegory (*secundum allegoriam*) the Church of Christ, according to anagogy (*secundum anagogen*) that celestial city of God, which is the mother of us all, according to tropology (*secundum tropologiam*) the human soul.[19]

As one of the recommended community readings of Benedictine monasticism, the *Collationes* was widely known in the Latin Middle Ages. This particular passage, however, became disproportionately influential in medieval exegesis; unlike the seven rules of Tyconius, or Augustine's four modes of interpretation, the four levels set forth by Cassian became the standard of medieval Latin exegesis. As Beryl Smalley puts it, this example "caught the fancy of the middle ages and became classical."[20]

Medieval exegesis of all biblical books, throughout many centuries, shows an awareness of this interpretive scheme, although usually in the order which de Lubac has characterized as the "second formula," where last things come last: historical, allegorical, tropological, anagogical.[21] This theory of "the four senses" was popularized in the later medieval and early modern periods through a little poem attributed to Nicholas of Lyra.

> littera gesta docet, quid credas allegoria,
> moralis quid agas, quo tendas anagogia.[22]

The jingle shows that Cassian's "tropological" sense was received as exclusively concerned with the human soul and moral life; and that "allegory," which Cassian defined specifically as the level of interpretation centered on Christ and the Church, was seen as essentially theological. Judson Allen has found a similar pattern in the "structural system" of the four-fold method: he argues that the allegorical level traditionally has to do with beliefs (on the level of idea/mind), the tropological with behavior (human action).[23]

Medieval Latin exegesis is striking in the flexibility with which Cassian's four-fold system is used. Many exegetes refer to "mystical," "allegorical," "moral," and "spiritual" senses of Scripture with anything but consistency, and they do not always distinguish allegory (as the Church in the world) from anagogy (as the Church in the age to come).[24] Yet there is always a self-consciousness in the use of these categories that implies a shared understanding of what they mean, even without explicit reference to the scheme.

Gregory the Great's famous *Moralia* on the Book of Job makes no overt mention of Cassian's four senses (although, as one familiar with the *Rule* of Benedict, he may well have been aware of the Jerusalem example); but he employs a method of interpretation which begins by distinguishing between the literal meaning of Scripture and the meanings which the Holy Spirit intended to be discovered there. As the title of the work suggests, Gregory understands Job's story as, basically, a tale of the moral life; nevertheless, he sometimes reads Job's tribulations as the adversities which have troubled the Church, and these are shown to rest visibly on the history of the Jews. In this way, the "historical" sense of the text can be said to be enriched by "spiritual" meanings, further divided into exegetical categories along Cassian's lines.[25] When Gregory began to write on the Song of Songs, he described allegory as a vehicle, literally as a "machine," which lifts the human soul across the vast distance separating this world from God, thus giving human understanding access to divine mystery.[26] Gregory characterizes the biblical text as God's "condescension" to human language, which is in turn elevated by allegory.

Modern critics familiar with this traditional language of Christian allegory have developed some insightful theoretical models for how the medieval allegorical system functioned. In an analysis of *The Quest of the Holy Grail*, a work which resonates with medieval biblical exegesis, Tzvetan Todorov shows how medieval allegory operates on two narrative levels, passing from one to the other by means of a commonly recognized code.[27] Todorov points out that the correspondence between levels of meaning is simple: "the sun is luminous, Jesus Christ is luminous; hence the sun can signify Jesus Christ." Yet, especially to a modern reader, the system of this code is bewilderingly complex and uncertain, since it opens up a seemingly limitless number of possible predicates that could be attached to any given subject, further increasing "the arbitrariness of ordinary language."[28]

In the medieval system of interpretation. Todorov says, this seeming arbitrariness is modified by two assumptions. First, the interpretation involves a priori thinking: "The overdetermined arbitrariness" of an allegorical text is "circumscribed and regularized by the fact that *we know what we will find.*" In Todorov's analysis of what he calls "patristic interpretation" as a hermeneutical strategy, the determination of this a priori meaning is clarified by the assumption of divine inspiration of the Bible, and by the demands of Christian doctrine.[29] Further, this mode of interpretation assumes a final unity among all the possible levels of meaning. Todorov reads *The Quest* as a text which strives to teach the deep connections of this hermeneutic, to show that "Every event has a literal meaning *and* an allegorical meaning . . . the dynamism of the narrative rests on this fusion of the two in one."[30]

Medieval allegory is, therefore, far more complicated than a simple substitution of the heavenly for the earthly; this is especially important and illuminating for the case of Latin exegesis of the Song of Songs. Judson Allen has made us aware that the late medieval tradition of commentary described the Song of Songs as one of a very few texts in which the *forma tractatus* is equal to the *forma tractandi*, for, as the ordering of the poems delights and soothes the soul, the inner meaning of the love between Christ and the soul expresses the same sweetness.[31] The medieval exegetical tradition approaches the Song of Songs as a revelation of "the real" love, God's love, but written in human words and using the more accessible language of human love. The Song of Songs is thus a message in code, and the key to the code is the complex hermeneutic of medieval Christian allegory.[32]

This glimpse into the mechanism of medieval interpretation helps to explain why the Song of Songs was able to generate such a wealth of commentary, why, indeed, it became the basis of a tradition of medieval literature. Surely, these sacred love poems present one of the most appealing, and difficult, examples of "heavenly discourse" in biblical language. They also present a challenge to the medieval literary impulse to mediate between what Todorov defines as "narrative and ritual, or, one might say, the profane and the religious."[33] Latin interpretation of the Song of Songs strives for narrative; the primary objective of breaking the code was to turn the text into a narrative plot.

The Song of Songs is striking in its unresolved hints of narrativity. Although the voice of the text is entirely in the first person, it actually seems that more than several characters are speaking. Consequently, even before the tradition of Christian commentary, the Song of Songs was copied with a series of rubrics which indicated the voices as *dramatis personae*. As early as the second-century Codex Sinaiticus, these voices turned the poems into a drama; in the Latin Bible tradition, such rubrics became increasingly elaborate and increasingly identified the interlocutors as Christ and the Church.[34] This may be one of the earliest examples of allegorical interpretation of the Song of Songs; it certainly is evidence of an interpretive strategy through which the text achieves a narrative coherence.

Many modern literary theorists have recognized that the nature of allegorical interpretation is to create narrative, a narrative, furthermore, that is by nature de-historicized. Paul de Man, for example, characterizes allegory as "sequential and narrative, yet the topic of its narration is not necessarily temporal at all."[35] Jacques Derrida suggests that this understanding highlights allegory as the power of language to speak at once of itself and of something else[36] And, in reference to the allegory of medieval secular literature. Paul Zumthor writes about the "syntaxical character" of allegory that develops "as a narrative counterpoint on a continuous background."[37]

Medieval and modern hermeneutics of allegory alike suggest several things that must be kept in mind as we turn to explicit examples of Latin exegesis of the Song of Songs. First of all, the gap between the "historical" sense of the text and various levels of allegorical interpretation is not a chasm; rather, all levels of meanings are directly linked to the text as it is read even before the process of allegory begins, with the assumption that there is a *complete* story to be told which must unfold on several levels. As Paul Zumthor has written about this method, it develops in relation to events defined on different points of a chronological (or perhaps cosmogonic) scale, conceptually linking past and future, thus, "the dynamism which, according to medieval cosmogony, attaches *natura* to *figura* justifies them intellectually."[38]

Since the text in question, the Song of Songs, is part of the biblical canon and attributed to Solomon, the a priori assumption of medieval interpretation is that the Song of Songs speaks of *God*'s love, in all its possible variety. Further, this process of determining meanings is not static, but develops according to the multivocal hermeneutic described by Augustine, strongly influenced by Cassian's four levels of biblical interpretation. Although the model came from Origen, the impetus for this lively tradition of medieval commentary on the Song of Songs was what

Todorov has called "a quest for narrative," a desire to turn an elliptical series of poems into a coherent *story* of God's love. Granting the nature of the Song of Songs, this quest for coherence could be argued to motivate even modern commentaries, but it is expressed with remarkable force through the vehicle of medieval allegory.

Medieval Allegory in Practice: Honorius Augustodunensis

One medieval Latin commentary in particular, the *Expositio in Cantica Canticorum* of Honorius Augustodunensis, is remarkable for its conscious and complex presentation of the levels of meaning to be found in the Song of Songs. This text is an extreme example of allegorical exegesis, and is presented here because it shows the complexity and vigor that could be manifested by the method. Honorius was, like Hugh of Saint-Victor and Hildegard of Bingen, a prolific and wide-ranging author of the early twelfth century; he wrote liturgical, dogmatic, and exegetical works, as well as a number of encyclopedic writings which covered topics from history to astrology.[39] The details of the life of Honorius are disputed by modern scholars, but the general consensus is that he came from England, where he may have been associated with Anselm of Canterbury, and probably entered religious life as an Augustinian canon. The greater part of Honorius's career, however, seems to have been spent as a Benedictine monk; he lived for many years in German lands, probably at the cloister of Scottish monks outside of Regensburg, but perhaps also (or instead) at Augsburg and (or) the Austrian abbey of Lambach.[40]

The *Expositio in Cantica Canticorum* was the second of Honorius's commentaries on the Song of Songs. An earlier work, the *Sigillum Beatae Mariae*, was written in England (perhaps at Worcester). It consists of commentaries on the liturgical readings for the Feast of the Assumption followed by a complete interpretation of the Song of Songs as related to the Virgin Mary, being one of the earliest texts to take this approach.[41] The *Expositio*, written in Germany sometime after 1132, is a more complicated and definitive interpretation, but it does not invalidate the earlier interpretation. Near the end of the *Expositio*, Honorius relates this text to his earlier treatment of the Song of Songs:

> Therefore, this book is read on the feast of Blessed Mary, for it shows the type of the Church, which is virgin and mother. Virgin, because uncorrupted by all heresy; mother, because through grace it always bears spiritual children. And therefore everything which is said about the Church can also be said about the Virgin, understood as both bride and mother of the bridegroom. There is a little book published by us, called *Sigillum S. Mariae*, in which all of the Song of Songs is specially adapted to her person.[42]

As this makes clear, the *Expositio* reads the Song of Songs primarily as the love between Christ and the personified Church, of which the Virgin is a type. Honorius's second interpretation was an influential text, extant in nearly one hundred manuscripts, seventeen of them from the twelfth century.[43] In several famous copies, the text is accompanied by a remarkable series of illustrations (see Plates 1–3) closely related to the interpretation. That such a text was popular is important evidence of the sophistication of medieval allegorical theory and exegesis, for this is an extremely detailed interpretation. Honorius attempted to build a simple didactic narrative on a wide range of sources, from classical rhetoric to the newly fashionable *Glossa ordinaria*, and including a bracing dose of apocalyptic in the development of the figure of the mandrake mentioned in passing in Song of Songs 7:13.[44]

But the most important feature of Honorius's work is the way in which it sets forth, and utilizes, a complex theory of allegorical interpretation to build up a coherent narrative from the mysteries of the Song of Songs. The methodical application of theory here is so remarkable that it stands as an exception to Zumthor's contention that Cassian's four senses were never consistently applied in medieval exegesis.[45] Because of its remarkable self-awareness about levels of meaning, a close analysis of Honorius's *Expositio* is in itself an education in the practice of medieval allegorical interpretation.

Honorius begins his treatise with two prologues, roughly equal in length, which describe his undertaking in detail, each in different rhetorical terms. The whole work is introduced by a dedicatory epistle, which sets the context of the work as a gift to the successor of Abbot Cuno of Regensburg, to whom Honorius had written an exposition of the Psalms.[46] The epistle ends with a piece of rhyming prose which, while calling attention to itself through the use of rhyme, alerts the reader to the difficulty of the work explicated:

> I therefore did as you requested, and I laid open in a plain style the book of Solomon entitled the Song of Songs, celebrated by the mouths of many, open

> to the minds of few; and so, enlightened by the Holy Spirit, I elucidated for all the studious a work obscure to the slothful, claiming for myself only the labor involved, and leaving the meanings to the authors.[47]

That such an intricate piece of rhetoric announces a work written *plano stylo* is a touch of irony compounded by the insistence on the inherent difficulty of the Song of Songs. The concluding denial of originality is exaggerated modesty, for Honorius's treatise on the Song of Songs develops an argument about the text which is entirely his own. Yet, in another way, it is not false modesty, since Honorius clearly depends on a rich tradition for aspects of interpretation ranging from broad theory to detailed explication.

The first prologue, for example, offers an impressive collage of methods of interpretation which take us around, and eventually up to, the text. Beginning with the words "In principio librorum," which may be taken to mean "at the beginning of books," or perhaps more philosophically "fundamental to books," Honorius posits three structural features: *auctor, materia, intentio*.[48] This set of categories, also found in Honorius's Psalms commentary, is part of the "Type C" academic prologue (called by students of the arts *accessus ad auctores*) which A. J. Minnis describes as "coming into use in Scriptural exegesis in the first quarter of the twelfth century."[49] Honorius defines the categories, adding *titulus* and *modus agendi*, in general terms, then with special reference to the Song of Songs.

Auctor

A distinction is quickly made between the *auctor* and the *scriptor*:

> The *author* of this book is the Holy Spirit, speaking by means of the vessel of wisdom, the *writer* of this book, Solomon, who was a most wise king and an extraordinary prophet.[50]

Honorius follows Origen in explaining that Solomon published (*edidit*) three books in heroic meter, distributed among the three parts of philosophy: Proverbs represents ethics (for obvious reasons), Ecclesiastes physics (since it explains the workings of nature), and Song of Songs represents logic, "in which the rational soul wishes to be joined to God through love."[51]

Equally curious is the observation with which Honorius closes his comments on authorship, in which he introduces for the first time the Aristotelian term, *aequivocum*:

> *Auctor* [that is, the word itself] is *aequivocum*. For *aequivocum* is a thing that is one in writing, but diverse in meaning, as lion.[52]

"Lion," an example taken directly from the "De categoris Aristotelis" of Isidore's *Etymologiarum*, can mean a constellation, a beast, a fish, the name of a pope or an emperor, or a sculpture or picture of a lion. This interesting mélange of proper and common nouns, of written and pictoral representation, of signifier and signifieds, leads into the various levels of meaning of the word *auctor*: founder (as Romulus of Rome), prinicipal actor (as Judas of Christ's death), or compositor of a book (as David of the Psalter, or Plato of *Timaeus*). Thus, even before the question of allegorical levels of interpretation is raised, Honorius has alerted the reader to the fact that words can mean different things.

Materia

This is a category which was generally understood to refer to the subject-matter of a text. Honorius describes the *materia* of the Songs of Songs with figurative language:

> the bridegroom and the bride, that is, Christ and the Church ... for Christ is said to be a bridegroom *per simile*, since just as a bridegroom and a bride are carnally joined, and thus made one, so Christ is associated with the Church through the assumption of flesh, and she is incorporated into him through eating his body.[53]

Modus agendi

Honorius then brings the reader to the level of the *modus agendi* or *modus tractandi* of the Song of Songs, which sets the didactic procedure of the commentary according to Cassian's four levels:

> This book is concerned with a wedding that is done in four *modis*, that is, historical, allegorical, tropological, anagogical.[54]

Each of these modes, he continues, is further divided into two parts, one more carnal, the other more spiritual: so, according to *history* there are two types of nuptuals, that of the flesh (Solomon and the daughter of the Pharoah) and that of betrothal alone (Joseph and Mary); the *allegorical* nuptuals are, more carnally, the Incarnation and, more poetically, the marriage of Christ and the Church,[55] the *tropological* nuptuals are those of the soul and Christ through desire and through a spiritual ascent; and those of *anagogy* the resurrection of Christ and the final Church of heavenly glory.[56] Three wedding stories in the Gospels (Matthew 22:2, Luke 23:36, and Matthew 25:1) are then explained as Christ's incarnation, ascension (to which Christians are convoked by the apostles) and the Heavenly Jerusalem, in fact, as the allegorical, moral, and anagogical modes. The *modus tractandi* reveals the *materia*: "the *materia* of this book," Honorius says, "is put together (*contexitur*) from these nuptuals, therefore it is called an epithalamium, that is, is a nuptual song."[57]

Intentio

This is the category which exemplifies the final didactic and edifying purpose, "the core" of the commentary "its *intentio* is the union through love (*dilectio*) of the Church or any soul as the bride of Christ to Christ the bridegroom."[58] This love, again, is of two kinds: human, which is bipartite (do not unto others—Tobit 4:16, do unto others—Matthew 7:12), and God's love, which is one: "If anyone love me, he will obey my word" (John 14:23).

By this point in the first prologue, Honorius has made use of the tradition of *accessus ad auctores* to underline the Song of Songs as divinely inspired text, written by the Holy Spirit through Solomon; its levels of interpretation seem to expand outward from the possible meanings of each word to a series of underlying biblical texts, drawn especially from the Gospels. In every instance (*auctor, materia, modus agendi, intentio*) the inherent multivalence of interpretation is stressed.

Titulus

The next section of the first prologue takes up the category which is usually the first subject of a "Type C" prologue; its concern is for the Song of Songs as a book of the Bible. Here there are overtones of the prologue to Origen's *Commentary*, such as the likening of the superlative title to the Holy of Holies. Honorius returns here to a discussion of the *modus agendi* of the Song of Songs; he advises the reader that this song should not be expected to scan like other poetry, since it is in the form of a hymn. The opening words, "Let him kiss me," "are not a song, but speak of a song, since they sing the good life of the just, that consists of love. The song is certainly the life of the just, and the Song of Songs is the life of the perfect."[59]

Then begins a series of interlocking definitions: the word *liber* is *aequivocum*; one meaning is a book. This book is a part of the Bible, which is divided into Old and New Testaments; the true author of each is the Holy Spirit. The Old Testament is divided into three parts: history, which deals with the past; prophets, who deal with the future; and the writings (*agiographiam*), which deal with eternity. The Song of Songs is the fifth book of the seven books of the writings, each of which is associated with one of the seven gifts of the Holy Spirit. The fifth gift of the Holy Spirit is *scientia*, knowledge, and "in the Canticles is included knowledge of all Scripture."[60] The Song of Songs is in the fifth place, Honorius explains, because of the concept of five grades of love common to medieval Latin poetry: look, speech, touch, kiss, deed *(visus, alloquium, contactus, osculum, factum)*, which represent Abraham, Moses, the Incarnation, the Resurrection, and the Final Judgement.[61] To Honorius, it is evident that the Song of Songs speaks of all of these.

At this point, Honorius demonstrates the intimate connection between the *modus agendi*, the *materia*, and the *intentio* of the Song of Songs; what follows is a synopsis of his imaginative understanding of the text, a vision which provides an allegorical framework for the entire exposition. The Song of Songs is first shown to divide into four parts, "because the Church, the bride of Christ of whom the poem sings, is gathered together from the four corners of the world, by the four Evangelists, into the wedding bed of the Bridegroom."[62] These four corners are equated with four ages: the Bride comes from the east *ante legem*, from the south *sub lege*, from the west *sub gratia*, and from the north *sub Antichristo*. In each age, the Bride is differently manifested: from the east she comes as the daughter of the Pharoah, in a chariot; from the south as the daughter of the King of Babylon or the Regina Austri, riding on a camel; from the west she comes as the Sunamita, in the four-wheeled cart of Aminadab; from the north as the Mandrake, who is picked by hand. The first three can be related to the historical brides and concubines of Solomon described in 1 Kings.[63] But even these Brides (and certainly the Mandrake) transcend the historical, they are associated with patriarchs, prophets, apostles, and the Antichrist, and represent the four ages: childhood, youth, old age, and the "*decrepita aetas*" of the world. Of course, they are also linked to the four levels of interpretation of the *modus agendi* of the text. A schematic representation of these four Brides highlights their characteristics and allocations.

Filia Pharaoni	*Filia Regis Babylonis* (*Regina Austri*)	*Sunamita*	*Mandragora*
in chariot	on camel	*in quadrigas Aminadab*	by hand
East	South	West	North
ante legem	*sub lege*	*sub gratia*	*sub Antichristo*
Patriarchs	Prophets	Apostles	Antichrist
puerilis	*juvenilis*	*senilis*	*decrepitas*
Historia	*Allegoria*	*Tropologia*	*Anagogia*

The broad association of the four cardinal directions with stages of salvation history, culminating in a time of tribulation coming from the north, seems to have been somewhat common, for a similar concept is described by Hildegard of Bingen in a letter to clerics of Trier.[64] Honorius was led to superimpose this strategy on the Song of Songs not only because of the wives of the historical Solomon, but also by a series of clues in the Song of Songs: 1:8 mentions the chariots of the Pharoah, 4:16 is an invocation of the south wind; 6:11–12 speaks of the four-wheeled chariot of Aminadab, and calls for the Sunamita (or Sulamita) to return; and 7:13 says that the mandrake gives forth its odor. This scheme of four Brides suggests a division of the text into four rather unequal sections: Song of Songs 1:1–2:17, 3:1–6:9, 6:10–7:10, and 7:11–8:14. The four books of the *Expositio* follow this division; each book deals with the story of one of the Brides.

There are several particularities of this scheme which should be mentioned in passing. First, of course, a geographical conception in which the daughter of the Pharoah comes from the east and the daughter of the King of Babylon from the south is surprising, especially from an author whose books of universal history make it quite clear that he understood the actual position of those lands.[65] Honorius abandons any sense of "realistic" direction; his four Brides from the four corners of the earth are meant to be understood in a purely cosmological sense.

The four-wheeled cart of Aminadab in which rides the Sunamita seems to be a conflation between the Vulgate reading of Song of Songs 6:11 ("nescivi anima mea conturbavit me propter quadrigas Aminadab"), the common but undistinguished Hebrew Bible name Aminadab, and *Abinadab*, who took the Ark of the Covenant out of his house in a cart when David carried it to Jerusalem (2 Samuel [Vulgate 2 Kings] 6:2–3).[66]

Finally, Honorius's particular reading of the Song of Songs as the tale of these four Brides inspired a series of illustrations (Plates 1–3) which appear in at least eight manuscripts, all copied in South German and Austrian monasteries. Four of these manuscripts begin the first book of the commentary with a traditional illustration of Christus and Ecclesia as the lovers of the Song of Songs (Plates 5 and 6).[67] All eight manuscripts, however, illustrate the last three Brides in postures and groupings that follow exactly the discussions of each given by Honorius at the beginning of Books 2, 3, and 4 of the *Expositio* (Plates 1–3), the illustrations are, in fact, positioned exactly at the beginning of each book. The Filia Babylonis, for example, comes riding on a camel led by philosophers and followed by apostles and martyrs. Likewise, the Sunamita, carrying a banner, rides in a chariot shaped like a tower; the four wheels are actually the four Evangelists: a man, an ox, a lion, an eagle; the cart is pulled by apostles and prophets, led by "Sacerdos Aminadab," while Jews stand in the background, looking on. At the beginning of book four, the Mandrake is pulled from the earth by Christ, who places *his own head* on her sexless body, while the severed head of the Antichrist rolls out of the frame of the illustration. A group of crowned women grasp the right arm of the Mandrake; behind them, in some manuscripts, stand a cluster of beardless youths. To the left, behind Christ, are a group of bearded men with halos. Underneath the Mandrake is an open-mouthed dragon, from which she has been extracted.[68]

This curious series of manuscript paintings, which deserves to be studied in its own right, bears an exact text to image relationship. These are illustrations of the commentary rather than of the biblical text; they could not have been conceived without some understanding of Honorius's interpretation. The series provides further evidence of the seriousness with which Honorius's treatise, and the elaborate interlocking series based on four developed in the first prologue, were received in the century after its composition.

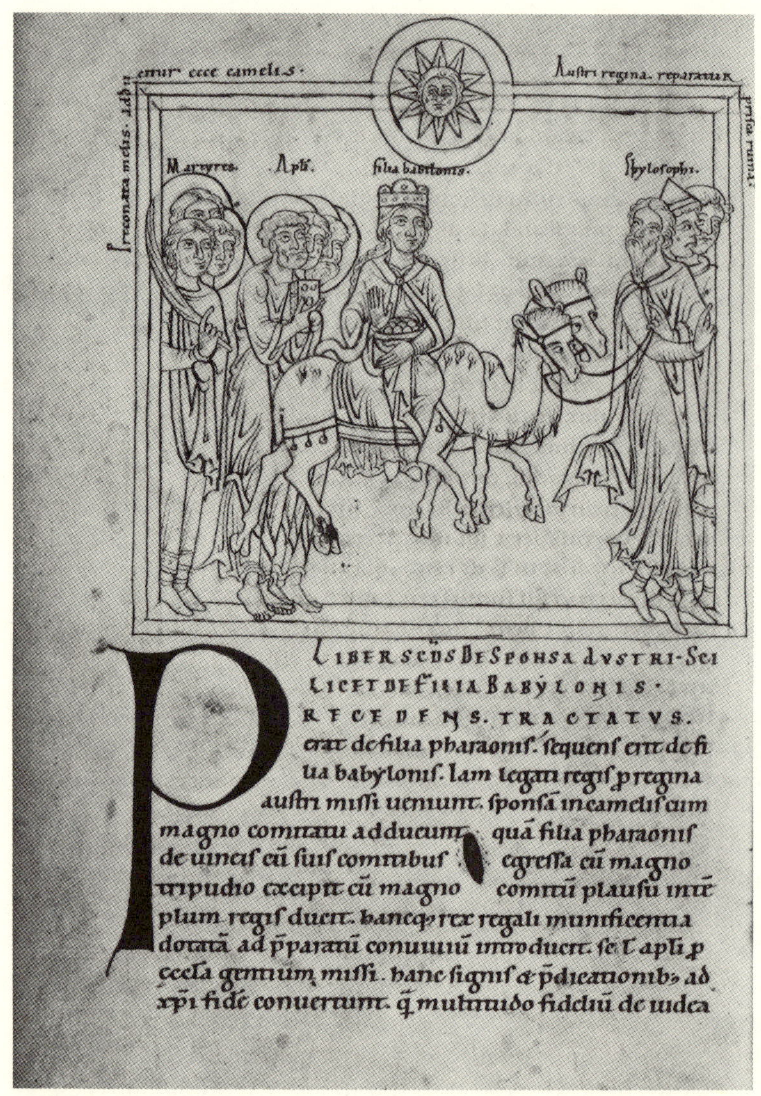

Plate 1. From Honorius Augustodunensis, *Expositio in Cantica Canticorum.* Vienna, Österreichische Nationalbibliothek, Codex 942. Salzburg, c. 12. Book Two: *Filia Babylonis* comes from the south on a camel, f. 38r. Reproduced by permission of Bild-Archiv der Österreichischen Nationalbibliothek, Vienna. Photo by Lichtbild Weskstätte "Alpenland".

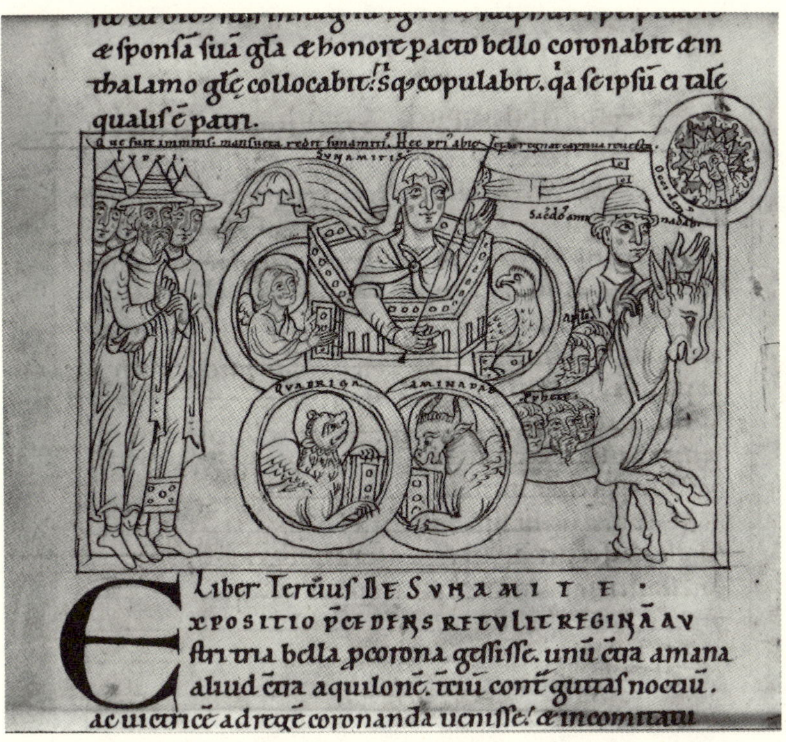

PLATE 2. From Honorius Augustodunensis, *Expositio in Cantica Canticorum*. Vienna, Österreichische Nationalbibliothek, Codex 942. Salzburg, c. 12. Book Three: *Sunamita* comes from the west *in quadrigas Aminadab*. Reproduced by permission of Bild-Archiv der Österreichischen Nationalbibliothek, Vienna. Photo by Lichtbild Weskstätte "Alpenland".

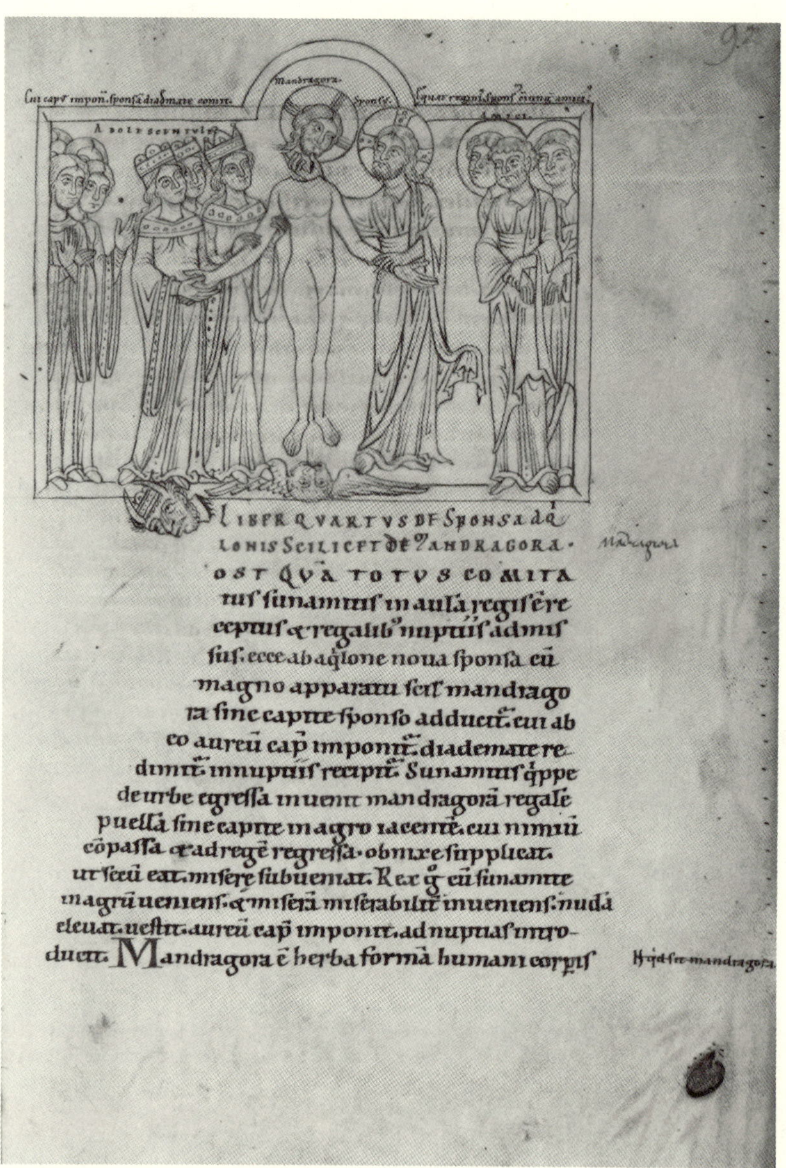

Plate 3. From Honorius Augustodunensis, *Expositio in Cantica Canticorum*. Vienna, Österreichische Nationalbibliothek, Codex 942. Salzburg, c. 12. Book Four: *Mandragora* (from the north) is picked by Christ, who gives her his head, f. 92. Reproduced by permission of Bild-Archiv der Österreichischen Nationalbibliothek, Vienna. Photo by Lichtbild Weskstätte "Alpenland".

The second prologue takes a complementary but profoundly different approach, attempting to explain by means of universal history why the Bridegroom found it necessary to take four such diverse Brides. The history of the world, as seen through the historical books of the Hebrew Bible, shows the ages clearly. The "Ecclesia primitiva" comes from Egypt with the Pharoah's daughter; this is the age of the patriarchs and prophets. The Church comes "de gentibus" with the return to Jerusalem from Babylon, this is the age of the Regina Austri. The Sunamita comes in the chariot of the Gospels, but is, nevertheless oppressed by the heresies and dissensions of the early Church; her reign lasts up to the death of the Antichrist who plagues her. Finally, the Mandrake rules after the death of the Antichrist.[69]

This prologue is full of onomastical allegory, by which each biblical figure bears witness to the coming kingdom of Christ. For example, "Jacob means 'warrior' or 'seeing God,' that is Christ, who always battles with the devil for the Bride and wins, and who always sees God."[70] There is an effort at the end to relate the whole to a more familiar system of six ages—from Adam to Noah, Noah to Abraham, Abraham to David, David to Babylon, Babylon to Christ, Christ to the End—but the overall scheme remains that of the four Brides and their respective ages.

Following these elaborate prologues, the first book begins by re-emphasizing the prophetic foreknowledge of the coming of the Bridegroom. Honorius tells a story about the son of the King of Jerusalem who sent four messengers to make a marriage contract with the daughter of the King of Babylon. She asked them seven questions about their master: Who is he? Is he handsome? Is he powerful? Is he rich? Is he honored? Who are his servants? How great is his praise? Each of these questions is answered by a quotation from the prophets or the Psalms, after which the woman responds:

> This Lord of yours, let him come and 'kiss me with the kiss of his mouth,' and speak to me those things which please him, and I will do his will. The celestial King of Jerusalem is God, whose son is Christ; the this-worldly King of Babylon is the devil, as it is written "the prince of this world is judged." (John 16:11) His daughter is human nature, made in the imitation of sin.[71]

"Father" is a concept which is understood in two ways, Honorius continues, by generation (as Adam or Abraham), and by imitation (as God and the devil). It is by imitation that the daughter of the devil, human nature, is taken to bride by the Son of God, who attained human flesh, and called the Church to himself. The Church is the one Bride, married to Christ through her human nature.

This leads Honorius actually to quote the first verse of the Song of Songs, "Osculetur me osculo oris sui." But before he addresses the text directly, he explains once more, and at some length, about the four *modis* by which Scripture is understood. These are related to the vision of Ezechiel (Ezechiel 1), in which four faces appeared in the wheel within the wheel. Then the senses are explicitly linked to the Song of Songs, through the repeating image of Solomon building the Temple in Jerusalem:

> *Historia* is that Solomon is called the peaceful one, and built the Temple in Jerusalem in seven years. *Allegoria* is that Solomon is called the peaceful one, that is Christ. For Jerusalem the vision of peace is the Church, which Christ built as his Temple from the seven gifts of the Holy Spirit. *Tropologia* is that, just as Solomon built the Temple from wood and stones, so every one of the faithful builds the Temple of God in his soul through good works and the example of the saints. And *Anagoge* is just as Solomon made the Temple in Jerusalem from precious stones, so Christ will institute the Temple in Heavenly Jerusalem with living jewels, that is, from all the elect.[72]

Each of these is explained with some complexity and detail, in the context of the interpretation of Song of Songs 1:1. A rubric "Sequitur cantus sponsi" introduces the second verse, "Quia meliora sunt ubera tua vino, fragrantia unguentis optimis," which begins the line-by-line exposition of the first book, by far the most detailed of the commentary. The exegesis of two words of this second verse, "unguentis optimis," demonstrates the highly schematic nature of Honorius's work. In this passage, the three stages of perfection (good, better, and best ointments) are conflated with the four modes of interpretation to give twelve types of ointment, ranging from that which heals outward wounds to the seven gifts of the Holy Spirit (Chart 1).[73]

The painstaking preparation of the two prologues, the analysis of the *intentio, materia*, and *modus agendi* of the Song of Songs, sets the literary parameters of the commentary, which follows the formula of Cassian's senses with some care. In the first book, the story of the daughter of the Pharoah, an obvious effort has been made to relate each verse to each of the four *modis* in turn. The terms, however, fluctuate in some fascinating ways: *historia* alternates easily with *ad litteram*, in a way reminiscent of

CHART 1. Honorius of Autun (PL 172, cols. 362 A–C) on Cant. 1.2, "unguentis optimis"

	bonum	ad litteram	exteriora vulnera sanat
		sensus spirituli	oleum infirmorum
		tropologice	lex naturalis
		allegorice	remissio peccatorum
unguentum	melius	ad literram	intercutaneum morbum sanat
		sensus spiritualis	oleum quo reges unguntur
		tropologice	lex scripta
		allegorice	bona vita post baptismum
	optimum	ad litteram	internos dolores fugat
		sensus spiritualis	chrisma quo christiani unguntur
		troplogice	sub gratia
		allegorice	septem dona Spiritus Sancti

Augustine's *De utilitate credendi*. In one place, the literal sense is separated from the historical, the second having to do specifically with the history of the Jewish people; in another, the historical sense is designated "tradunt Hebraei."[74] The allegorical sense, having to do with Christ and the Church, is sometimes given in various ways for the same passage, and so tends to dominate the exposition. Honorius's discussion of the little foxes of 2:12–15 is an elaborate ecclesiological interpretation for which no other interpretive options are offered.[75] The great importance of the allegorical sense is underlined by the fact that at 1:2 and 1:4, it is called "spiritualem intelligentiam," the spiritual understanding. As anagogy is treated last, it is occasionally refered to as the "altiorem sensum," the other sense.

The interpretations of the first book are quite standard, following the newly-popular *Glossa ordinaria*, and drawing on established authorities such as Justus of Urguel, Bede and Alcuin, as well as contemporary twelfth-century authors like Ralph of Laon. At 1:2, "Your name is oil poured out," the interpretation follows Origen.[76] The ecclesiological interpretation is directly coded to the understanding that this section of the Song of Songs speaks of the Primitive Church; following an extended metaphor of Christ as a deer (commenting of 2:9, "my Beloved is like a goat or the young of a stag"), Honorius addresses an open apostrophe to the Primitive Church.[77] The biblical text used throughout is the Vulgate, but Honorius is also aware of other Bible versions, and quotes from a non-Vulgate text ("alia translatio") at 1:11, introducing an extra passage about the royal gold and silver of the Bridegroom.[78]

Book two, the longest section of the *Expositio* and the story of the daughter of the King of Babylon, continues this method, but with considerably less rigor. The historical/literal sense of the text is often not directly pointed out, and there is a parallel increase of attention to the anagogical sense, often in conjunction with moral interpretation; an example of this is the treatment of 3:7–8, where the *lectulum* of Solomon is discussed in a passage in which the tropological and anagogical senses are saved for the very end. But at 5:9, when the daughters of Jerusalem ask the Bride, "Of what sort is your beloved that you so adjure us?" the interpretation is entirely about the Church, an interpretation Honorius calls "mystica doctrina." He continues: "and notice that here this chapter is missing *historia* and *anagoge*. But truly *allegoria* and *tropologia* shine, as it [the passage] refers only to Christ and his members."[79].

This section of the commentary makes use of the extended descriptions of the Bride and Bridegroom, interpreting all the praise bestowed on specific anatomical parts as descriptive of the orders of the Church. For example, the teeth mentioned in Song of Songs 4:2 are the confessors and expositors of Scripture, white from baptism, who bite heretics. The ten parts of the body of the Bridegroom (Song of Songs 5:11–16) are equated to ten orders of the Church, even though Honorius has already used *seven* orders of the Church in Song of Songs 1:2. He explains that this is by design: the seven orders are the body of Christ when the Church is militant in the face of persecution, armed with the seven gifts of the Holy Spirit, the ten orders make up the body of Christ, the Church, at peace. There is a strange parallel between the way Honorius reads the bodily descriptions of the beloved as the anatomy of the Church, and medieval Jewish mystical traditions of reading these lists as a description of the physical being of divinity.[80].

At the beginning of the second book, the Church is portrayed asleep on the bed of infidelity; gradually, the stage is set for the Incarnation. Verse 4:8 is presented in a strict allegorical framework, the names *Libano, Amana, Sanir* presented with common allegories of etymology, as meaning "whitening," "unquiet," "a stink or a nocturnal bird," there the Bridegroom calls the Bride over the tops of mountains, away from the carnal dens of the lions and leopards.[81] Towards the end, the discussion becomes more theological, moving to a stage for the introduction of the age of grace, and including a discussion of the Incarnation which reproduces Anselm's argument of the *felix culpa.*[82] The book ends with a description of twelve wars, six fought in biblical times, by the Ecclesia Primitiva, six fought *sub gratia*, including battles with early Christian heresies, and ending in the final war between God and the devil, after the conquest of Antichrist.

Books three and four are structured rather differently. In the third book, the story of the Sunamita is divided into three parts: the first (6:10–7:5) relates, in the voice of the Bridegroom, the descent into the nut grove, that his soul was disturbed ("conturbavit") because of the four-wheeled cart of Aminadab, the call to the Sunamite to return, and a description of the Bride. This is treated as one unit: first, historically, the nut grove is the Synagogué, then, allegorically, it is the Primitive Church; tropologically, it is the cloister and anagogically it is the womb of the Virgin Mary, the mother of Christ.[83] The next section (7:6–7:9a), in which the Bride is compared to a tall palm tree, is first interpreted, in a combination of historical and allegorical senses, as the triumph of the Church over the Synagogue; including an analysis of five songs of praise found in the text, then according to tropology and anagogy.[84] The final unit of text, considered by Honorius (7:9b–10) has only allegorical, tropological and anagogical interpretations.

The structure of the commentary enforces an overall ecclesiological understanding of this section of the Song of Songs. At the center is verse 7:2 an overtly sensual description of the Bride's navel. Honorius points out that the navel is at the center of the body, having six parts (head, eyes, nose, mouth, neck, breast) above it, and six parts (feet, shin, shank, hip, thigh, belly) below it, "the seventh is the navel, which signifies those who, through the seven acts of mercy, aspire to the seven-fold day or place of rest (*septenarium requiei*), which are given through the seven gifts of the Holy Spirit."[85] Again, as at other descriptions of the body of the Bride or the Bridegroom, each part of the body is associated with one order of the Church: the belly, for example, signifies married people, the breast the doctors, the head those in the contemplative life. Following the definition of the head, with no immediately visible relation to the Song of Songs, is an enumeration of the ten stages of the Church, five before the advent of Christ (paradise, natural law, circumcision, written law, prophets), five after the Incarnation (Gospels, martyrs, confessors, religious, Antichrist). This leads into the allegorical discussion of the same pericope, which gives the etymology of Sunamita as "captive," and describes how the Primitive Church gradually broke its bonds. In the tropological interpretation, the "captive" Sunamita is held to represent the soul held by the devil in the bondage of sin.

The five songs of praise which here link the historical and allegorical sense are those of the Primitive Church, the Church of the gentiles, the Church "sweating in persecution," the Church living in peace, and the Synagogue converted to the faith. The tropological interpretation stresses the palm of victory of the martyrs, the emblem of the pious soul victorious over sin. In the anagogical sense, the Church receives the palm of victory after the final battle. The last verse of this section "I am my Beloved's, and his turning is towards me," is an open introduction of the Bride of the fourth book, the Mandrake.

The fourth book follows a similar method of four-fold exegesis by pericope rather than by verse; here the text is divided into four parts. The first (7:11–8:4) gives a description of a flowering garden (including the Mandrake) into which the Beloved comes. Again, the historical and allegorical senses are merged, and quite deliberately so. The daughters of Jerusalem invoked in 8:4 are three:

> This verse is repeated three times, noted first for the Primitive Church, second for the Church of the Gentiles, third for the converted Synagogue, and the concordance of all in one faith in the Trinity is indicated. The thing which "rather historically" (*quasi historice*) is said of the Synagogue is also allegorically (*allegorice*) understood of the Church.[86]

The second part (8:5–7) continues in this vein, with an overall understanding of the Incarnation. The seal of 8:6 evokes the classical Christian metaphor of Christ taking on human nature like an impression in wax.[87]

In the third and last section of book four (8:8–12), a young girl without breasts inspires a number of ecclesiological interpretations: she is the Church after the ravages of Antichrist, or the Church missing the doctors, indicated by the breasts. If the Church builds a wall (8:9), the wall will be those strong in the faith. This will be a time of great peace, the greatest the world has ever known, after the destruction of Antichrist. Again, the allegorical sense refers to the Primitive Church, the tropological speaks particularly of the monastic life, invoking Augustine and Benedict as particular examples. The ecclesiological interpretation which pervades the entire treatise is in itself multifaceted, for it is in the exposition of the final section (8:13–14) that Honorius relates all of this elaborate exegesis to the Virgin Mary, the type of the Church.

The four books of Honorius's *Expositio in Cantica Canticorum* show a disciplined, almost relentless application of the four levels of biblical interpretation described by Cassian, yet they display a number of variations on this theme, all in service to Honorius's overall understanding of the Song of Songs as the four brides of the four ages of the Church. The progression of allegorical interpretation throughout the treatise is didactic, beginning with a careful line-by-line demonstration of the technique, ending with more sweeping interpretation of the senses, which are, nevertheless, ommipresent. The framework is set forth in great rhetorical detail by the first prologue, and explained historically, in relation to the ages of the world, in the second. The repetition of the four senses at the beginning of book one may have been a practical move in the anticipation that copies of the *Expositio* would be made without the prologues, as was indeed the case.[88] The four levels of Scripture thus operate in every verse of the Song of Songs, yet the interpretation of Honorius is overwhelmingly in the allegorical mode, having to do with the love between Christ and the Church.

The complexity with which modes of meaning modulate into one another in this treatise is cautionary for an attempt to describe any medieval commentary as representative of only one level of meaning. Even though the next three chapters of this book will discuss Song of Songs commentaries which are primarily allegorical, tropological, and mariological in their orientations, Honorius has demonstrated how intrinsically these are all linked to one another. His assertion that, after all, the whole of the Song of Songs is also the song of the Virgin Mary shows that even this painstaking commentary does not pretend to have exhausted all of the possible meanings of the text.

Rhetorical and thematic devices by which Honorius interpreted the Song of Songs in this treatise demonstrate the multivocality which critics describe as the heart and soul of medieval allegorical interpretation. The commentary also gives ample testimony to the medieval fascination with categories and lists, by means of which certain passages of a text are easily associated with cosmological ages and gifts of the Holy Spirit. Such lists also made up key elements of the biblical code. All of these techniques, from the prologues to the interpretation of the final verse, are virtuosic applications of common medieval approaches to the Bible. Yet the basic insight into the Song of Songs, the perception of four Brides from the four ages of the world, is superimposed on the text because of an imaginative insight that is uniquely the author's. This flash of Honorius's imagination was transposed into representational images through a series of illustrations which defied logic and perspective to show us, for example, the flattened-out wheels of the *quadrigas* of Aminadab as the faces of the four evangelists.

Thus, by means of an extremely stylized framework, Honorius opened up the cryptic poems of the Song of Songs as a narrative pulsing with life. This commentary is an extraordinarily complicated and successful example of the use of allegorical exegesis to create a coherent narrative from the Song of Songs. Honorius demonstrated on many levels the multifaceted nature of God's love in the drama of human salvation. Other Song of Songs commentaries will employ similar strategies in seeking the key to the code, but none will surpass the seriousness and complexity of this work.

Notes

1. Robert Gordis, *The Song of Songs: A Study, Modern Translation, and Commentary* (New York: Jewish Theological Seminary Press, 1954), second edition: *The Song of Songs and Lamentations: A Study, Modern Translation, and Commentary* (New York: Jewish Theological Seminary Press, 1974). All quotations are from the first edition. For the connection between the allegorical method and canoncity, see pp. 2, 43. For a convincing study of metaphor in the Song of Songs

itself, see Robert Alter, "The Garden of Metaphor," in *The Art of Biblical Poetry* (New York: Basic Books., 1985) pp. 185–203.

2. Roland E. Murphy, "Canticle of Canticles," in *The Jerome Biblical Commentary*, ed. R. E. Brown et al. (Englewood Cliffs, N.J.: Prentice-Hall, 1968) pp. 506–510. In Christian exegesis, interpretations of the Song of Songs as a human love story were bolstered by the influential work of H. H. Rowley, especially "The Interpretation of the Song of Songs," JTS 38 (1937) 337–363.

3. Phyllis Trible, "Depatriarchalizing in Biblical Interpretation," JAAR 41 (1973) 30–48; further developed in *God and the Rhetoric of Sexuality* (Philadelphia: Fortress Press, 1978).

4. Gordis says that this theory was "most vigorously propagated" in the 1920s by T. J. Meek, p. 4 note 17,

5. Pope gives excellent summaries of various ancient and modern interpretations, pp. 89–288.

6. A recent study which portrays the text as "entertainment" is Michael V. Fox, *The Song of Songs and the Ancient Egyptian Love Songs* (Madison: University of Wisconsin Press, 1985).

7. Gordis, p. 8; discussion of the cult theory, pp. 4–10; the Song of Songs as national literature, pp. 24–30.

8. A. Robert and R. Tournay, *Le Cantique des cantiques; traduction et commentaire* (Paris: J. Gabalda, 1963). The commentary was prepared for publication by Tournay after Robert's death; therefore many of the conclusions are actually by the second author.

9. Robert, p. 145 (on 3:17); p. 285 (on 8:1), and the preface of Tournay, pp. 22–23.

10. Arthur Green, "The Song of Songs in Early Jewish Mysticism," *Orim* 2, no. 2 (Spring, 1987), reprinted in *Modern Critical Interpretation: The Song of Songs*, ed. Harold Bloom (New York: Chelsea House Publishers, 1988) pp. 141–153. See also *Midrash Rabbah, Aggadat Shir Ha-Shirim*, trans. H. Freedman and M. Simon, vol. 9 (London: Soncino, 1939), *The Targum to the Song of Songs*, ed. H. Gollancz (London: Luzac, 1908), U. Neri, *Il Cantico dei cantici. Antica interpretazione ebraica* (Rome: Citta nuova, 1976, second edition, 1987), and Raphael Loewe, "Apologetic Motifs in the Targum to the Song of Songs," in *Biblical Motifs: Origins and Transformations*, ed. A. Altmann, Brandeis University, Studies and Texts III (Cambridge, Mass.: Harvard University Press, 1966) pp. 159–196. The quotation attributed to Rabbi Akiba is from the *Mishnah, Yadayim* III.5; other comments on sanctity of the text attributed to Akiba are found in *Tosefta, Sanhedrin* XII, 10 and *Babylonian Talmud, Sanhedrin* 101a.

11. The most elaborate study of this function is by Henri de Lubac, especially "Mira profunditas," I,1 (1959) pp. 119–128.

12. G. R. Evans, *The Language and Logic of the Bible: The Earlier Middle Ages* (Cambridge: Cambridge University Press, 1984) pp. 1–10; Tzvetan Todorov, "A Finalist Interpretation: Patristic Exegesis," in *Symbolism and Interpretation*,

trans. Catherine Porter (Ithaca, N.Y.: Cornell University Press, 1982) pp. 97–130, and "La Synthèse Augustinienne," in *Théories du symbole* (Paris: Éditions du Seuil, 1977) pp. 34–55; Umberto Eco, " L'Epistola XIII e l'Allegorismo Medievale," *Carte Semiotiche*, Rivista dell'Associazione Italiana di Studi Semiotici O (October, 1984) 13–31. For medieval transmission of *De doctrina Christiana*, see Michael M. Gorman, "The Diffusion of the Manuscripts of Saint Augustine's 'De Doctrina Christiana' in the Early Middle Ages," RB 95 (1985) 12–24.

13. *Augustine, On Christian Doctrine*, trans. D. W. Robertson (Indianapolis, Ind.: Bobbs Merrill, 1958) IV. 8. 22, p. 132. The critical edition is edited by J. Martin, CCSL 32 (1962).

14. Augustine, I.4.4, ed. Martin, p. 8; Robertson p. 9.

15. Augustine, III. 27. 38, ed. Martin, pp. 99–100; Robertson pp. 101–102.

16. Augustine, III.30.42, ed. Martin, pp. 102–103; Robertson, p. 104. For Tyconius, see F. C. Burkitt, *The Rules of Tyconius* (Cambridge, Cambridge University Press, 1894). Tyconius was cited by early medieval authors, notably Paschasius Radbertus, but through Augustine and Bede, see E. Ann Matter, "The Lamentations Commentaries of Hrabanus Maurus and Paschasius Radbertus," *Traditio* 38 (1982) p. 155 n. 72.

17. Angelomus of Luxeuil, *Enarrationes in Libros Regum*, PL 115:245–246; see Smalley, pp. 41–42. M. L. W. Laistner suggests that Tyconius may have been a very limited source for Angelomus, "Some Early Medieval Commentaries on the Old Testament," in *The Intellectual Heritage of the Early Middle Ages*, ed. C. G. Starr (Ithaca, N.Y.: Cornell University Press, 1957) p. 185 n. 4 (originally published in HTR 46 (1953) 27–46).

18. Augustine, *De utilitate credendi*, III.5, ed. J. Zycham, CSEL 25 (1891) pp. 7–8; translated by John H. S. Burleigh, *Augustine: Earlier Writings*, Library of Christian Classics VI (Philadelphia: Westminister Press, 1953) pp. 294–295. These levels are put to practical use in *De genesi ad litteram imperfectus liber*, 2, PL 34:222A.

19. "Hierusalem quadrifarie possit intellegi: secundum historiam civitas Iudaeorum, secundum allegoriam ecclesia Christi, secundum anagogen civitas dei illa caelestis, "quae est mater omnium nostrum," (Galatians 4:26) secundum tropologiam anima hominis." John Cassian, *Collationes* XIV.8, SC 54, ed. E. Pichery (Paris, 1958) p. 190.

20. Smalley, p. 28.

21. de Lubac, I,1 (1959) pp. 190–193.

22.

> The letter teaches the act, what you should believe allegory, moral, what you should do, where you should be heading, anagogy.

Quoted from Eco, p. 14. The rhyme is also attributed to Augustine of Dacia.

23. Judson Boyce Allen, *The Ethical Poetic of the Later Middle Ages: A Decorum*

of Convenient Distinction (Toronto: University of Toronto Press, 1982) pp. 212–214.

24. Matter, pp. 146–147 for levels of interpretation in Hrabanus Maurus on Lamentations, p. 156 n. 62 for examples from the Lamentations commentary of Paschasius Radbertus. Allen's insistence on "medieval terminology" (p. 214) thus does not always remove confusion, at least not in early medieval texts.

25. See, for example, Gregory the Great, *Moralia in Iob*, ed. M. Adriaen, (1979): XIII.xii.15, CCSL 143A, pp. 792–793; V.xxxi.55, CCSL 143, pp. 256–258; XV.lvii.68; CCSL 143A, pp. 792–793.

26. "Allegoria enim animae longe a deo positae quasi quandam machinam facit, ut per illam leuetur ad deum," Gregory the Great, *Expositio in Canticum Canticorum*, 2, ed. P. Verbraken, CCSL 144 (1963) p. 3.

27. Tzvetan Todorov, "The Quest of Narrative," in *The Poetics of Prose*, trans. Richard Howard (Ithaca, N.Y.: Cornell University Press, 1977), pp. 125–126.

28. Todorov, "The Quest," pp. 126–127.

29. Todorov, *Symbolism and Interpretation*, p. 98.

30. Todorov, "The Quest," pp. 127–129;, see also *Symbolism and Interpretation*, pp. 106–107.

31. Allen, pp. 91–92, citing the Gloss and Aegidius Romanus, *In librum Solomonis qui Cantica Canticorum inscribitur Commentaria* (Rome: apud Antonium Bladum, 1555).

32. The concept of Bible as code has been developed by Northrop Frye in *The Great Code, The Bible and Literature* (New York: Harcourt Brace Jovanovich, 1982). He relates the bridal imagery of the Song of Songs to the tension between covenant and harlotry in the Hebrew Bible.

33. Todorov, "The Quest," p. 132.

34. For the Codex Sinaiticus, see the facsimile edition of Constantinus Tischendorf, *Codex sinaiticus petropolitanus* (St. Petersburg, 1862) vol. 3; on the rubrics in the Middle Ages, see D. de Bruyne, "Les anciennes versions latines du Cantique des Cantiques," RB 38 (1926). 118–122. I am guided by Jay Treat's unpublished study of these rubrics. See Gordis, pp. 10–13 for a discussion of "the dramatic theory."

35. Paul de Man, "Pascal's Allegory of Persuasion," in *Allegory and Representation*, ed. Stephen Greenblatt (Baltimore: Johns Hopkins University Press, 1981) p. 1.

36. Jacques Derrida, *Memoires for Paul de Man*, The Wellek Library Lectures at the University of California, Irvine (New York: Columbia University Press, 1986) p. 11.

37.

> l'allégorie présente un caractère syntaxique, plutôt que lexical: l'effet poétique provient en effet, plutôt que du sujet, de son prédicat verbal. L'allégorie est ainsi perçue au niveau de la phrase plutôt que du nom: celle-la révèle celui-ci, le promeut à son niveau significant. Tel est, on l'a dit, le charme de l'allégorie

qu'elle semble créée de rien. Elle se dégage comme un contrepoint narratif sur un arrière-plan continu dont elle se distingue en perspective par des marques aisément reconnaissables mais d'une grande légèreté.

Paul Zumthor, *Essai de poétique médiévale* (Paris: Éditions de Seuil, 1972) p. 127. Zumthor here quotes Morton Bloomfield, "A Grammatical Approach to Personification Allegory," *Medieval Philology* 66 (1963) 163–166.

38.

l'esprit établit une relation d'identité historique entre deux événements conçus comme également réels, mais situés à des points différents de la durée et se définissant l'un par rapport à l'autre comme respectivement passé et futur. . . . Le lien qui les unit ainsi est de nature conceptuelle: le dynamisme qui, dans la cosmogonie médiévale, attache *natura* à *figura* le justifie intellectuellement.

Zumthor, pp. 124–125. Zumthor argues that this tradition derives ultimately from the *Psychomachia* of Prudentius. See also Erich Auerbach, "Odysseus' Scar," in *Mimesis; The Representation of Reality in Western Literature*, trans. Willard R. Trask (Princeton, N.J.: Princeton University Press, 1953) pp. 3–23.

39. The works of Honorius collected in PL 172 are divided into the categories "Didascalia et Historica," "Exegetica," "Liturgica," and "Dogmatica et Ascetica." Important discussions of these treatises are Valerie I. J. Flint, "The Chronology of the Works of Honorius Augustodunensis," RB 82 (1972) 215–242, "The Place and Purpose of the works of Honorius Augustodunensis," RB 87 (1987) 97–127, and Marie-Odile Garrigues, "Quelques recherches sur l'oeuvre d'Honorius Augustodunensis," RHE 70 (1975) 388–425. I would like to thank Paul Dietrich for his advice concerning Honorius.

40. Generally, Valerie Flint has argued that Honorius was an English Canon who became a Benedictine and spent most of his career in southeast Germany and Austria ("The Career of Honorius Augustodunensis, Some Fresh Evidence," RB 82 (1972) 63–86), while Garrigues places him in a house of Canons Regular in Augsburg ("Honorius était-il bénédictin?" StMon 19 (1977) 27–46). Flint has more recently deviated from her former view in "Heinricus of Augsburg and Honorius Augustodunensis: Are They the Same Person," RB 92 (1982) 148–158, to which question she answers yes.

41. Honorius, *Sigillum Beatae Mariae*, PL 172:495–518, see also Valerie I. J. Flint, "The Commentaries of Honorius Augustodunensis on the Song of Songs," RB 84 (1974) 196–211, especially 197–204. The *Sigillum* will be considered more fully below in chapter six.

42.

Hic liber ideo legitur de festo S. Mariae, qua ipsa gessit typum ecclesiae, quae virgo est et mater. Virgo, quia ab omni haeresi incorrupta; mater, quia parit semper spirituales filios ex gratia. Et ideo omnia quae de Ecclesia dicta sunt, possunt etiam de ipsa Virgine, sponsa et matre sponsi intelligi. Exstat libellus

> a nobis editus, qui intitulatur Sigillum S. Mariae, in quo tota Cantica specialiter adaptata sunt ejus personae.

PL 172:494C–D.

43. The full text is printed in PL 172:347–496. For manuscripts, see Stegmüller, vol. 3 (1951) 3573; for twelfth-century manuscripts, mostly from Austria and south Germany, see Flint, "The Place and Purpose," pp. 119–120.

44. For studies of Honorius, see Ohly, pp. 251–262; Riedlinger, pp. 136–139, 212–214. Flint's list of sources for the beginning of the *Expositio* ("The Commentaries," pp. 210–211) considers only other formal commentary texts. The mandrake symbolism has been studied by Horst Dieter Rauh, *Das Bild des Antichrist im Mittelalter: Von Tyconius zum deutschen Symbolismus* (Munster: Aschendorff, 1973), pp. 235–268.

45. Zumthor, p. 125.

46. Dedicatory epistle in PL 172: 347C–D, discussed by Flint, "The Chronology," p. 234.

47.

> Feci itaque quod jussisti, et librum Salomonis qui intitulatur Cantica canticorum multorum ore celebratum, paucorum intellectui reseratum, plano stylo reseravi; ac opus desidiosis obscurum, omnibus studiosis Spiritu sancto illustrante elucidavi, nihil mihi praeter solum laborem ascribens, sententias vero auctoribus [*al.* auctoritati sanctorum] relinquens.

PL 172:347 C–D.

48. "In principiis librorum tria requiruntur, scilicet, auctor, materia, intentio." PL 172:347D.

49. A. J. Minnis, *Medieval Theory of Authorship: Scholastic Literary Attitudes in the Later Middle Ages* (London: Scolar Press, 1984; second edition Philadelphia: University of Pennsylvania Press, 1988) p. 41; for an outline of the "Type C" prologue (so defined by Richard Hunt), see pp. 18–19. The categories given by Minnis are in the order: *titulus, nomen auctoris, intentio auctoris, materia libri, modus agendi*; Honorius here discusses the categories in the order: *auctor, materia, modus, intentio, titulus*. Compare to "De titulo, intentione, materia, et auctore," Honorius, *Selectorum psalmorum expositio*, PL 172: 270C.

50. "Auctor libri hujus est Spiritus sanctus, loquens per vas sapientiae, Salomonem hujus libri scriptorem qui fuit rex sapientissimus et propheta praecipuus." PL 172:347D–348C. See Minnis, p. 132, for late medieval explanations of why Solomon's name does not appear in the title.

51.

> qui Salomon tria volumina heroico metro edidit, quae in tres partes philosophiae, scilicet ethicam, physicam, logicam distribuit. . . . Cantica Canticorum logicae contulit, in quibus rationalem animam per dilectionem Deo conjugi voluit, vel docuit ut ibi: 'Fortis est mors dilectio. Aquae multae non potuerunt extingere charitatem.' (Song of Songs 7:6,7)

PL 172:348C. Compare to Origen's prologue to the Commentary, ed. Baehrens, *Origenes Werke* 8, CGS 33 (1926) pp. 75–76. In his commentary on the Psalms, Honorius relates physics to Genesis, ethics to Paul, logic to Psalms, PL 172: 270B. See also Minnis, p. 26.

52. "Aequivocum autem dicitur quod unum est in litteratura, sed diversum in significatione, ut leo." PL 172:348D. The discussion continues to the end of the column. Compare to Isidore of Seville, "Aequivoca sunt, quando multarum rerum nomen unum est, sed non eadem definitio, ut *leo*. Nam quantum ad nomen pertinet, et verus, et pictus, et coelestis leo dicitur." *Etymologiarum* II.26, "De categoriis Aristotelis," PL 82:144A. A definition of *aequivocum*, but without this example, is also given by Boethius, *In categorias Aristotelis*, PL 64:163–167. Other examples of the term are found in Honorius's explanation of the word *liber* (PL 172:350C), *acies* (Song of Songs 6:3, 446D), and *chorus* (Song of Songs 7:1, 456A).

53.

> Materia libri est sponsus et sponsa, id est Christus et Ecclesia, ut in Evangelio legitur: "Qui habet sponsam sponsus est (John 3:29)," et item: "Decem virgines exierunt obviam sponso et sponsae (Matthew 25:1)." Christus namque per simile dicitur sponsus, quia sicut sponsus sponsae carnaliter conjungitur, et unum cum ea efficitur, ita Christus per assumptam carnem Ecclesiae associatur, et ipsa per comestionem corporis ejus ei incorporatur.

PL 172:349A. See also Minnis, p. 21.

54. "Hic liber agit de nuptiis quae fiunt quatuor modis, scilicet historice, allegorice, tropologice, anagogice." PL 172:349A–B; Minnis, pp. 21–22.

55. PL 172:349B, once again in rhyming prose: "per commistionem corporis sui sibi sociavit. Quam et suo sanguine, et lavacro baptismatis lavit, et variis Spiritus sancti charismatibus dotavit."

56. PL 172:349C, ending: "quo anima quod est inferior vis interioris hominis spiritui, quo est superior vir ejus per consensum divinae legis conjungitur, de quo conjugio spiritalis proles, id est bonum opus gignitur."

57. "De his nuptiis materia hujus libri contexitur, ideo et epithalamium, id est nuptiale carmen dicitur." PL 172:349D–350A.

58. PL 172:350 A.

59. "non sunt canticum, sed de cantico agunt, quia bonam vitam justorum, quae in dilectione constat, canunt. Canticum quippe est vita justorum. Canticum canticorum est vita perfectorum." PL 172:350C. Minnis, pp. 19–20; and p. 132 for Nicholas of Lyra's statement that the *forma tractandi* of the Song of Songs should be understood as a promise.

60. PL 172:350C–351A, ending "Et notandum quod Cantica spiritui sapientiae assignantur, quia scientia totius Scripturae Canticis includitur." PL 172:350D–351A. Perhaps *sapientiae* here is a miscopying of *scientiae*? On the tradition of texts relating a variety of biblical sevens to the seven gifts of the Holy Spirit, see E. Ann Matter, "The Pseudo-Alcuinian 'De Septem Sigillis': An

Early Latin Apocalypse Exegesis," *Traditio* 36 (1980) 111–137; and Roger E. Reynolds, *The Ordinals of Christ from their Origins to the Twelfth Century* (Berlin; N. de Gruyter 1978).

61. PL 172:351A–C. This list of five signs of love is found in Latin poetry from Horace to the *Carmina Burana*, see Ohly, pp. 256–257.

62. PL 172:351C–353C, beginning "Hic autem liber in quatuor partes dividitur, quia Ecclesia sponsa Christi quam canit, de quatuor plagis mundi, per quatuor Evangelia in thalamum sponsi colligitur."

63. 1 Kings (Vulgate 3 Kings) 1:3 and 2:17, 21–22 tell the story of Abishag the Shunamite, the young girl Solomon took to bed to warm his old bones; 1 Kings 3:1 speaks of Solomon's marriage to "the daughter of Pharoah;" 1 Kings 11:1 lists Solomon's foreign wives as the daughter of the Pharoah, and Moabite, Ammonite, Edomite, Sidonian, and Hittite women.

64. Hildegard of Bingen, Epistola 49, PL 197:251A–B. For Hildegard's cosmology, see Barbara Newman, *Sister of Wisdom: St. Hildegard's Theology of the Feminine* (Berkeley: University of California Press, 1987).

65. See Honorius, *De imagine mundi* I.15–18, PL 172:125–127.

66. Pope, pp. 584–592 (verse numbered 6:2 in his translation).

67. 1) Munich B.S. clm, 4550 (c.12 Benediktbeuren); 2) Munich, B.S. clm 5118 (c.12 Beuerberg); 3) Munich, B.S. clm 18125 (c.12 Tegernsee); 4) Baltimore, Walters 29 (c.12 Lambach); 5) Sankt Paul in Lavanttal 441 (c.14. Sankt Blasien); 6) Sankt Florian XI.80 (dated 1301); 7) Vienna Ö.N.B. 942 (c.12 Salzburg); 8) Augsburg, Universitätsbiblothek 1 2 2° 13 (dated 1180 Southwest Germany). 1, 3, 5, and 8 all have full-page illustrations of Christus and a crowned Ecclesia on f.1. The Augsburg manuscript was rediscovered by Michael Curschmann; for an analysis of these images, see his "Imagined Exegesis: Text and Picture in the Exegetical Works of Rupert of Deutz, Honorius Augustodunensis, and Gerhoch of Reichersberg," *Traditio* 44 (1988). My thanks to Professor Curschmann for making a copy of this article available to me before its publication. I am also grateful to the staff of the Index of Christian Art at Princeton University for help with these references.

68. See G. Swarzenski, *Die Salzburger Malerei* (Leipzig, 1908), plate 402 for the Vienna manuscript; A. Strange, *Deutsche Malerei der Gotik* vol. (Ledeln, Liechtenstein: Kraus, 1969), plate 134 for the Sankt Florian manuscript; G. A. Welten, "Sponsa Christi: Het Absismozaïek van de Santa Maria in Trastevere te Rome en het Hooglied," *Feestbundel F. Van der Meer* (Amsterdam and Brussels, Elsevier 1966) p. 153 for Munich clm 4550 and its relationship to the apse mosaic of Santa Maria in Trastevere. I am grateful to Dale Kinney for this reference.

69. PL 172:353–358.

70. "Jacob qui dicitur 'luctator' vel 'videns Deum,' est Christus, qui cum diabolo pro sponsa luctamen iniit et vicit, et semper Deum Patrem videt." PL 172:355B.

71. PL 172:357D–358A. The questions of the daughter of the King of Ba-

bylon are: 1) Quis est? 2) Est pulcher? 3) Est potens? 4) Est dives? 5) Honoratur muneribus? 6) Quae est ejus servitus? 7) Quae est laus ejus?

72.

> Historia est quod Salomon dicitur pacificus, et fecit templum in Jerusalem septem annis. Allegoria est quod Salomon dicitur pacificus et est Christus. Jerusalem visio pacis et est Ecclesia, quam Christus fecit sibi templum ex septem donis Spiritus sancti. Tropologia autem est quod sicut Salomon ex lignis et lapidibus templum construxit, ita quisque fidelis in anima sua templum Deo ex bonis operibus et exemplis sanctorum facit. Anagoge vero est quod sicut Salomon ex pretiosis lapidibus templum in Jerusalem fecit, ita Christus in coelesti Jerusalem ex vivis lapidibus, id est ex omnibus electis templum instituit.

PL 172:359C–D.

73. PL 172:362A–C. My thanks to Paul Meyvaert for identifying this scheme. Similar schematic exegesis is common in Honorius's *Clavis physicae*, ed. Paolo Lucentini, TT 21 (1974); see Plates VI and VII.

74. PL 172:366C (1:3); PL 172:373C (1:8) for an interpretation in which the historical and literal senses are separated.

75. It is interesting to note that this passage includes verse 2:15, beginning "Capite nobis vulpeculas parvulas," which is always read as the foxy heretics besetting the Church, whatever the hermeneutical direction of the commentary.

76. For a study of the commentary sources to 370B, see Flint, "The Commentaries," pp. 210–211. Flint argues that there is no clear trace of Origen in this text, but the similarities at 1:2 (364B), 1:11 (377A), 1:14 (379B), and 2:6 (386D) are obvious, if not word-for-word.

77.

> O primitiva Ecclesia, quae diu cessasti a praedicatione, surge a quiete tua, id est praepara te ad laborem, ad praedicatione gentibus, propera, quia tempus breve est. Et, si hoc feceris, eris amica mea, faciens mihi amicos per fidem, qui sunt inimici per infidelitatem.

PL 172:(389–) 391C.

78. PL 172:376C, adding at 1:10 "Similitudines auri fabrefaciemus tibi, cum distinctionibus argenti, quoad usque rex in accubitu suo est," which is the reading of Vaccari, p. 20. The verse (1:11 in Vaccari's text) was also used by Jerome and Augustine, see notes in Vaccari.

79. "Et hoc notandum quod istud capitulum ab historia et ab anagoge deficit. Allegoria vero et tropologia splendescit, quia id solum Christum et sua membrum respicit." PL 172:440B.

80. PL 172:444 for the ten members/orders of peace (Song of Songs 5:11–16), 361 for the seven of war (Song of Songs 1:2); another example is 457B–460A (Song of Songs 7:2–5, this time fifteen members associated with "ordines justorum.") For the Jewish mystical tradition of reading these passages as a description of the divinity, see Gershom Scholem, *Major Trends in Jewish Mysticism*

(New York: Schocken Books, 1969), and *On the Kabbalah and Its Symbolism*, trans. Ralph Manheim (New York: Schocken Books, 1965).

81. PL 172:417–421. The major name allegory texts used for this type of medieval interpretation are attributed to important theologians and exegetes: Jerome, Bede, Alcuin, Hrabanus Maurus. Honorius's readings are closest to those in the *Allegoriae in sacram scripturam* (PL 112:849–1088) attributed to Hrabanus Maurus. Extensive use of these lists in an anonymous commentary from the twelfth century will be discussed below in chapter five.

82. PL 172:433B, a rather scholastic passage which begins "Item quaeritur utrum Filius Dei esset incarnatus, si homo non fuisset lapsus." Flint has demonstrated the influence Anselm had on Honorius, stemming from his years in England, "The Chronology," pp. 219–227. For a broad view of Anslem's influence, see Gillian R. Evans, "A Theology of Change in the Writings of St.Anselm and His Contemporaries," RTAM 47 (1980) 53–76.

83. PL 172:453–461 for historical, 461–463 for allegorical, 463–466 for moral, 466 for anagogical.

84. PL 172:466–469 for historical/allegorical, 469–470 for tropological, 470 for anagogical.

85. "septimus est umbilicus, qui significat illos, qui per septem opera misericordiae aspirant ad septenarium requiei, quae dabitur per septem dona Spiritus sancti." PL 172:457C.

86. "Iste versus jam tertio est repetitus, primo primitivae Ecclsiae, secundo Ecclesiae gentium, tertio Synagogae conversae adnotatur, et concordia omnino in una fide Trinitatis notatur. Istud quasi historice de Synogoga dictum allegorice quoque de Ecclesia gentium intelligitur." PL 172:474D.

87. "Sigillo est imago insculpta, quae cerae impressae imaginem reddit. Sigillum est Christi humanitas, cui imago insculpta est Christi divinitas, cera vero humana anima, ad imaginem Dei formata." PL 172:479C.

88 Examples of this common happenstance of the medieval scriptorium are: Salzburg, Studienbibliothek V.2.E.42, f. 161 beginning "Filius regis" (PL 172:357C, "Tractatus Primus"); and Warsaw, National Library Abtl. II, Chart. Lat. Fol. I.229, f. 1 beginning at the same place.

Chapter Four

The Song of Songs as the Changing Portrait of the Church

The second commentary of Honorius demonstrates in action some of the outstanding characteristics of medieval allegory of the Song of Songs: the elaborate schematization which nevertheless allows for fluidity of movement between modes of interpretation, and the manipulation of these levels of interpretation to construct a narrative about the Church out of the fragmentary images of the text. The sophistication with which Honorius put his theoretical models to work is the result of a long process of development in applying to the Song of Songs Cassian's allegorical level of interpretation, that is, the level of interpretation centered on Christ and the Church. This chapter will discuss several important Song of Songs commentaries in that allegorical mode, all written before the twelfth century. Since this was the most common understanding of the Song of Songs in medieval exegesis, the most obvious sense of the text, such analysis will offer insight into the development of the genre of Song of Songs commentary. Each author who wrote in the allegorical mode reworked the assumptions of interpretation which he had inherited to explain to each Christian century how the Song of Songs is the portrait of love between God and the Church.

This mode of interpretation can actually be found in all medieval Christian Song of Songs commentaries, for the love between God and the Church lies latent in the other main forms of interpretation. That is to say, the tropological understanding of the Song of Songs as the love between Christ and the soul is intimately connected to the life of the Christian community; even mariological readings never forget that the figure of the Virgin Mary is the type of the Church. But the reverse is also true: few Song of Songs commentaries are *only* about the Church, since other levels of interpretation were also, and increasingly, understood by authors and audiences alike. Nevertheless, the great number of interpretations which apply the ecclesiological understanding, one of the senses which Origen developed from Jewish exegesis, can teach us about the way medieval authors responded to demands about the form and mission of the Church as it was understood by each generation; how, that is, the genre of commentary continued to reflect changing realities.

The Song of Songs in the Age of the Great Councils

Medieval Latin ecclesiological exegesis of the Song of Songs was indebted to Origen both directly and by way of two expositions of the text from the years between the Councils of Nicaea (325) and Chalcedon (451), the works of Gregory of Elvira and Apponius, authors lost in the shadow of such contemporary theological giants as Ambrose, Augustine, and Jerome. Gregory, who died around 392, was the bishop of Elvira (Granada) in southern Spain. He wrote a number of works which were known in the Middle Ages under the names of more famous authors, most commonly, that of Origen of Alexandria. In fact, Gregory of Elvira did draw heavily on Origen in an exposition of Psalm 91 (according to the Vulgate numbers), the *Tractatus de archa Noe*, and the work known simply as *Tractatus Origenis*, a compendium of selected passages on Genesis which shares material with Augustine's *City of God*.[1] Gregory's treatise on the Song of Songs is entitled in the manuscripts *Tractatus de epithalamio*.[2] It is, with some lacunae, a five-book interpretation of an Old Latin text of verses 1:1–3:4; it appears in two manuscript traditions, a short and a long version, the latter considered the original.[3] Gregory shows the first stage of development from the Latin translations of Origen on the Song of Songs, for his commentary is original in scope and structure and in its overall purpose: polemic against heretics.

Gregory was squarely in the middle of the controversies over the nature of the Church, especially in its relationship to imperial power, controversies that rocked the Christian world in the aftermath of the condemnation of Arian Christology at the Council of Nicaea. His position was emphatically, fanatically, Nicene, so much so that he supported Lucifer of Cagliari against the more moderate anti-Arian position of Athanasius.[4] Unlike Athanasius, Gregory of Elvira opposed allowing those who had made a liaison of convenience with Arianism to re-enter the Nicene ranks by a simple profession of faith; like the Donatist party in the next century, he believed that only those who had not been led astray by false teachers could make up the spotless body of Christ. Gregory of Elvira's treatise on the wedding-hymn of Christ and the Church develops the allegorical interpretation of the Song of Songs as a justification for this polemical orthodoxy.

The *Tractatus de epithalamio* begins with a short preface, very reminiscent of Origen, which sets out the characters of the poems "under the figure" of a wedding-hymn, a figure which suffices for the reader to understand what Solomon has written "under an aenigma."[5] This is Gregory's justification for taking the commentary in a new direction. In details of interpretation the *Tractatus* sticks quite close to Origen, but neither the five short books into which it is divided, nor its furious attacks on those outside a certain definition of faith sound anything like the Alexandrian exegete.[6] The *Tractatus* of Gregory of Elvira shows how quickly the genre of Song of Songs commentary had begun to develop or was developing.

Gregory of Elvira perceived all of those outside of Nicene Christianity as equally inimical. At Song of Songs 1:2, "for your breasts are better than wine," he launches an attack on the Jews which will become a major theme of his treatise. Instead of the two breasts of the she-goat of the Law, written on tablets of stone by the finger of God, Christians, like cows, have the four breasts of the Evangelists, full of the sweet milk of wisdom. This rather unlikely image preserves a theme from Origen, that the Gospels supersede the Prophets, but with a fervor that is totally new.[7] The antithesis here set up between Judaism and Christianity is repeated most notably in the denunciation of Jewish observance (circumcision, the Sabbath, rites of purification) which explicates part of Song of Songs 1:5, "they have placed me as a guard in the vineyards, my own vineyard I have not kept."[8] The Jews, in other words, have been preoccupied with external observance, and have therefore not properly cared for the promises they were given.

But, although Gregory lists the people of Israel among those who, in the words of Song of Songs 1:6, "wander after the flocks of your companions," it is the *Christians* who wander and lead others astray that most exercise him. In his explication of 1:6, he lashes out against "the many pseudo-apostles" who masquerade as leaders of the faithful and, like wolves in sheep's clothing, corrupt the virginity of that simple dove, the church. This reading shows Gregory's preoccupation with the allegorical mode as the inherited content of exegesis, for both Origen's

Homilies and his *Commentary* elaborate at this point on the theme of interior knowledge.[9] Gregory of Elvira's particular concern for the purity of the Church is made clearer, perhaps even dangerously clear, in his commentary on 2:15, "catch for us the foxes, the little foxes who destroy the vineyards." The foxes are the heretics who destroy the Church in flower; but these are *little* foxes (in his version, *vulpes pusillas*), for the ragings of powerful princes are worse than the seductions of heretics.[10] In many passages of the *Tractatus*, it is easy to hear echoes of the struggle between the Nicene and Arian Christians, and here, perhaps, a sly allusion to the bane of the Nicene school, the Emperor Constantius II.

Besides his virtually complete elaboration of the Song of Songs as an allegory of the immediate tribulations of institutional Christianity, Gregory of Elvira also gives a hint of another development in Latin Song of Songs interpretation: the connection between the Song of Songs and the Apocalypse as related allegories of the Church. At Song of Songs 1:14, he says, the Church is called a dove because the Greek word for dove, "peristera," has the same numerical value as the letters alpha and omega, which, as Apocalypse 22:13 testifies, signify Christ, the beginning and the end.[11] A numerical connection between alpha and omega and the dove is also found in early Latin commentaries on the Apocalypse, which by the fourth century was read as a prophecy of the eventual triumph of the spotless Church over various heretical sects.[12] The Song of Songs and the Apocalypse were thus increasingly read together, as two accounts of the same divine plan; as we have seen, an apocalyptic theme in Song of Songs exegesis is well developed by Honorius in the twelfth century.[13]

The *Tractatus de epithalamio* of Gregory of Elvira thus provided a model for exegesis of the Song of Songs which made the narrative of God's love for the Church into a polemic for orthodoxy. This is also true to some extent though not exclusively, of other commentaries from the age of the great councils. The influential commentary of Apponius, for example, while relying on the same sources as Gregory of Elvira, makes a striking contrast to this strident exclusivity. Apponius is an obscure author whose major (and perhaps only) work, *In Canticum Canticorum expositionem* was not printed until 1843, and has only recently appeared in a critical edition.[14] As Grillmeier has shown, this interpretation of the Song of Songs presents itself squarely within the Christian polemics of the age: it argues Christ's divinity against the Arians and Christ's humanity against the Gnostics, and echoes Origen's stress on the soul of Christ and the human soul.[15]

Apponius emerges from the difficult pages of this work as a complicated and rather cosmopolitan figure. His attitude towards the disputes of fourth-century Christianity is far more tolerant and sophisticated than that of the Bishop of Elvira, yet the reasons for this tolerance are obscure. In fact, many things about Apponius are obscure. He has been credited with knowledge of Greek and several Semitic languages, but this has been disputed.[16] He has been described as a native of fifth-century Syria or of seventh-century Ireland, or as a converted Jew, all with little evidence. Recent scholarship has suggested that the Song of Songs commentary of Apponius was written between 398 and 404, perhaps in Italy, or among an Italian literary circle.[17] His commentary on the Song of Songs seems to show knowledge of Jewish biblical interpretation, but this may be secondary, as he is heavily dependent on Jerome. Apponius also cites from the Latin translations of Origen on the Song of Songs, and a number of grammatical and scientific texts of late antiquity.[18] Like Jerome, Apponius may be most accurately described as a Christian who lived and studied in Italy and/or Palestine, and perhaps had some connection with an intellectual center such as Caesarea, where many worlds—East and West, Christian and Jewish, Semitic, Greek, and Latin—came together.[19]

It is not surprising, therefore, that Apponius's work on the Song of Songs is most widely known in the Latin Middle Ages in the form of an adaptation into twelve homilies attributed to Jerome. This version, known by its *incipit*, "Veri amoris," is found in twice as many manuscripts as the original, significantly, in copies associated with monastic houses in France and the Low Countries.[20] This compendium or one like it may explain how Apponius came to be cited, with and without attribution, by northern authors of the eight to the twelfth century, among them the Venerable Bede and Angelomus of Luxeuil.

At the beginning of the commentary, Apponius promises to show the hidden wit of the rough text of the Song of Songs, "following in the tracks of ancient teachers," and "by using the examples of the Hebrews." The latter may refer to rabbinic interpretation, or it may indicate use of the Vulgate Bible translation of Jerome, which Apponius consulted along with other Latin translations.[21] Whether or not Apponius actually knew

Hebrew, there are hints throughout of his awareness of the Jewish tradition of Song of Songs interpretation. Near the beginning of Book I, he recalls Akiba's defense of the Song of Songs, stating that it speaks not at all of carnal love ("which the Gentiles call cupidity") but is "totally spiritual, totally worthy of God, and totally the salvation of souls;" just below is a remarkably clear reference to the commonplace of rabbinic interpretation that the Song of Songs "was shown *in figura* to Moses on Mount Sinai so that he could make the Tabernacle of like beauty and measure."[22] At Song of Songs 1:7–8, Apponius gives an elaborate (though trinitarian) exegesis of Deuteronomy 6:5, part of the central Jewish prayer known as the Sh'ma.[23]

This knowledge and acceptance of Judaism is in striking contrast to the vituperations of Gregory of Elvira, and indeed, to other contemporary Christian authors. Clark rightly claims that Apponius even "outstrips Origen in his positive evaluation of ancient Israel."[24] But Apponius's most frequent type of reference to Judaism is not to contemporary Jews, but to the role the Hebrew people played in keeping the Law before the proclamation of the Gospel. The entire commentary is structured around the ultimate triumph of the Church, against great odds, as the people of God. Apponius praises the ancient Hebrews as forerunners of the Church: they were, for example, the only ancient people to anoint with oil, and they anticipated the coming of Christ, who was praised by God's faithful servant, Moses. The triumphalism of this message must be stressed, for to contemporary Jews, Apponius preached conversion.[25]

However more cosmopolitan and tolerant Apponius may have been, he is most like Gregory of Elvira in his firm defense of the Church militant. He shows the highest regard for both the secular and religious power of the Roman Empire, which he links to the triumph of Christianity. Like contemporary Syrian authors, but unlike the Roman Church of the fourth century, Apponius understood the Feast of the Epiphany as the birthdate of Christ; using a tradition dating from Tertullian, he emphasized the congruence of the Nativity and the foundation of the Empire under Augustus, both evidence of divine providence.[26] This variant on Roman liturgical customs thus paradoxically serves to emphasize the importance of Rome for Christian leadership.

The commentaries of Gregory and Apponius, then, pass on to medieval exegetes a vision of the Song of Songs as a narrative about the true, pure, and ultimately triumphant Church, led through persecutions by the Bridegroom, Christ. They show the development of the commentary genre from Origen in this concern for the true *institutional* Church, a concept which was also becoming current in Latin Apocalypse interpretation, and was perhaps a natural consequence of this period of intra-Christian strife. It is true that, in drawing the boundary line between the beloved of Christ and those outside this narrative, Apponius and Gregory of Elvira differ greatly, especially in their respective treatments of the Jewish tradition. Here, the question is whether the figure "Synagoga," especially as one of the interlocutors of the Song of Songs, is best understood as the holy forerunner of the Church or as just another meddlesome heresy nipping at Christian unity. In either case, these commentaries lay the ground for artistic representations, accompanying the Song of Songs in a number of manuscripts, which show Christ in judgment with the crowned Church at his right and the repudiated Synagogue pushed down (or already underfoot) on his left (Plate 4).[27] For both authors, there is no question that the Song of Songs is the hymn that celebrates the marriage of God with an institution of worldly as well as spiritual power.

Monastic Idealism and the Song of Songs

With the commentary of Gregory the Great, the ecclesiological interpretation of the Song of Songs began to reflect a new set of preoccupations with the sanctity of the institutional Church. Gregory the Great, a Roman of the senatorial class, was born ca. 550, more than a generation after the deposition of the last Roman emperor in the west. He spent most of his adult life under the threat of Rome's absorption into the kingdom of the Lombard invaders; in 573, when Gregory held the positions of president of the Senate and Prefect of Rome, the Lombards had advanced to Benevento. In the next year, Gregory abandoned secular political life and devoted himself to the Church, turning his family home on the Caelian hill into a monastery dedicated to Saint Andrew. From this point on, he was an advocate of the monastic life, with its emphasis on withdrawal from the world. But this change of life spared Gregory neither power nor responsibility: for sixteen years he served in such posts as papal deacon and secretary to Constantinople, and in 590 he was elected Pope.[28]

Gregory's most famous work, the *Moralia in Job*, was begun in

PLATE 4. Crowned Ecclesia on Christ's right hand, *Synagoga* underfoot. Montalcino, Museo Civico, "Biblia atlantica," f. 56. Twelfth century. Reproduced by permission of the Sovrintendenza dei Beni Culturali ed Artistici, Siena. Photo by Lensini.

Constantinople and finished in the first years of his pontificate. In these beginning years in the role of Pope, Gregory also wrote the *Regula pastoralis* and the fragmentary text *Expositio in Canticorum*. The commentary on the Song of Songs may have been originally delivered orally before being revised, by Claudius of Ravenna, a few years before Gregory's death in 604.[29] Gregory's commentary may have gone to verse 4:5 of the Song (at least, the Irish missionary Columbanus refers to a text of this length), but the extant treatise breaks off suddenly after 1:8. The vicissitudes of the scriptorium may be responsible for this break, as well as for the fact that many manuscripts divide the text into two homilies.[30] Even in this truncated version, Gregory's exposition of the Song of Songs was widely read and admired.[31] It became the most important medieval source for later Song of Songs exegetes, partly because of Gregory's authority as a model Pope, partly because of his role as a promulgator of Latin Christianity throughout Europe, but perhaps most of all because of the imagination and charm of the work.

Gregory begins with a long prologue which uses a number of images to play on the theme of allegory as the bridge between divine and human realms. This is the most theoretical discussion of allegory in the early Middle Ages; rather than concentrating on categories, it reflects poetically on the means by which allegory reveals the divine truth hidden *sub umbra et figura*. Gregory says that allegory is the hint of the former bliss of paradise in this pilgrimage of life; it is a machine which draws human senses up to God; it is the means by which we are stirred to spiritual love through such fleshly images as kisses and breasts; it is the mist over the sacred mountain of Scripture, through which God descends to human hearts and understanding.[32] Although expressed through his own rich set of metaphors, Gregory's reflection on allegory is clearly influenced by Origen, whose presence is gently felt throughout.[33]

Gregory's Bible text reflects his many sources, which include, besides Origen, Augustine, and Apponius, his own earlier works.[34] Like Origen, Gregory worked with levels of interpretation that fluctuate with some flexibility, according to the passage. His approach to allegory is thus far more open-ended than the rigorous system of Honorius Augustodunensis; it is modeled on the examples of Origen and Ambrose, and clearly reflects an awareness of the four-fold scheme Cassian set forth in the *Collationes*, which Gregory may have known through his contact with the Benedictine Rule followed at the monastery of the Lateran.[35] Taking two or three lines of text at a time, Gregory expounds a series of running narratives in different modes of interpretation, which are related but never congruent. Nor are these levels strictly parallel, for they fade in and out, according to the sense he finds most prominent in each passage. Gregory the Great did not just speculate on the nature of allegory, he also worked, or rather played, with the potential of allegory to say more than one thing at a time.

For example, the first verse, "Let him kiss me with the kiss of his mouth," is interpreted in two ways: first, "more generally," as the Church sighing for the coming of Jesus, then, "more specially," as "the longing for God in each of our hearts." The spiritual interpretation is cast in the mold of monastic spirituality, with a stress on the monastic virtue *compunctio*, the double-edged fear of and longing for God, as the way to the kiss of the entire soul.[36]

For Song of Songs 1:4–6, however, Gregory gives *three* interpretations, parallel to the historical, allegorical, and tropological modes of Cassian. First the "Synagogue," then the Church, then the soul confesses to being "black but beautiful . . . for the sun has discolored me." In this discussion, the "Synagogue" is a conflation of the ancient Hebrews (the tents of Solomon make up one part of the discussion) with the *ecclesia primitiva* or *synagoga fideles*, the Jews who came to believe in Christ and were rejected by the *synagoga infidelitatis*. The "blackness" of the Church recalls the commentaries of the conciliar age, as the interpretation portrays the Apostles, sons of the Heavenly Jerusalem, fighting against the errors of the old heretics Arius, Sabellius, and Montanus.[37] But the understanding of this passage according to the tropological mode takes the commentary, in tone and purpose, far from the vision of Gregory of Elvira and Apponius, into the psychological drama of the monastic ideal.

In this same passage, to give an eloquent example, Gregory explains that every human being is made up of two "rational spirits," human and angelic, in constant struggle:

> "The sons of my mother fought against me." Behold, while these rational spirits fight, these spirits, sons of the mother, while they fight against the soul, they make her lean on earthly things, be free for worldly acts, seek transitory things. . . . "My vineyard," that is, my soul, my life, my mind, I have neglected to keep.[38]

Gregory thus does not limit his concern to the institutional Church, led astray by "the flocks of your companions," but shows a new *pastoral* concern for individual Christians, who can be led astray even by those *within* the hierarchy of the Church. In a passage echoing the themes of the *Regula pastoralis*, he says:

> For many little ones among the faithful of the Church hunger to live well. They wish to have a life of rectitude. They consider the life of the priests who are put above them; and, since the priests themselves do not live well, and those who are before them do not live right, so those who follow after dissolve in error.[39]

These passages demonstrate a shift in perception of "the Church," from a triumphant institution on earth battling the external enemy, to a mystical body with brooding potential for corruption from within. Gregory's exegesis always turns on the tension between inner and outer manifestations, and often tends towards mystical rapture. It is this inner vision of perfection, as well as a pessimism about the external correlation of Church and Empire, that marks the shift into early medieval Song of Songs commentary. In his most positive portrayals of the Church, Gregory emphasizes this mystical end-point. For example, the Church is like a king's house: it has a door, stairs, a dining room, a bedroom. The door is opened by faith, the stairs climbed by hope, the dining room entered by charity; but anyone with the disposition to seek after sublime secrets and secret discernment enters "almost into the bedroom," that is, into the mystical embrace. This is a familiar progression; in the *Moralia*, discussing Song of Songs 5:2, "I sleep and my soul keeps watch," Gregory explains that the heart that clings to God internally is able to function at once *in mundo* and *extra mundum*, just as Gregory was called to do.[40]

The desire for God that echoes through this commentary is unmistakably monastic; it shows the perfectionism of the monastic ideal extended out onto the Church and to every human soul. Unfortunately, the Church, at least the Church on earth, often falls short of this ideal. A striking difference in the ways that Gregory the Great and the fourth-century commentators read the Song of Songs is that Gregory used the text to criticize, as well as to praise, the institutional Church. He by no means saw the enemies of the Church as primarily external. This work introduces into genre of commentary on the Song of Songs the theme of distrust of temporal power, and was especially forceful coming from one who had himself repudiated that power. This message was welcome to monastic authors for centuries to come because it lent authority to their spiritual perception of reality, through the words of that very monk who had renounced the world to become the strongest leader the western Church could remember. From this point on, the tension between the monastic ideal and the structures of temporal power, secular and ecclesiastical alike, becomes an important theme of commentary on the Song of Songs.

For the Venerable Bede, who lived from ca. 673 to 735, Gregory the Great was a much-admired figure, the model for monastic life, an ideal at the center of his self-understanding. Bede's life was spent almost totally within the world of the cloister: he was dedicated to the monastery of Wearmouth in Northumbria at the age of seven, and spent the rest of his days there and in the related community at Jarrow. Book 2 of Bede's famous *Ecclesiastical History of the English People* begins with a life of Gregory, especially praising him for sending missionaries to convert the English to Christianity.[41] The *Ecclesiastical History* describes a number of Gregory's writings, but does not mention the commentary on the Song of Songs, nor is this text cited in Bede's commentary on the same book.[42]

Bede's commentary on the Song of Songs is a strange work, incorporating many sources and, on first consideration, directed towards a number of goals. This appearance may be a consequence of how it was written. Paul Meyvaert suggests that it passed through several stages of composition before attaining the final form in which it has been handed down to us.[43] Certainly, what appears to be the final redaction has an odd shape. It is made up of seven books: the first a polemic against the Pelagian author Julian of Eclanum; the second through sixth a running commentary on the Song of Songs; the seventh a compendium of passages on the Song of Songs from various works of Gregory other than his commentary on the Song of Songs. This schematic representation, completely peculiar to this work, has challenged both medieval and modern readers. The problem of how to treat Bede's opening barrage against Pelagianism led many medieval scribes (and the modern editor) to treat the first book as a prologue followed by books one through six. For the sake of clarity, I will follow this division of the text in my references to the critical edition, although not in my interpretation of the treatise, since it is clear that Bede intended the opening section as "book one."[44]

Bede seems to have been moved to the attack by a lost treatise of Julian on the Song of Songs, perhaps called *De amore*.[45] We know nothing of the history of this text outside of Bede's discussion and quotations. Julian was the bishop of Eclanum (Aeclanum), in southern Italy, the son of a notable Christian family, friends of Augustine. In 418, he was exiled by Pope Zosimus for refusing to condemn the intrepid Irish monk Pelagius, whose writings in defense of free will motivated Augustine's formulation of the doctrine of original sin. Julian wrote a number of attacks on the related doctrine of predestination, and was Augustine's final opponent.[46] Part of Julian's exile was spent in the company of Theodore of Mopsuestia, who influenced the way he understood several biblical books, including the Psalms, Job, and the Song of Songs.[47]

Bede's refutation of Julian can thus be read as an apologetic for allegorical exegesis of the Song of Songs, but it is much more than this, for Julian's interpretation of the Song of Songs, as reconstructed from Bede, was not merely an exercise in Antiochene literalism. It seems to have been, rather, an apology for human love specifically directed against the idea of original sin. Bede does criticize Julian's literal understanding of several verses of the Song of Songs, namely 1:1 "your breasts are better than wine," 1:9 "your neck like necklaces," 5:11 "his hair exalted like of palms," which Julian seems to have taken as physical descriptions.[48] But his animus against Julian is more directed against a perceived advocacy for the basic goodness of human sexuality than against issues of biblical hermeneutics. It is on this theological issue that Bede begins "book one" with a warning against the "snake in the grass" (*anguis in herba*) Julian, whose interpretation must be invalidated before Bede's can begin. Bede is scornful of the Pelagian understanding of the relationship between human sexuality and moral culpability, and angrily dismisses Julian's claim that, except for open lust, the flesh holds no inherent sin.[49]

In response to Julian's exegesis of Song of Songs 8:2 "I will seize you and lead you into the house of my mother, there you will teach me," Bede gives a passionate defense of Augustinian anthropology:

> For Scripture testifies that sin is congenital to man, saying: "a heavy yoke is upon the children of Adam, from the day of their coming out of their mother's womb, until the day of burial into the mother of all." (Ecclesiasticus 40:1) Indeed, holy Job testifies that this is as old as the conception of man itself, when supplicating God he says: "who can make clean one conceived from unclean seed? are you not the only one who is?" (Job 14:4) And what could be the consequence of saying that there is no congenital sin in men born of the joining of male and female, since the Son of God, who himself was created from the Virgin without the service of the body of a man, was both surrounded by the truth of the flesh, and came out free of stain?[50]

The reference to the spotless birth of Christ is essential for Bede's argument because it stresses the distance between the human state of sin and the extraordinary fact of the incarnation. For the rest of "book one," Bede continues to develop two related ideals: the inherent depravity of human life as classically manifested in sexuality, and the utter necessity for the freely given grace of God as the only antidote to this situation. All of this background is important to the proper understanding of the Song of Songs because Bede wants to follow Gregory's lead in reading the text as a joyous celebration of God's pure love for both the Church and the soul, a love that is especially apparent in the monastic life. This is an ideal which Julian, who married the daughter of the bishop of Benevento, obviously did not espouse.[51] In preserving the allegorical reading of the Song of Songs, Bede is also defending the monastic life and the view of human nature on which it is based. This is certainly the rationale for "book one," which ends with a promise to interpret the Song of Songs "following in the tracks of the fathers," and defending the grace of God.[52]

Between "book one" and the outright exposition, Bede goes through the entire Song of Songs twice, presenting it as the love between God and the Church according to two rhetorical strategies. The first of these short texts, which most manuscripts entitle "Capitula in Canticum Canticorum," divides the Song of Songs into thirty-nine events, each described in one sentence, for example:

> I. The Synagogue wishes the Lord to come in the flesh, and runs up to meet him in devoted love.
>
> II. Hiding herself from the persecution of the unfaithful Jews, the Primitive Church laments from that place, and, trembling, asks the help of her beloved Redeemer.
>
> III. The Lord, scolding the frightened Church, reminds her of the graces given by him against all the snares of the enemy.[53]

The "Capitula" give an easily accessible overall narrative of the Song of Songs, presupposing the allegorical level of interpretation. Following this section is the Vulgate text of the Song of Songs, here rendered in a dramatic form by means of forty-one rubrics. These identify the speakers as the Synagogue, the Church, and Christ, sometimes with accompanying descriptions of attributes or actions. Bede is here making use of the ancient custom of presenting the Song of Songs as a drama in order to complement the "Capitula." Both of these short summaries enforce the overall allegorical mode of reading the text: the first describes the story;

set against it is the Song of Songs itself, in a rubricated text which identifies the interlocutors.[54]

Then begin the five books of commentary. Of course, after these elaborate preliminaries, the reader has no doubt about the interpretation Bede will pursue. And, indeed, he follows through with an elaborate explication of the Song of Songs as the love between God and the Church, carefully incorporating many sources. Bede's "book two" shows the influence of Origen in several places, although he does not name him. He does, however, quote an "ancient translation" of Song of Songs 1:10 that is congruent with Rufinus's text in book two of the *Commentary*; and he ends this book at 2:13, which is also the stopping point of Origen's second *Homily*.[55] Bede draws from a number of classical authors (Horace, Juvenal, Pliny, Vergil), and even more Christian ones, but especially from Gregory and Jerome. More specific to the tradition of Song of Songs commentary, he is aware of several Bible translations, and loosely quotes passages from Gregory the Great and Apponius on the Song of Songs, citing both by name.[56] The intermediate books of Bede's running commentary begin at Song of Songs 4:6, 5:13, and 7:5; this division of the text does not suggest a particular rhetorical motivation (indeed, 5:13 is right in the middle of a description of the Beloved) but rather emphasizes the continuity of the exegesis by dividing the Song of Songs into somewhat equal passages. The "Capitula" and the rubricated text of the Song of Songs are divided more thematically, and perhaps are meant to supply the narrative outline of the commentary proper.

The final book, which Bede calls the seventh, offers a collection of quotations from Gregory the Great on the Song of Songs. Bede explains that he has heard about a compendium of Gregory's interpretations of the entire Bible put together by the disciple Paterius, but does not have a copy, and so has compiled this florilegium to fill the void. The collection shows Bede's familiarity with Gregory's *Moralia in Job*, homilies on the Gospels and Ezechiel, and the *Regula pastoralis*.[57] This final section of Bede's commentary makes it very clear that, just as Julian misinterpreted it entirely, Gregory understood the Song of Songs especially well. Like the other authors examined in this chapter, Bede used the Song of Songs to comment on the situation of the Church as he knew it. His contrast of Julian (at the beginning) and Gregory (at the end) makes use of two long-dead authors to highlight some contemporary issues, especially his support of the Roman primacy, over against what he saw as "Pelagian" notions in traditional Celtic Christianity.[58] The consequent defense of Augustinian anthropology is the most important theological issue of the commentary, the monastic life of prayer and contemplation is the human ideal urged by this vision of human nature.

Bede's *In Cantica Canticorum* thus employs its unusual structure in the service of one coherent interpretation, and on consideration does not seem so ungainly. It was surely the most rhetorically complicated work on the Song of Songs in the early Middle Ages. Its complexity highlights a familiar theme: that the Song of Songs is about heavenly rather than earthly love, about the marriage of Christ and the Church—but in Bede's own terms. An emphasis on the spiritual life can be found even in Bede's commentary on the Apocalypse (which essentially focuses on the triumph of the Church militant), in the damnation of the "impious city," and the final vision of the heavenly Jerusalem "bedecked as the wife of the Lamb."[59] In his commentary on the Song of Songs, Bede continually balances the outward action of the Church with monastic virtues. For example, *Capitulum XXIII*, in allegorically paraphrasing the vignette of the awakened lover of Song of Songs 5:2–7, speaks of the Church both in contemplative repose and in apostolic action. It is the former concept that is most forcefully expressed in the illuminated capital of a Cambridge manuscript of Bede's commentary, which exploits the O of "osculetur" by portraying a mouth in which Christ and the Church sit locked in a kiss.[60] (Plate 5)

The next stage of adaptation of the allegorical understanding of the Song of Songs to the changing portrait of the Church served to reinforce this mode of understanding while avoiding the theoretical and rhetorical complexities of Gregory the Great and Bede. Compared to these earlier treatises, the commentaries of Alcuin and Haimo are more striking in form than in content. They strive to produce short text-book versions of previous exegesis, in response to the multinational, expansive, yet highly centralized Carolingian Church.[61] It is precisely in the three generations from Alcuin to Haimo, and primarily in the realm of biblical exegesis, that the glossed school text which became so important to later medieval Christian literature began to take its classical form.

Alcuin, a native Northumbrian who died in 804 after decades of service to the Frankish kings, wrote a *Compendium in Canticum Canticorum* that completely abandons Bede's argument about Julian and Gregory, yet remains essentially an expanded version of Bede's "Capitula" with fre-

PLATE 5. Christ and the Church kiss in the middle of a kiss. From Bede, *In Cantica Canticorum*, Cambridge, King's College MS. 19 f. 12v. St. Alban's, twelfth century. Reproduced by permission of the King's College Library.

quent rubrics to indicate the speakers. At least one manuscript affixes an original (and characteristically Alcuinian) poem recommending the Song of Songs above Vergil.[62] Alcuin's commentary on the Apocalypse follows a similar path, mixing excerpts from Bede and Ambrosius Autpertus.[63] Both texts are beautiful examples of the adaptation of already-existing interpretations into shorter reference works intended for an audience still primarily monastic, but not always highly skilled in Latin grammar, syntax, and rhetoric.

This straightforward, easily accessible style is also the hallmark of the most popular Song of Songs commentary of the Middle Ages, that of Haimo of Auxerre. Haimo (for many years confused with Alcuin's pupil, Haimo of Halberstadt) was one of the brightest figures of the ninth-century school at the monastery of Saint-Germain of Auxerre, and was appointed abbot of the nearby monastery of Sasceium in 865.[64] Haimo was a prolific exegete, even though his literary profile is still unclear, awaiting the difficult task of separating his works from those of later authors, especially Remigius of Auxerre.[65] We know a bit more about Haimo's intellectual environment than about his life. Auxerre was an especially important center in the late Carolingian practice of making composite texts, a process which hints at the development of the scholastic method. Haimo's biblical commentaries are more complicated than Alcuin's, but show many of the same educational motivations: they incorporate many sources, often seemingly contradictory ones, into short synopses of great clarity. The method at which Haimo excelled caught on to such an extent that extracts from his works were in circulation as school texts during his own lifetime.[66]

Haimo's *Commentarium in Cantica Canticorum* is a masterful compendium, incorporating selections from classical authors, including Plato and Aristotle, Origen, Gregory the Great, Bede, and even Alcuin, from whom he borrowed the sensible structure of a chapter of commentary for each chapter of the Song of Songs.[67] In this he seems quite characteristic of his generation, which also produced the tour-de-force *catena* on the Song of Songs of Angelomus of Luxeuil, which was dedicated to Carolingian royalty.[68] The far greater popularity of Haimo's commentary can be explained by several structural characteristics which made it especially easy to use. For one thing, it retains the dramatic form outlined by Bede, introducing nearly every verse by a rubric identifying the speaker. This application of these rubrics to a running commentary was a brilliant touch which was so popularly received that Haimo's commentary influenced the rubrics commonly added not to commentaries but to *Bibles* copied in the eleventh and twelfth centuries.[69] Haimo makes his commentary accessible by following a regular structure, beginning each explication with a literal meaning (often because of the necessity of explaining an obscure word), then moving to a mode he, following Justus of Urguel, called "mystice" or "spiritualiter," both terms for the allegorical level of exegesis.[70] For example, in his comments on Song of Songs 7:13, "the mandrakes give out fragrance in our gates," Haimo first explains the mandrakes as a plant used in the ancient world for medicinal purposes, relating it to the delectable "Matian fruit" described by Macrobius and Pliny; and then goes on to the "mystical" meaning of the apostles and their successors setting out through the gates of the Church. Much of this is found in Bede, but in the opposite order.[71]

Haimo's consistent pattern of allegorical interpretation, plunging in with no theoretical discussion of the method, shows to what extent the application of multiple senses was an assumed part of his intellectual world, asking for no comment. By the ninth century, Cassian's theory of four levels of exegesis had become commonplace, deeply ingrained in the commentary tradition. Although Haimo here interprets the Song of Songs according to a consistently allegorical understanding, examples of his acceptance of Cassian's method abound, providing the soil in which Honorius's elaborate application of the theory could take root. For example, whereas Bede used the verse "your lips drip honeycomb" (4:11) as an opportunity to digress on Cassian's four senses, complete with the example of Jerusalem, Haimo gives only the bare bones of the system:

> Therefore Divine Scripture is correctly called dripping honeycomb, because it is understood in many ways and expounded by various senses, now according to the letter, now according to allegory, now according to morality, now according to anagogy, which is the superior sense.[72]

The final comment about the superiority of the anagogical sense may well be intended to emphasize the "true" Church as the mystical body of the elect. A similar idea is found in Haimo's interpretation of Song of Songs 5:2, where he describes the triple knocking on the door by which Christ awakens the Primitive Church for her labor: by the first, he exhorts her to virtue and by the second, to preach conversion; by the third, the Lord calls his elect, "since the vexation of sickness shows that

PLATE 6. "Vox optantis Christi adventum" (A voice hoping for the advent of Christ). *Christus* and *Ecclesia* in Embrace. Valenciennes, Biblioteque Municipale, MS. 10, f. 113. Twelfth century. Reproduced by permission of the library. Photo by ETS Gerard.

death is near."[73] Haimo's text is at once more direct than Bede's and more vivid than Alcuin's. If Alcuin removed Bede's interpretation of the Song of Songs from the Pelagian controversy, Haimo cast it in a more emotional tone, still very much in the context of the monastic ideal, but so condensed that it could take on a more universal form.

From Allegory to Anagogy to Tropology

The personal immediacy of Haimo's text opened the way for yet another internal transformation of the genre, a series of commentaries which especially stress the understanding of the Song of Songs as the love between Christ and the individual human soul. This idea became especially current in the twelfth century, but its roots can be seen several generations earlier, in the increasingly common perception of the relation between the Song of Songs and the Apocalypse. The Apocalypse is a biblical book which, by its very nature, elides the allegorical, tropological, and anagogical senses; read as an allegory of the Church, it points towards the importance of the elect in God's plan for the end-times. It is hardly surprising that Haimo, like Alcuin, put together an Apocalypse commentary from the works of Bede and Ambrosius Autpertus; many medieval exegetes commented on both the Apocalypse and the Song of Songs.[74]

The softening of boundaries between Apocalypse and Song of Songs interpretation became especially evident as external ecclesiastical turmoil raised more doubts about the purity of the Church. Several eleventh-century commentaries on the Song of Songs consequently developed an interpretation of the text in direct response to the Gregorian Reform and the Investiture Controversy. Especially interesting examples of this phenomenon are the three related texts of Robert of Tombelaine, Bruno of Segni, and John of Mantua, all authors associated with the court of Gregory VII. These three commentaries stress the theme of the hidden Church of the pure, a concept found in Augustine's treaties against the Donatists.[75] All three exhort the reader as the Bride, while aiming at quite different audiences. John of Mantua's text, written specifically for the Countess Matilda of Tuscany, does not seem to have been widely known in the Middle Ages; Robert's commentary, in contrast, became a medieval classic.[76] A description of the history, premises, and goals of the commentary on the Song of Songs by Robert of Tombelaine will show yet another way in which allegorical readings of the Song of Songs mirrored the changing medieval Church.

Robert of Tombelaine was a Benedictine monk whose career was buffeted by the storms of the Gregorian Reform. Ardent in his dream of an institutional Church pure from corruption, he spent most of his life attacking monastic laxity and ecclesiastical abuses. Robert first entered the powerful island monastery of Mont-Saint-Michel, but retreated to a hermitage on the nearby island of Tombelaine in protest against the simony of his abbot. In 1066, Bishop Odo of Bayeux appointed him the first abbot of Saint-Vigor-le-Grand; when Odo was disgraced and imprisoned in 1082, Robert sought refuge in Rome, where he died (ca. 1090) in the service of the reforming pope, Gregory VII.[77]

Robert's *Commentariorum in Cantica Canticorum* was probably written on Tombelaine, since the dedicatory epistle to Ansfrid of Préaux speaks of writing "in a solitary cell."[78] Robert here speaks of a division of the commentary into two somewhat unequal books, the first ending at 4:6, the second taking up at the next verse. The commentary has a complicated textual history which has never been resolved with a critical edition: it appears in the *Patrologia Latina* in two partial versions, one in Robert's name, the other attributed to Gregory the Great. The text also makes up a great part of one version of the *Glossa ordinaria* on the Song of Songs.[79] Medieval attribution of this text to Gregory, the greatest theoretician of Song of Songs allegory since Origen, was a great tribute. This becomes apparent by comparison: Alcuin's Song of Songs compendium was instead confused with Isidore of Seville, Haimo's with Cassiodorus. In fact, Robert's allegory is far more subtle and multivalent than any Song of Songs commentary of the ninth century. The fact that Robert's exposition was taken up in the gloss shows that it also resonated with a vision of the Church that was developing in the early twelfth century. Robert of Tombelaine thus gives a rare glance into the inner transformation of the Songs of Songs commentary genre.

Robert's interpretations are founded on the traditional ecclesiological readings of Paterius (for Gregory the Great), Bede, Alcuin, Angelomus, and, most of all, Haimo; but they differ from all of these in that they shade consistently into ascetic perfectionism. In his prologue, Robert explains that the Song of Songs is the last of Solomon's works, not according to the convention that it represents logic, but because "the perfected man, treading the world underfoot, is joined to the Bridegroom by an embrace."[80] Of 4:10, "a garden enclosed, my sister my bride," which Haimo saw simply as the Church, Robert stipulates:

> Here is rightly said a garden enclosed, because it is fortified all around by a rampart of charity, lest some reprobate should enter among the number of the elect within.[81]

The enjoining of monastic perfection on the Church is reminiscent of, and explains why Robert's commentary was attributed to, Gregory the Great. But, while Gregory's reading of the Song of Songs generally moves from ecclesiology to pastoral guidance, Robert's consistently goes farther, to mystical unity. On Song of Songs 1:6, "lest I begin to wander after the flocks of your companions," Robert adds to Gregory's fears about bad Christian leadership:

> Truly, one in whom Christ does not repose will wander, for his mind, which that sweet and weighty Spirit of Christ does not fill, is dissolute, moved around by many thoughts. But who are the companions of Christ, through whose flocks the Bride greatly fears to wander, except all the false Christians? They, either by reason of the name alone, or even the communion of the sacraments, will be called brothers of Christ, because he himself called his chosen his brothers, and, living together in the Church they associate with the elect. These multitudes are rightly called flocks in reproach, since they live like irrational animals, without order, they are given over to the devouring by seducer spirits.[82]

This skepticism about the "false Christians" who are part of "even the communion of the sacraments" is a logical extension of the doubts first articulated by Augustine against the Donatists and echoed by Gregory the Great: that the "true" Church might not be the one immediately visible. Robert continues the monastic tradition of reading the Song of Songs as the love between Christ and the Church of those given over to contemplative life, but he suggests that the relationship between these esoteric and exoteric churches had deteriorated since the time of Gregory the Great. Even with a new Pope Gregory working to cleanse the external Church of impurities, Robert had little hope for the wedding of Christ and the Church on earth. By the image of the elect (those in whom Christ reposes) wandering through the flocks of those "given over to the devouring by seducer spirits," Robert hints at the cataclysmic end awaiting false "companions of Christ." The Song of Songs commentary of Robert of Tombelaine is full of apocalyptic expectations for the final wedding of the lamb with the Church of the elect.

Robert of Tombelaine by no means represents the end of the tradition of ecclesiological interpretation of the Song of Songs. He did not signal the end of commentaries which portray the text primarily as the love between Christ and the Church, but he did cast that marriage in a decidedly unearthly light. His commentary is a useful stopping point for my analysis, since its stress on the spiritual cleansing of the Church which will take place through individual souls shows this mode of understanding verging towards the moral or tropological sense which is the subject of the next chapter.

But, just at the time that the commentary genre begins to reflect an increasing emphasis on monastic purity, artistic representations of the Song of Songs confirm the primacy of the ecclesiological mode of reading the text, clearly demonstrated by illuminations accompanying twelfth-century texts of and commentaries on the Song of Songs. Song of Songs commentaries in the ecclesiological mode influenced the development of a widespread iconographical system through which, for example, the Church was represented as a woman with an architectural or a triple-pointed crown. In one twelfth-century series of illuminated Bibles, this crowned woman makes use of Song of Songs 8:2, "I will seize you and lead you," to emphasize the fact that Christ's sufferings were for her sake.[83] (Plate 7) The striking illustrations of the commentary of Honorius Augustodunensis discussed in chapter three (Plates 1–3) are exceptions to a general artistic convention that made no distinction between the Song of Songs and its various interpretations. These more common artistic representations are not based on one commentary, but have instead a well-articulated tradition of interpretation behind them.

Allegorical exegesis of the Song of Songs, the most popular medieval expression of the commentary genre, is perhaps a difficult mode for modern readers to understand. Sympathetic confrontation with these commentaries must begin with the disconcerting fact that here the passionate lovers of the Song of Songs are turned into Christ and the Church. This may seem the coldest allegory of a hot poem, yet there was nothing dispassionate about the medieval perception of the Church as Bride of Christ. The Church, as an earthly institution but also as a heavenly ideal, could so easily attain personification precisely because these ecclesiological commentaries model medieval reality. This chapter has traced the ways in which Song of Songs commentaries reflect changes in the per-

PLATE 7. "Coniugis in morem permiscetur per amorem Ecclesiae Christus perit hinc dolor et quoque fastus" (Joined together in customs mixed together by love Christ dies for the Church from this pain and also pride). On Christ's scroll, Song of Songs 2:1–"Ego flos campi" (I am the flower of the field). On Ecclesia's scroll, Song of Songs 7:13, 8:2–"Dilecte mi aprehendam te" (My beloved I will seize you). Engelberg, Stiftsbibliothek MS. 32 f. 2v. Twelfth century. Reproduced by permission of the library.

ception of *Ecclesia* and "her" major impediments in each period. There is a movement from a sense of "inside/outside" to "inside/*truly* inside," in concert with the growing impact of the monastic ideal and related readings of the Apocalypse. It is no historical accident that so many medieval exegetes commented on both the Apocalypse and the Song of Songs.[84] Doubtless, interpretation of the Song of Songs in the allegorical mode was so popular because of the flexibility of method which allowed for continual, subtle, changes of reading. This very flexibility led to a more fundamental "internal transformation"[85] of the genre, the twelfth-century commentaries which saw in the Song of Songs the marriage between God and the soul.

Notes

1. All of these have been studied by A. Wilmart, "Fragments du Ps-Origène sur le psaume XCI dans une collection espagnole," RB 29 (1912) 274–293; "Archa Noe," RB 26 (1909) 1–12; "Un manuscrit du Tractatus du faux Origène espagnol sur l'arche de Noé," RB 29 (1912) 47–59. Texts edited by J. Fraipont in CCSL 69 (1967).

2. Gregory of Elvira, *Tractatus de epithalamio (in Canticum Canticorum libri quinque)*, ed. J. Fraipont, CCSL 69 (1967) pp. 67–210.

3. A. Wilmart, "L'ancienne version latine du cantique I–III,4," RB 28 (1911) 11–36, for missing verses cf. note 2; A. Wilmart, "Les 'Tractatus' sur le cantique attribués à Grégoire d'Elvire," BLE (1906) 233–299; followed by Fraipont in CCSL 69, p. 167. The edition of G. Heine, *Bibliotheca anecdotorum* I (Leipzig, 1848) pp. 132–166, discounted manuscript "Rotensis," Lérida, Archivo de la Catedral 2, ff. 108v–118v (c.10, Saint Vincent of Ronda), which Wilmart showed to be the best copy. The commentary seems always to have been attributed to Gregory, although the incipit twice calls it a work of "Gregorius Papa" (meaning simply bishop), which may have been misleading after the time of Gregory the Great (d. 604).

4. For Lucifer of Cagliari, and his struggle with Constantius II, see W.H.C. Frend, *The Rise of Christianity* (Philadelphia: Fortress Press, 1984) pp. 534–543, and J. N. D. Kelly, *Jerome: His Life, Writings, and Controversies* (New York: Harper and Row, 1975) p. 63.

5. "Iam uero in canticis canticorum figuraliter sub epithalamii carmine quattuor Salomon introducit personas ... Haec pauca de operibus Salomonis sub aenigmatibus dicta lectori in prologo exposuisse sufficiat. Explicit prologus." Preface, ed. Fraipont, p. 169. This is clearly, but not slavishly, following Origen, *Homily* I, 1, ed. Baehrens, GCS 33, Origen, vol. 8 (1925) p. 29.

6. For the influence of Origen, Wilmart, "Les 'Tractatus'," and the discussion

of Ohly, pp. 28–31. The five books are divided as follows: I = 1:1–1:5; II = 1:6–1:11; III = 1:12–2:6; IV = 2:7–2:17, V = 3:1–3:4. Book IV expounds a longer section of the text, but in less space.

7. "Habuit quidem prisca lex duo ubera in duabus tabulis lapideis quae digito dei impressae candidum lac disiplinae populo Israelitico praebuerunt; sed nunc ubera domini iam non duo, sed quattour esse cognouimus; quattuor enim euangeliorum fontes dulce lac sapientiae credentibus tribuunt." I, 9, ed. Fraipont, p. 173; also in Origen, *Commentary* I, ed. Baehrens, p. 97; but not in *Homily* I, 3, pp. 32–33.

8. II, 4, ed. Fraipont, p. 180. See also the portrayal of the Jews as an inferior offering to God, ed. Fraipont, p. 173, and the *Tractatus Origenis*, Wilmart, "Un manuscrit du *Tractatus*," pp. 56–57; CCSL 69 (1967) pp. 26–146.

9. II, 11–18, ed. Fraipont, pp. 183–185. The sexual imagery of II, 15 is remarkable: "Cum enim sancta et inuiolata simplex columba ecclesia falsos et iam dixi doctores et corruptores uirginitatis suae grauiter pertimesceret, qui sub uelamine sacerdotum dei, h. e. qui sub uestitu ouium lupi rapaces ut praedixerat dominus uenturi erant, et certa definitione euangelicae ueritatis requireret rationem" p. 184. Compare to Origen, *Homily* I, 9, ed. Baehrens, pp. 40–41; *Commentary* Book II, pp. 141–149.

10. "Maiores sunt utique principes saeculi potestates ad seuiendum quam haereticorum fallaciae ad seducendum," IV, 25, ed. Fraipont, p. 205.

11. "Columba apud Graecos peristera dicitur, cuius nominis litterae per computum Graecum in summam redactae unum et octigentos faciunt; unum autem et DCCC α et ω graece signantur; unde et ipse dominus, cuius est caro eccelesiae, "ego sum: inquit α et ω, quo numero nomen columbae signatur" III, 10–11, ed. Fraipont, p. 195.

12. Already in the fourth century Jerome had moderated the chiliasm of the Apocalypse commentary of Victorinus of Pettau, cf. *Commentarii in Apocalypsin*, ed. Johannes Haussleiter, CSEL 49 (1916) The dove is also related to α and ω by Primasius, *Commentariorum super Apocalypsin B. Joannis*, PL 68:932 D–33A.

13. See above, chapter 3, note 44.

14. The *In Canticum Canticorum Expositionem* of Apponius is edited by B. de Vregille and L. Neyrand, CCSL 19 (1986). Apponius may also have been the author of *De induratione cordis Pharaonis*, a short text attributed to Pelagius, see Vregille and Neyrand's introduction, pp. xcix–cv. The spelling "Apponius" is favored by the manuscripts and by ancient witnesses.

15. See the discussion of Apponius by Aloys Grillmeier, *Christ in Christian Tradition*, second edition, vol.1, trans. John Bowden (Atlanta: John Knox Press, 1975) pp. 384–388, under the title "Origenist Christology in the West." Apponius lashes out at a list of heretics in Book II, ed. Vregille and Neyrand, p. 44.

16. Johannes Witte, *Der Kommentar des Aponius zum Hohelied. Untersuchung über die Zeit und den Ort seiner Abfassung* (Erlangen: Junge & Sohn, 1903) argues

that Apponius knew Hebrew and Syriac, pp. 22, 40–46, but Vregille and Neyrand dismiss any knowledge of Semitic languages as superficial, pp. lxviii–lxx.

17. Witte, pp. 64–77, first advanced the thesis that Apponius was a converted Jew from Syria; this claim is simply stated by Ohly, p. 51, and more cautiously by Riedlinger, p. 7. Clark is frankly skeptical, p. 399, and Vregille and Neyrand deny it, p. cxl, noting his confusion about the geography of Palestine, "parfois déconcertante, même lorsqu'il s'agit de lieux bibliques," p. lxxiii. The suggestion that Apponius was instead a seventh-century native of Ireland was made by Grosjean and Baxter in CPL; Riedlinger argues to the contrary, p. 47, note 1. For dating of the commentary, see ed. Vregille and Neyrand, pp. cviii–cx.

18. Among the authors known to Apponius were Vergil, Servius, Terence, Pliny Major, Pomponius Mela, and a herbal of Pseudo-Apuleius. In Book V (ed. Vregille and Neyrand, pp. 123–124) there is a discussion of the beliefs of "Platonici" and "Stoici." Vregille and Neyrand argue that Apponius's knowledge of Origen was secondary, while admitting substantial parallels between his commentary on the Song of Songs and the *Commentary* and *Homilies* of Origen translated by Rufinus and Jerome, pp. lxxxvii–lxxxix.

19. I would like to thank Mary Rose D'Angelo for this suggestion. It certainly seems that Apponius moved in the same circles as Jerome and Rufinus. An interesting account of Caesarea as an intellectual center is Lee I. Levine, *Caesarea Under Roman Rule* (Leiden: E. J. Brill, 1975).

20. Paolino Bellet, "La forma homilética del comentario de Aponio al Cantar de los Cantares," *Estudios Bíblicos* 12 (1953) 28–39. Vregille and Neyrand also edit the homiletic redaction of Apponius's commentary, pp. 315–462, from seven manuscripts, six dating before the year 900. In contrast, the full commentary is extant in four manuscripts, only one from before 1000.

21. "et hispidus sermo, si habet in se reconditum sal, non syllogismorum resonantia uerba, sed sensum requirat . . . uestigia antiquorum magistrorum secutos . . . utentes exemplaria Hebraeorum." Prologue, ed. Vregille and Neyrand, p. 2. Apponius's varying Bible texts were taken by Witte as evidence to date the commentary near the beginning of the fifth century, when the Vulgate was beginning to be used, p. 22. This is in agreement with the study of Vregille and Neyrand, pp. lxxxvii–lxxix.

22. "In quo utique nihil de carnali amore, quem Gentiles cupidinem appellant, qui insania potius intelligi potest quam amor, sed totum spiritale, totum dignum Deo, totumque animae salutare." "in Monte Sina, beato Moysi ostensum est in figura cuius pulchritudinis uel mensurae tabernaculum faceret." I, 44–46, ed. Vregille and Neyrand, p. 4. For these motifs in rabbinic exegesis, see above, chapter three, note 10.

23. "Diliges Dominum Deum tuum in toto corde tuo . . . in toto corde, in toto anima, et in tota uirtute deligit," II, 9–5; 110–111, ed. Vregille and Neyrand, pp. 40–41. This verse appears ten times in the commentary.

24. Clark, pp. 399–400.

25. "quod in solo populo Israel erat notum per chrismatis unctionem" I, 366–367, ed. Vregille and Neyrand, p. 16; "omnibus pulchrior gens hebraea est nominata. Quae in illa plebe, quae Christum cognoscens, quasi legitimum virum in propria domo suscepit, ubi Moses famulus fidelis laudatur," II, 300–303, p. 48. But: "Per haec utique *egreditur ad agrum*, gentium conuersationem, de plebe arrogante et praesumente de sapientia legis mosaicae, de civitate, ubi in propria uenit et sui eum non receperunt. Et cum eum ciuitas sua non recepisset, cui lamentando improperat: 'Hierusalem, Hierusalem, quae occidis prophetas, et lapidas eos qui mittuntur ad te' (Matthew 23:37)." XI, 57–63, p. 257. For an outline of the plan of the commentary as God's plan for the Church, see ed. Vregille and Neyrand, pp. lxxxiv–lxxxvii.

26. This idea has been studied by Theodor E. Mommsen, "Aponius and Orosius on the Significance of the Epiphany," in *Late Classical and Medieval Studies in Honor of Albert Mathias Friend, Jr.* (Princeton, N.J.: Princeton University Press, 1955) pp. 96–111. See also K. S. Frank, "Aponius, in Canticum Canticorum Explanatio," *Vigiliae Christianae* 39 (1985) 370–383.

27. For example, the twelfth-century Bible of Stephen Harding, now Dijon, B.M. 14, and the Biblia atlantica, now in Montalcino, see Marie-Louise Thérel, "L'origine du thème de la "synagogue répudiée" *Scriptorium* 25 (1971) 285–289, and plates 13–14.

28. For Gregory's life and chronology, see J. Richards, *Consul of God: The Life and Times of Gregory the Great* (London: Routledge & Kegan Paul, 1980). On Gregory as an exegete, see Claude Dagens, *Saint Grégoire le Grand: culture et expérience chrétiennes* (Paris: Études Augustiniennes, 1977) pp. 55–81.

29. This is the situation described in a letter of 602 from Gregory to John of Ravenna, MGH Epist. II, p. 352. Verbraken thinks that Gregory would not have had the time or the strength to revise the lectures himself, *Sancti Gregorii Magni Expositio in Canticum Cantiorum*, ed. P. Verbraken, CCSL 144 (1963) p. vii. See also Rodrigue Bélanger, *Grégoire le Grand Commentaire sur le Cantique des Cantiques*, SC 314 1984) pp. 22–28, and Paul Meyvaert, "The Date of Gregory the Great's Commentaries on the Canticle of Canticles and I Kings," *Sacris Erudiri* 23 (1978–1979) 191–216.

30. Columbanus, Epistle 1 (602), MGH Epist. III[3] p. 159, ed. Verbraken, p. viii. The homiletic rescension breaks the text in the middle of 1:3, at "introduxit me rex in cubiculum [Vulgate cellaria] sua," ed. Verbraken, p. 27, ed. Bélanger 112. Verbraken surmises that the original work was in two books, and that a set of rubrics prompted the division of what survives. Ohly, p. 60, and Riedlinger, p. 64, refer to the text as two homilies. See Bélanger, pp. 16–22, for an analysis of the redactions.

31. Verbraken used twenty-one manuscripts in his critical edition, and indicated several more in his articles, "La Tradition manuscrite du Commentaire de saint Grégoire sur le Cantique des Cantiques," RB 73 (1963) 277–288, and "Un nouveau manuscrit du Commentaire de S. Grégoire sur le Cantique des Cantiques," RB 75 (1965) 143–145.

32. "Allegoria enim animae longe a deo positae quasi quandam machinam facit, ut per illam leuetur ad deum," ed. Verbraken, p. 3, ed. Bélanger, p. 68; "Nominantur enim in hoc libro oscula, nominatur ubera, nominatur genae, nominatur femora, in quibus uerbis non irridenda est sacra descriptio, sed maior dei misericordia consideranda et," ed. Verbraken, p. 4, ed. Bélanger, p. 70; "Iste mons et condensus est per sententias et umbrosus per allegorias," ed. Verbraken, p. 7, ed. Bélanger, p. 76.

33. Unfortunately, as Paul Meyvaert has pointed out, Verbraken indicates only biblical sources to the text: "The most serious omission from the list is the name of Origen. . . . A comparison makes it clear that Gregory carefully studied and borrowed from Latin versions of Origen's homilies on the Canticle, from his Commentary on the Canticle, and from a homily on 1 Samuel . . . references to Origen could be added on almost every page." "A New Edition of Gregory the Great's Commentaries on the Canticle and 1 Kings," JTS n.s 19 (1968) p. 220, reprinted in *Benedict, Gregory, Bede and Others* (London: Variorum Reprints, 1977), VII.

34. See ed. Bélanger, pp. 43–49, for a helpful discussion of Gregory's use of Origen, Augustine, and Apponius.

35. *Regula Sancti Benedicti*, 42, ed. R. Hanslik, CSEL 75 (Vienna, 1960). In general, Gregory's preferred mode of exegesis was the tropological sense, but all four of Cassian's levels can be found in his writings; see, for example, *Moralia in Iob*, ed. M. Adriaen, CCSL 143, p. 25 for the historical sense; and CCSL 143A, p. 793 for the anagogical. See chapter one, note 14 and chapter 3, note 35 above. See also Vincenzo Recchia, *L'esegesi di Gregorio Magno al Cantico dei Cantici* (Torino: SEI, 1967).

36. "Suspirans enim sancta ecclesia pro aduentu mediatoris dei et hominum. . . . Hoc autem, quod generaliter de cuncta ecclesia diximus, nunc specialiter de unaquaeque anima sentiamus." ed. Verbraken, pp. 14, 17, ed. Bélanger, pp. 88, 92. For *compunctio*, see Carole Straw, *Gregory the Great: Perfection in Imperfection* (Berkeley: University of California Press, 1988) pp. 223–226, and the famous discussion of Jean Leclercq, *The Love of Learning and the Desire for God: A Study of Monastic Culture*, trans. Catharine Misrahi (New York: Fordham University Press, revised edition 1974) pp. 37–41. For the influence of the monastic ideal on Gregory's papal policies, see Frend, pp. 883–892, and Judith Herrin, *The Formation of Christendom* (Princeton N.J.: Princeton University Press, 1987) pp. 175–177.

37. For the "Synagogue," see ed. Verbraken, pp. 32–35, ed. Bélanger, pp. 124–125; for the Church, ed. Verbraken pp. 35–38, ed. Bélanger, pp. 125–128; for the soul, ed. Verbraken, pp. 38–39, ed. Bélanger, pp. 128–130. See also ed. Verbraken, pp. 40–41, ed. Bélanger, pp. 130–132, for Arius, Sabelius, and Montanus, the heretics who lead astray.

38.

> "Filii matris meae pugnauerunt contra me." Ecce dum pugnant isti spiritus rationales, isti spiritus filii matris, dum pugnant contra animam, faciunt eam

> rebus terrenis incumbere, actionibus saecularibus uacare, res transitorias quaerere. . . . "Vineam meam, id est animam meam, uitam meam, mentem meam, custodire neglexi."

Ed. Verbraken, p. 39, ed. Bélanger, p. 128.

39.

> Multi enim paruuli intra ecclesiam fideles appetunt bene uiuere, uolunt uitam rectitudinis tenere, considerant uitam sacerdotum, qui eis praepositi sunt: et, dum sacerdotes ipsi non bene uiuunt, dum hi qui praesunt non recte uiuunt, hi qui subsequuntur in errorem dilabuntur.

Ed. Verbraken, p. 41, ed. Bélanger, p. 132.

40. "Omnis, qui in ecclesia positus iam sublima secreta rimatur, iam occulta iudicia considerat, quasi in cubiculum intrauit." ed. Verbraken, p. 27, Bélanger, p. 108. See also the analysis of Gregory's exegetical method by de Lubac I, 1 pp. 187–90; and Straw, p. 253, for discussion of *Moralia* 23.20.35.

41. See *Bede's Ecclesiastical History of the English People*, edited and translated by Bertram Colgrave and R.A. B Mynors (Oxford: Clarendon Press, 1969). See also Paul Meyvaert, "Bede and Gregory the Great," *Jarrow Lecture* 1964, reprinted in *Benedict, Gregory, Bede and Others* (London: Variorum Reprints, 1977), VIII, p. 4.

42. J. D. A. Ogilvy, "The Place of Wearmouth and Jarrow in Western Cultural History," *Jarrow Lecture* 1968, p. 4, "his [Gregory's] *In Cantica and In Primum Regum* seem to have been unknown to Bede." The new critical edition of D. Hurst, *Bedae Venerabilis in Cantica Canticorum*, CCSL 119B (1985), rather, lists seven references specifically to Gregory's treatise on the Song of Songs, but all of these should be traced instead to Origen, Apponius, or Justis of Urguel; see Hurst's indications of Origen on pp. 190, 191, 197.

43. Paul Meyvaert, "Bede the Scholar," in *Famulus Christi. Essays in Commemoration of the Thirteenth Centenary of the Birth of the Venerable Bede*, ed. G. Bonner (London: S.P.C.K., 1976), reprinted in *Benedict, Gregory, Bede and Others*, IX, p. 45. The six eighth-to eleventh-century manuscripts from which Hurst edits the text all represent the final redaction.

44. See the *apparatus criticus* to Hurst's edition, pp. 169, 223, 358. Bede explicitly calls the discussion of Julian "book one" at the beginning of the last book, his catena from Gregory, ed. Hurst, p. 359.

45. "Cuius causa duelli primum de amore libellum composuit," ed. Hurst, p. 167. The text of Julian's works edited by Lucas De Coninck and Maria Josepha D'Hont reproduces Bede's excerpts as *Commentarius in Canticum Canticorum*, CCSL 88 (1977), pp. 398–401. It is followed by another work, *De Bono Constantiae*, also only found in Bede on the Song of Songs, ed. De Coninck and D'Hont, pp. 400–401.

46. For the career of Julian, see the introduction to the edition of De Coninck and D'Hont, and Peter Brown, *Augustine of Hippo* (Berkeley: University of California Press, 1969) pp. 381–397. For Augustine's struggle with Pelagius and Pelagianism, see Brown, pp. 340–375.

47. Julian was also the author of a Latin translation of Theodore on the Psalms, and of a commentary on Job (a book Theodore thought uncanonical), edited by De Coninck and D'Hont, pp. 1–109. For a general discussion of Theodore's influence, see M. L. W. Laistner, "Antiochene Exegesis in Western Europe During the Middle Ages," HTR 40 (1947) 19–31.

48. Edited by De Conninck and D'Hont as Julian, pp. 399, 400; as Bede by Hurst, pp. 170–171, 172, 285. Julian interprets the last verse as a reference to curly red hair.

49. Bede begins:

> Scripturus iuuante gratia superna in cantica canticorum primo ammonendum putaui lectorem ut opuscula Iuliani Eclanensis episcopi de Campania quae in eundem librum confecit cautissime legat ne per copiam eloquentiae blandientis foueam incidat doctrinae nocentis sed ut dici solet ita botrum carpat ut de spinam caueat, id est ita in dictis eius sanos sensus scrutetur et eligat ut non minus uitet insanos, uel potius illud faciat Maronis:
> Quis legitis flores et humi nascentia fraga,
> frigidus, o pueri, fugite hinc, latet anguis in herba.

Ed. Hurst, p. 167. The poem is Vergil's *Eclogue* III, 92–93, which Bede may have known from intermediary sources, see Peter Hunter Blair, "From Bede to Alcuin," in *Famulus Christi*, ed. Bonner, pp. 248–249.
A bit further on, Bede says:

> Dicit eandem quamdiu de genitali uoluptate desiderat quasi ad solius animi moueri arbitrium ita et in actibus suis habere iocunditatem ut perturbationis immunem ita etiam libertate gaudentem. Ed. Hurst, pp. 168–169.

50.

> Nam peccatum esse homini congenitum testatur scriptura quae dicit: Graue iugum super filios Adam a die exitus de uentre matris eorum usque in diem sepulturae in matrem omnium. Immo hoc ab ipsa conceptione esse homini coaeuum testatur beatus Iob cum domino supplicans ait: Quis potest facere mundum de inmundo conceptum semine? nonne tu qui solus es? Et quae poterit esse consequentia ut ideo dicatur nullum peccatum hominibus ex masculi et feminae coniunctione nascentibus esse congenitum quoniam filius Dei qui sibi sine ministerio uiri corpus ex uirgine fabricauit et carnis ueritate circumdatus et maculae immunis extitit?

Ed. Hurst, p. 173.

51. The source for Julian's marriage is Poem 25 of another distinguished family friend, Paulinus of Nola. Julian's father, Memoratus, had also been a bishop, and probably sent his son to study with Augustine in Carthage sometime after 408, see the introduction of De Coninck and D'Hont, p. vii.

52. "Hinc ad expositionem stylum uertamus cantici canticorum et in libro ad intelligendum difficillimo seduli patrum uestigia sequentes quicquid iuuante

ea quam defindimus gratia Dei ualemus studii salutaris impendamus." Ed. Hurst, p. 180.

53.

> I. Sinagoga dominum uenire in carne desiderat ac uenienti deuota caritate occurrit.
>
> II. Obscuratam se persecutione infidelium Iudaeorum primitiua queritur ecclesia unde et dilecti sui redemptoris tremens inuocat auxilium.
>
> III. Dominus obiurgans ecclesiam pauentem ammonet datae sibi gratiae aduersus omnes hostium insidias.

Ed. Hurst, p. 181.

54. Ed. Hurst, pp. 185–189. For the tradition of rubricated copies of the Song of Songs in dramatic form, see above, chapter three, note 34.

55. "Hunc locum antiqua translatio sic habet: 'Similitudines auri faciemus tibi cum distinctionibus argenti quoad usque rex in recubitu suo est'," ed. Hurst, p. 203; compare to Origen, *Commentary*, book II, ed. Baehrens GCS 33, Origen 8 (1925) p. 157. This is not the Bible text of the *Homilies*, but compare the end of Bede's book I, ed. Hurst, p. 223, with the end of Jerome's translation of Origen, *Homily* II, ed. Baehrens, pp. 59–60. References to Origen are given in Hurst's *apparatus fontium*.

56. For a summary of Bede's tradition of Latin Bible study, see Peter Hunter Blair, "The Northumbrian Bible," in *The World of Bede* (New York: Saint Martin's Press, 1970) pp. 221–236. Several works of Gregory appear in Hurst's notes, *passim*. See pp. 223, and p. 285, where Apponius's interpretation of the palm tree of 5:11 is compared to that of Julian. If Bede knew Apponius from a homiletic redaction, at least the particular manuscript he used had the proper attribution, see note 20 above.

57.

> Audiui autem quia Paterius eiusdem beati papae Gregorii discipulus de tota sancta scriptura quaeque ille per partes in suis operibus explanauit collecta ex ordine in unum uolumen coegerit, quod opus si haberem ad manus facilius multo ac perfectius studium meae uoluntatis implerem.

Ed. Hurst, p. 359; Ohly lists the verses covered, p. 65, note 3. For the compendium of Paterius, and those of Taio and Lathcen, which Bede does not mention, see above, chapter one, note 14.

58. Dáibhí O'Crónín, "New Heresy for Old': Pelagianism in Ireland and the Papal Letter of 640," *Speculum* 60 (1985) 505–516, argues that the term "Pelagian" meant to Bede, among other things, a follower of the Irish rather than the Roman date for Easter.

59. Bede, *Explanatio Apocalypsis*, PL 93:129–206. In the preface, Bede uses the categories of Tyconius to set up the Apocalypse as a tale of seven ages of the Church; the last two are "damnationem meretricis magnae, id est, impiae

civitatis," and "ornatum uxoris Agni sanctae videlicet Jerusalem de coelo a Deo descendentis ostendit," 131B.

60. Ed. Hurst, p. 182. See Riedlinger's discussion, pp. 87–88. For the kiss, see Cambridge, King's College Ms. 19, f. 21v, at the beginning of Bede's commentary on the Song of Songs. Mary Rose D'Angelo first suggested to me the relationship between the "O" and the kiss.

61. Described by E. Ann Matter, "Exegesis and Christian Education: The Carolingian Model," in *Schools of Thought in the Christian Tradition*, ed. Patrick Henry (Philadelphia: Fortress Press, 1984) pp. 90–105.

62. PL 100:641–666. Ohly, pp. 70–71, estimates that Alcuin includes about an eighth of Bede's treatise. The text is so condensed that it also circulated as a work of Isidore of Seville, *Expositio in Canticum canticorum* PL 83: 1119–1132, cf. Ohly, p. 71, note 4. For the poem, see PL 100:641–642, "In Codice Vaticani," the edition of E. Dümmler, MGH PLAC 1, 299, Ohly, p. 72, and Hunter Blair, "From Bede to Alcuin," pp. 250–255.

63. Alcuin, *Commentariorum in Apocalypsin*, PL 100:1085–1156, taken from Bede, *Explanatio Apocalypsis*, PL 93:129–206, and Ambrosius Autpertus, *Expositionis in Apocalypsin*, ed. R. Weber, CCCM 27, 27A (1975).

64. Haimo is identified as a monk of Auxerre by the twelfth-century chronicle of "Anonymous of Melk," but conflated with Haimo of Halberstadt by the late medieval scholar Johannes Trithemius. Wilmart called attention to this "erreur désastreuse" in "Un commentaire des Psaumes restitué à Anselme de Laon," RTAM 8 (1936) 325–344. See also R. Quadri, "Aimone di Auxerre alla luce dei 'Collectanea' de Heiric di Auxerre," *Italia medioevale e umanistica* 6 (Padova, 1963) 1–48, and John J. Contreni, "Haimo of Auxerre, Abbot of Sasceium (Cessy-les-Bois) and a New Sermon of 1 John V, 4–10," RB 85 (1975) 303–320.

65. A number of Haimo's works are published in PL 116–118, under the name of Haimo of Halberstadt. See also H. Barré, *Les homéliaries carolingiens de l'école d'Auxerre*, ST 224 (Vatican, 1962). The Song of Songs commentary is attributed in manuscripts to Remigius, Cassiodorus, and Thomas Aquinas as well as Haimo, see Ohly, pp. 73–75. Burton Van Name Edwards is currently editing a Genesis commentary which has been attributed to both Haimo and Remigius.

66. For a detailed account of the use of biblical glosses as school texts, see John J. Contreni, "The Biblical Glosses of Haimo of Auxerre and John Scottus Eriugena," *Speculum* 51 (1976) 411–434. For a general account of this process in the second half of the ninth century, see Matter, pp. 96–102.

67. PL 117:295–358, also under the name of Cassiodorus, PL 70:1055–1106. For Haimo's use of Origen, see chapter three above.

68. The *Enarrationes in Cantica Canticorum* of Angelomus, dedicated to Lothar I (d. 855), is found in PL 115:551–628. For a close analysis of its many sources, including Apponius, Gregory the Great, and Alcuin, see Ohly, pp. 80–85.

69. Compare Haimo's opening line, "Desiderantis vox est Synagogae adventum Christi," to the opening rubric "Vox optantis Christi adventum" found, for example, in the Alardus Bible of Saint-Amand (Valenciennes, B.M. Ms. 10, c. 1100) f. 113 (Plate 6, see also Walter Cahn, *Romanesque Bible Illumination* [Ithaca, N.Y.: Cornell University Press, 1982] p. 113), the related Bible of Saint-Bénigne (Dijon, B.M. 2, c.11–12) f.301, and Bible of Stephen Harding (Dijon, B.M. 14, c.12) f.50, in Thérel, pp. 285–289, and plates 13–14. This phrase is also the title, although not the incipit, of the Song of Songs commentary of Lucas of Mont Cornillon (d. 1178–79), PL 203:489–592.

70. The term "mysticus" was regularly used by early medieval authors to refer to ecclesiological (not moral) commentary; see for example, Justus of Urguel, *In Canticum Salomonis explicatio mystica*, PL 67:963–994, beginning "Vox Ecclesiae haec est venientis ad Christum in osculo."

71. PL 117:349: "Poma ejus optimi sunt odoris, in similitudinem pomi Matiani, quod nostri terrae malum vocant," glossed by the 1529 Cologne edition from which this text is printed "Poma Matiana Romae maximo in honore fuisse, advecta e quodam pago, in Alpibus sito prope Aquileiam," with references. Compare to Bede's treatment, ed. Hurst, p. 335, where the description of the plant comes last.

72.

> Recte ergo divina Scriptura favus distillans vocatur, quia multipliciter intelligitur et variis sensibus exponitur, nunc juxta litteram, nunc juxta allegoriam, nunc juxta moralitatem, nunc juxta anagogen, id est superiorem sensum.

PL 117: 321C, compare to Bede, ed. Hurst, p. 260.

73. PL 117:327, ending: "Est et tertia pulsatio, qua pulsat electos suos Dominus, cum aegritudinis molestiam esse mortem vicinam designat."

74. Haimo, *Expositionis in Apocalypsin B. Joannis*, PL 117:937–1220.

75. For the idea of the hidden Church as the faithful in Augustine, see Peter Brown, *Augustine of Hippo* (Berkeley: University of California Press, 1967) pp. 222–225.

76. *Johannis Mantuani in Cantica Canticorum et de Sancta Maria tractatus ad Comitissam Matildam*, ed. Bernhard Bischoff and Burkhard Taeger, SpF 19 (1973), with extensive introductions. The sole extant manuscript is Berlin, Staatsbibliothek der Stiftung Preussischer Kulturbesitz, Ms. Theol. lat. oct. 167, written around 1100. Bischoff and Taeger note that Robert's arrival in Rome (ca. 1080) may have sparked the composition of this text. Bruno of Segni's *Expositio in Cantica Canticorum*, PL 164:1233–1288 was written around the same time. It is discussed by Ann W. Astell, *The Song of Songs in the Middle Ages* (Ithaca, N.Y.: Cornell University Press, forthcoming). John, Robert, Bruno, and Peter Damian were all among the party of Gregory VII.

77. On Robert's life, see Ohly, pp. 95–97; Riedlinger, pp. 101–104; and P. Quivy and J. Thiron, "Robert de Tombelaine et son commentaire sur le Cantique

des Cantiques," in *Millénaire monastique de Mont-Saint-Michel*, vol. II (Paris, 1967) pp. 347–356. For the complicated story of Odo, see D. R. Bates, "The Character and Career of Odo, Bishop of Bayeux (1049/50–1097)," *Speculum* 50 (1975) 1–20.

78. "Dum enim ego in cella solitaria positus Cantica canticorum exponerem," PL 150:1363B. Ansfrid became abbot of Preáux in 1044, Robert probably went to Tombelaine before 1048, Ohly, p. 95.

79. PL 150:1361–1370 for the text to only Song of Songs 1:11, under the name of Robert; PL 79:493–548 for 1:12 to the end, as Gregory. For the text history, see Ohly, p. 95, note 4. Robert's commentary became the main source of the *Glossa ordinaria* version printed in PL 113, see above, chapter two, note 62.

80. "Ad extremum, jam consummatum virum, et calcato saeculo praeparatum, in Cantico canticorum Sponsi jugit amplexibus." PL 150:1364.

81. "Qui hortus conclusus bene esse dicitur, quia caritatis vallo circumquaque munitur, ne intro numerum electorum reprobus aliquis ingrediatur." PL 79:513D. Contrast to the universality of Haimo, PL 117:322B–C.

82.

> Vere, in quo Christus non cubat, vagatur, quia mens, quam ille suavis et ponderosus Christi Spiritus non implet, multis cogitationibus dissoluta circumfertur. Sed qui sunt sodales Christi, per quorum greges sponsa vagari pertimescit, nisi falsi quique Christiani? Qui aut ob nominis solius, aut etiam sacramentorum communionem, fratres Christi vocantur, quia electis quos ipse fratres vocavit, in Ecclesia cohabitando, sociantur. Quorum multitudines bene per exprobrationem greges appellantur, quia, dum quasi irrationabilia animalia sine ordine vivunt, seductoribus spiritibus ad devorandum traduntur.

PL 150:1368B. Compare to Gregory on the same passage, note 39 above. Notice Robert's consistent use of the future tense, which lends an apocalyptic shade to the passage.

83. I refer here to two twelfth-century manuscripts from the Swiss monastery of Engelberg (4, f.69v and 32, f.2v = Plate 7), see F. Fosca (G. Troz), *L'Art Roman en Suisse* (Geneva: Rato-Sadog, 1943), and A. Brückner, *Scriptoria Medii: aevi helvetica* VIII (Geneva: Rato-Sadog, 1950). The crowned *Ecclesia* is also found in the Bible of Stephen Harding (note 69 above), the "Biblia atlantica" (note 27 above and Plate 4) and the opening of "Anselm of Canterbury," (Anselm of Laon) on the Song of Songs (Admont 37 (255) written c. 1180) f. 12, in P. Buberl, *Die illuminierten Handschiften in Steirmark* vol. 1 (Leipzig: Hiersemann 1911) figure 70. Other illustrations use words rather than this iconographic system, for example the Alardus Bible of Saint-Amand (note 69 above and Plate 6), and the twelfth-century *Lectionarium matutinale* of Ellwangen (Stuttgart: Landesbibliothek Bibl. fol. 55, f. 180vb), which identifies the figures as "Christus sponsus" and "Sponsa ecclesia," see K. Löffler, *Schwäbische Buchmalerei im Ro-*

manischer Zeit (Augsburg: B. Filser, 1928) table 45. I am grateful to the Graduate Seminar of the Department of History of Art at the University of Pennsylvania for an invitation to discuss these manuscript paintings, and for insightful comments on their interpretation.

84. Besides Bede, Alcuin, and Haimo, Anselm of Laon and Rupert of Deutz also wrote on both the Apocalypse and the Song of Songs. Lost treatises on the Song of Songs are attributed by medieval testimony to Victorinus of Pettau and Apringius of Beja (see Ohly, pp. 27, 60). The subject is certainly worthy of extended study.

85. For the definition of "internal transformation" of genres as described by Maria Corti, see chapter one above, notes 12 and 17.

Chapter Five

The Marriage of the Soul

The association of the Song of Songs with the love between God and the individual soul is present in the Christian tradition from the beginning; as we have seen, it is present in Origen, and remains a secondary possibility for the text throughout the long tradition of ecclesiological exegesis. As a primary mode of interpretation, however, this way of reading the Song of Songs came into its own in the twelfth century. Latin exegetes of this period of evangelical fervor and monastic reform tended to emphasize a personalistic spirituality, in which the Song of Songs was increasingly read as a dynamic guide to the quest of each human being for union with God. This chapter will show that the level of understanding the Song of Songs which Cassian termed tropological or moral was not limited to the spiritually elite world of the cloister. However, the tradition was greatly influenced, and may be said to be classically represented, by a text written especially for a monastic context, the famous sermons of the Cistercian abbot, Bernard of Clairvaux.

The Monastic Perfectionism of the Cistercian Tradition

Bernard's interpretation of the Song of Songs has been studied very carefully by twentieth-century scholars, especially Jean Leclercq, who has painstakingly reconstructed the history of the text both during Bernard's lifetime and in the following centuries. One of the most difficult problems raised by this scholarship is the form in which these "sermons" were originally presented. Many twelfth-century witnesses, including the author himself, referred to the work as the "Sermones Super Cantica Canticorum," and others called it "Homiliae," but the collection was also often given titles which suggest a more literary than verbal character: "Tractatus, Expositio, Liber, Opus" (Treatise, Exposition, Book, Work)[1]

There is evidence that Bernard spoke on the Song of Songs to the community of Clairvaux. Leclercq, however, warns against taking too literally a sermon of Bernard's contemporary, Guerric of lgny, which testified that the abbot of Clairvaux "has planned to *speak* on the whole nuptial canticle," since the passage continues with a reference to what has been already *published* (*edidit*).[2] The literary terms used to describe the creation of this commentary suggest a process by which the exegesis of specific verses was "dictated" (*dictare*) to a secretary who "transcribed" (*transcribere*) copies to be "edited" (*edere*) by the author, a system which suggests a deliberately literary work.[3] Yet, this process probably began with teaching lectures to the community of Clairvaux, perhaps during the daily "conferences" in chapter, a context which explains occasional references in the sermons to the daily round of sacred teaching. Out of these talks, which were never transcribed in their original form, Bernard may have crafted both the famous series of "Sermones" on the Song of Songs and a lesser-known work, the *Brevis Commentatio in Cantica Canticorum*.[4]

The sermons, which number 86 in their final redaction, were written over a period of eighteen years, starting in Advent of 1135. Bernard had commented on the Song of Songs only to the beginning of chapter 3 when he died in August 1153. Sermon 86 remains incomplete, without the customary concluding benediction.[5] Bernard's trip to Italy at the end of 1136 interrupted the task at Sermon 24, in the middle of Song of Songs 1:3. A second version of Sermon 24 was written after his return and preserved separately in some manuscripts, but the later recensions copied in England and at Clairvaux combined these into one long sermon.[6] It is possible to date other sermons through references to contemporary events: Sermon 26 was written in response to the death of Bernard's brother Gerard, a fellow monk of Clairvaux; Sermons 65 and 66 were probably written after the trials of Cathars in Cologne in 1143, but before Bernard's investigatory trip to Languedoc in the summer of 1145; and sermon 80 was written shortly after the condemnation of the trinitarian teaching of Gilbert of Poitiers at the Council of Reims in March-April, 1148.[7]

These "sermons," written at different times and reflecting different theological debates, do not have an overall plan of exposition of the Song of Songs. It seems that Bernard did not mean them to be a comprehensive, formal interpretation of the biblical text, but rather used the Song of Songs as an ongoing occasion for commentary on the issues of Christian life he found most pressing. His interpretations follow the pattern of earlier exegetes, moving between the well-known allegorical and tropological modes; especially in the first sermon, Bernard stays close to Origen.[8] Yet the *Sermones* are often strikingly original. And, in spite of the references to the busy world in which Bernard was a major political figure, his understanding of the biblical text is worked out in a primarily spiritual mode, and nicely shows the internal transformation of the commentary genre to the tropological level. It is for their insight into the life of the soul, especially in the quest for union with God, that these sermons were so revered.

Bernard clearly understands this quest as a special prerogative of the monastic elite. Sermon 1 begins, in fact, with a distinction between the "spiritual food" offered to those of the cloister but not to laypeople:

> To you, brothers, different things should be said than to those of the world, and certainly in a different way. Indeed, to them milk is given to drink, but not food, as is the method of the Apostle in teaching. For to the spiritual a more solid [food] ought to be given, as that same one teaches by his example: "We speak," he says, not in the words of those trained in human wisdom, but in the doctrine of the Spirit, bringing together spiritual things with spiritual people." (1 Corinthians 2:13) And again: "We speak wisdom among the perfect," (1 Corinthians 2:6) among whom, I am confident, you are to be found, unless in vain you have long been occupied with heavenly studies, trained your senses, and meditated on the law of God by night and day.[9]

Bernard's first sermon thus reveals the transformation of Song of Songs commentary to a totally monastic reading. Here the Song of Songs is understood as a guide to ultimate goal of Cistercian spiritual discipline, union with God. Sermon 3 offers an elaborate explication of the opening verse, "Let him kiss me with the kiss of his mouth," as an elliptical description of three stages of mystical ascent. The sermon begins with a metaphor of textuality, of experience as book:

> Today we read in the book of experience. You must turn your attention inwards, each one must take note of his own particular awareness of the things which are about to be discussed. I wish to discover if it has been given to any of you to say from in his own words (*ex sententia*), "Let him kiss me with the kiss of his mouth." For it is not given to just any man to say this with emotion (*ex affectu*), but if anyone has received this mystical kiss (*spirituale osculum*) from the mouth of Christ even one time, he seeks again that intimate experience, and repeats it willingly.[10]

Bernard's point here is that the book of the Song of Songs is conflated with the "book" of personal experience of those who are chosen to say, *ex sententia* and *ex affectu*, out of their own words and emotions, "Let him kiss me with the kiss of his mouth." The immediate, personal, nature of this reading does not begin with other levels of interpretation, but goes straight to mystical union.

The kiss of union, the "kiss of the mouth," is not attained immediately, however, but rather through a series of ascending spiritual kisses: Bernard describes moving from the "kiss of the feet" to the "kiss of the hand," before attaining the "kiss of the mouth." His warrant for this interpretation is the Latin text, which repeats related words for kiss and mouth three times: "*Os*culetur me *os*culo *oris* sui." This insight is essentially untranslatable, but a comparable sense of the possibilities of the text could be rendered in English by a translation such as "Let him kiss me with the kiss of his kisser."

Working from this insight, Bernard develops the kiss of the foot as the beginning stage of penitential devotion: "but at the feet of the most severe Lord let them.... Prostrate yourself on the ground, embrace his feet, soothe them with kisses, sprinkle them with your tears, so that you wash not them but yourself."[11] The intervening "kiss of the hand" is a necessary step that becomes possible by God's helping hand, which Bernard explicates in Sermon 2 as possible through the intercession of Jesus. The "kiss of the hand" is thus linked to the practice of a holy life:

> It is a long and formidable leap from the foot to the mouth, a manner of approach that is not commendable. What then? Only recently tarnished with the dust of sin, you would dare to touch those scared lips? Yesterday you were lifted from the mud, today you wish to encounter the glory of his face? By the hand you must be transported. First that [hand] must cleanse your stains, then it must raise you up. How raise you? By giving you that by which you may aspire. What is this? The beauty of continence and the fruits worthy of penitence (Luke 3:8) which are the works of piety.[12]

The first two kisses prepare the soul to aspire to the ultimate gift of spiritual grace, the "kiss of the mouth." Bernard stresses that this union can only be attained through the purification of the first kiss and the helping hand of the second, which "will steady our trembling knees." But the final kiss, even coming after many prayers and tears, is yet more awe-full, eliciting from Bernard the consciously poetic style and the apparent rhetorical contradictions characteristic of his most emotionally-charged prose passages:

tunc demum
audemus forsitan
ad ipsum os gloriae
caput attollere,
pavens et tremens dico,
non solum speculandum,
sed etiam osculandum."

Then, at last
let us (perhaps) dare
raise up the head
to that mouth of glory
(I speak fearfully and trembling)
not only to catch sight of it,
but even to be kissed.[13]

Having attained this rhetorical peak of affective spiritual zeal, Bernard ends the homily with a reference to guests who have "just then" arrived at the gates of the monastery, calling him from the pleasures of discourse on the holy mysteries to the concrete obligations of the rule of monastic charity. In view of Leclercq's conclusions about the primarily literary nature of the *Sermones*, this may be a clever device by which an immediate sense of the monastic daily rhythm is consciously adduced to a carefully *composed* text. Of course, the ending of Sermon 3 may also reflect actual moments in the teaching life of a Cistercian abbot; but the guests function mostly as bearers of the anticlimatic mood which Christine Mohrmann sees following closely upon (and gradually subsuming) Bernard's discussions of actual mystical experience.[14]

Given that the *Sermones* were written over several decades and without an overall rhetorical scheme, the best method of analysis of major themes is close study of individual sermons or related groups of sermons. Sometimes Bernard's interpretation of a given verse is contained in one sermon, as is the case in Sermon 43, on Song of Songs 1:12, "a little bundle of myrrh is my beloved to me, between the breasts he shall linger." In this brief but remarkably passionate discussion of the spiritual life, the harshness of myrrh is likened to afflictions and trials, yet the soul is counseled to gather the myrrh with love, to hold it close to the heart, in front where it can be seen and its fragrance smelled, for carried on the back it becomes a burden and weighs the soul down.[15]

In contrast to the clear expository focus of Sermon 43 are long and digressionary discussions such as that of Song of Songs 1:6, "Show me, you whom my soul loves, where you pasture, where you lie down at midday, lest I begin to wander after the flocks of your companions." Bernard divides the verse into two sections, and subjects each to close scrutiny. The request that the beloved show his place of repose at midday is expounded in Sermons 31 to 33, which are worth analyzing in detail to see one elaborate example of Bernard's moral exposition of the Song of Songs. As we saw in the last chapter, this verse provided an opportunity for many exegetes to warn about the dangers of heretics. Although this idea is not totally missing in Bernard's interpretation (a reference to the "enemies of grace" in Sermon 32 is directed against Peter Abelard, likened by Bernard to Pelagius),[16] this series of three sermons offers a substantially different, and largely spiritual, interpretation of the passage.

Sermon 31 uses a series of Neoplatonic images to contrast the immutable and eternal nature of God to human understanding. Human souls, trapped in past, present, and future, cannot know eternity, nor see God "just as he is" (*sicuti est*):

> Neither the wise man nor the saint nor the prophet, can or could see him just as he is in this mortal body; but whoever may be worthy will be able to in the immortal. For he is seen here, but as he sees fit, and not just as he is.[17]

The Sun of Justice is seen to humans on earth through the "rays of God" (*radii Deitatis*) not "just as he is," just as the sun is seen by the eye through reflections of light, but not directly.

The imagery of light, heat, and vision is continued in the next paragraph, in which Bernard speaks of the sweetness of communion with God even in these temporal and partial manifestations. Echoing Origen, Bernard ascribes to each human soul a special angel, "a faithful companion," (*fidelis paranymphus*) who entices the soul towards union with God by quickening the affections.[18] Yet this union of the imperfect with Perfection itself is not to be understood in a corporeal sense:

> But beware, lest you conclude that we see in this union of the Word and the soul something corporeal or perceptible. We speak of that which the Apostle said, since "whoever is united to God becomes one spirit with him." (1 Corinthians 6:17) As much as we can, we express in words the ecstasy of the pure mind in God, or rather the loving descent of God into the soul, matching spiritual things to the spiritual.[19]

This warning, built around Paul's remote language of the third person, sets a frame for the passionate love language which follows, in which the soul is addressed with a conscious emphasis on grammatically feminine gender as the Bride to whom the Bridegroom comes:

> by a special privilege, she receives him flowing from heaven into her intimate affections, and even into the innermost part of her heart, and she has present the one she desires, not in a shape (*non figuratum*) but in an infusion (*sed infusum*,) not in appearance, but in affect; and without doubt it is more delightful because it is inward, not outward.[20]

The remainder of Sermon 31 extends the warning against carnal understanding of this passion by emphasizing the imaginative creativity with which God takes on a number of charming guises in showing his love for the soul. Using imagery from the Gospels as well as the Song of Songs, Bernard explains that God not only appears as bridegroom, but also as physician, traveler, silver-tongued companion, wealthy father, and magnificent and powerful king. Sermon 32 elaborates on these forms, explaining that each is perfectly suited to particular stages of the spiritual life. Christ appears in the Song of Songs as a shepherd for the benefit of those who have the task of spiritual leadership, those who give food to others as well as feed themselves. The last part of verse 6, "lest I begin to wander after the flocks of your companions," stresses the need to guard against false leaders, with an allusion we have already noted to Bernard's nemesis, Peter Abelard.[21] The end of Sermon 32 consciously acknowledges that this interpretation has concentrated on the "letter" of the text, the imagery of the Song of Songs; Bernard thus promises that the next sermon will turn to the "spiritual sense which lies hidden" in these images.[22]

Bernard's Sermon 33 on the Song of Songs is a masterful exposition of the mystical noontide, the never-ending light in which the contemplative soul is invited to take its repose. Bernard first draws attention to the "elegance" with which the phrase "you whom my soul loves" distinguishes between spiritual and carnal affections.[23] Nor, he says, must one overlook the significance of the full noon in which the flock lies down to feed, in which this embrace takes place. The feeding is the spiritual food of the Eucharist, and "that noon is the whole day that knows no evening."[24]

The imagery which follows is at once mystical and apocalyptic: the dawn began, Bernard says, with the rising of the Sun of Justice at the birth of Christ, and, although this sun will be with us to the end of the world:

> The light will nevertheless not attain noontide, nor be seen here below in that plentitude which it will exhibit hereafter, at least to those who are destined for the privilege of this vision. O true noontide, fullness of warmth and light, resting-place of the sun; blotting out of shadows, drying up of marshes, banishing of evil odors! O perpetual solstice, when day will never decline to evening![25]

This spiritual noon, the full presence of God, is thus more a characteristic of the next life than of this one, although some holy ones (Jacob, Moses, Isaiah, Paul) have experienced its warmth on earth. The spiritual understanding of the text leads to an elaborate warning against four types of temptation that beset the soul: weakness of the spirit ("the terror of the night"), flattery ("the arrow that flies by day"), hypocrisy ("the pestilence that stalks about in darkness"), and "the noontide devil" which lays traps for the perfect. As these temptations are related to stages of spiritual development, Bernard then shows how each operated in universal history. The Primitive Church, beset by "terrors of the night," showed a strength which led the Enemy to shift tactics to the "arrow of the day," sectarian heresy. But the Church survived both of these trials. Bernard sees his contemporary Church afflicted by the pestilence that stalks in darkness, for "today a putrid corruption creeps (*serpit*) through the whole body of the Church."[26] This corruption, caused by riches and simony, paves the way for the noontide devil, who is the Antichrist.

This last interpretation is, of course, in the allegorical mode. The discussion is reminiscent of the stages of the Church discussed in the second Song of Songs commentary of Honorius Augustodunensis (chapter three), and totally in agreement with the assessment of ecclesiastical corruption of Robert of Tombelaine (chapter four). The expectaion of the coming of Antichrist evokes the apocalyptic fervor of Cassian's anagogical model which we have seen (chapter four) as part of the tradition of medieval interpretation of the Song of Songs on the allegorical level. These striking correlations lead to the perception that, while Bernard's *Sermones* provide many stirring examples of moral exegesis, they never focus solely on that level, nor consistently present the soul as an entity separate from the Church. Like the ecclesiological commentaries, tropological readings of the Song of Songs often show the implicit relation of all the familiar modes of interpretation.

Bernard's spiritual interpretation of the Song of Songs is even more marked in his shorter and less famous work, the *Brevis commentatio in Cantica*, but even this text does not divorce the tropological reading from other levels of understanding. The *Brevis commentatio*, a line-by-line exposition to Song of Songs 2:8, bears striking similarities to the exegetical pattern of William of Saint-Thierry's commentary, (see below) and may actually be the result of a dialogue between these two great Cistercian authors.[27] The text begins with a discussion of "three states of the love of God" (*tres status amoris dei*) found in the Christian soul: the sensual or animal, the rational, and the spiritual or intellectual; these are represented in the Song of Songs by the young men, the companions, and the Bride and Bridegroom.[28] In the interpretation of the first verse, the three states are linked to the three kisses:

> Now, according to the three states of love, there are three kisses of the lover. First, atonement or reconciliation; second, merit; third, contemplation. The first is of the feet, the second of the hand, the third of the mouth.[29]

The pattern of three is repeated many times: the kisses are related to the love both between and flowing out of the three Persons of the Trinity; while the "best ointments" of Song of Songs 1:2a are the three monastic ideals of compunction, devotion, and piety. This use of repeating numerical series is characteristic of Bernard's exegetical method.[30]

Although short and highly schematic, the *Brevis commentatio* gives evidence of profound grappling with the textual intricacies of the Song of Songs. The line "Your name is oil poured out" (1:2b) is first considered as if spoken by the Bridegroom, then by the Bride; then an "anagogical" meaning describes the love of God spreading out from the Jews to the Church of the Gentiles; finally, the "moral sense" relates this effusion to the progressively intimate spiritual states of faith, hope, and charity.[31] This is a complex interpretation, which reads almost like notes for a systematic moral interpretation, an interpretation which was not the purpose of Bernard's *Sermones*.

This interpretation of the Song of Songs seems never to have been fully developed by Bernard. Indeed, since even Bernard's much longer *Sermones* only comment on the text to 3:1, a number of Cistercians in the late twelfth century attempted to "finish" his interpretation, with questionable success. One of Bernard's secretaries, Geoffrey of Auxerre, declined the "official" completion of Bernard's homilies, but produced instead a compendium and a short gloss; Gilbert of Hoyland attempted a continuation of Bernard's treatment of the Song of Songs to 5:9; and John of Ford, beginning with 5:8, went to the end of the biblical text.[32] But the Cistercian commentary which moves most surely in an equal depth of spiritual insight is one written concurrently with Bernard's interpretations, the only original Song of Songs commentary of his close friend, William of Saint-Thierry. William's *Expositio super Cantica Canticorum* is thought to have been conceived during a period of convalescence spent at Clairvaux in the company of Bernard.[33] From this point of view, both Bernard's *Brevis commentatio* and William's *Expositio* manifest a vision of the Song of Songs confidentially forged in a Cistercian infirmary by two experts on the spiritual life. Although this story may seem rather romantic, it does help to explain the consistently personal and esoteric focus of William's only original treatment of the Song of Songs. The extant version of William's commentary is incomplete and probably unfinished, commenting on the text only to 3:4a, "when I had hardly passed by them / I found him whom my soul loves." William seems to have divided the Song of Songs into four parts (which he called "Songs"), of which the extant text preserves the first and almost all of the second.[34]

In the preface to the work as a whole, William speaks revealingly of the allegorical task he has set himself:

> We do not attempt those deeper mysteries which it [the Song of Songs] contains with regard to Christ and the Church; but restraining ourselves within ourselves and measuring ourselves by means of ourselves, we shall, in the poverty of our understanding—as anyone may venture to do—touch lightly on the Bridegroom and Bride, Christ and the Christian soul, in a certain moral sense. For our labor we ask no other fruit than one befitting our subject, namely, love itself.[35]

Perhaps the most surprising aspect of this confession is the perception that "a certain" tropological or moral interpretation (*sensum tantummodo moralem aliquam*) is circumscribed by the measure of human potential, whereas the allegories of Christ and the Church are "deeper mysteries" (*Profundiora illa mysteria*). This statement reveals William's sense of the supremacy of the tradition of ecclesiological exposition of the Song of

Songs as surely as it expresses doubts about the spiritual possibilities of human beings.

William's text is centered around the assumption of the same three levels of human potential found in Bernard's *Brevis commentatio*: the animal, the rational, and the spiritual. These stages also resonate with the three-fold kiss of Bernard's Sermon, 3, as both Bernard and William share a conception of the remote reflection of the Trinity in the human soul, ultimately based on the anthropology of Augustine.[36] In commenting on 1:15, "our bed is flowery," William says:

> Meanwhile, in the pressures of this life, as a help in her [the Bride's] labors and a comfort in her waiting, a paradise is set out for the Bride's good soul and, for her good conscience, a little flowery bed, and here is attained not that eternal kiss and perfect union, but a certain imitation of that kiss and perfection, and a certain similitude of that union and likeness. For by the action of the Holy Spirit, man's spirit and the sense of enlightened love sometimes, fleetingly, attain to it. Then that something, whatever it is—something loved rather than thought, and tasted rather than understood—grows sweet and ravishes the lover. And for a time, for an hour, this affects the lover, and shapes his efforts; and then it seems to him that no longer in hope, but almost in reality, he sees with his eyes, and holds and handles with his hands, by a sort of evidence of experimental faith, the very substance of things to be hoped for of the Word of Life.[37]

Cistercian readings of the Song of Songs as the wedding-hymn between Christ and the soul are thus strongly colored by a sense of the unworthiness of the soul, which leads to the necessity for spiritual ascent, the ultimate goal of the monastic life. In this, the Cistercians seem particularly aware of the limitations of not just the body, but even the *soul* in this world, and look ahead, with trembling of love and fear, to a hoped-for mystical consummation of the world to come.

The Monastic Ideal Adapted to the Life of the World

But the Cistercians were not the only twelfth-century Christians to emphasize the Song of Songs as the love between Christ and the soul. Rosemarie Herde has shown that the tropological interpretation of the Song of Songs informed a vast range of Latin religious poetry and prose from this period.[38] An interesting comparison to the Cistercian perspective can be seen in a treatise on Song of Songs 4:6b–8 which medieval readers knew as the *Eulogium sponsi de sponsa*.[39] The *Eulogium* is linked to the world of the Canons Regular, and especially to the famous Parisian teacher, Hugh of Saint-Victor.[40] It is an extremely short text, barely six columns of the *Patrologia Latina*; the profusion of manuscripts suggests that it enjoyed the sort of popularity that turns serious textual study into a punishing task. There are at least eighteen twelfth-and thirteenth-century copies in the Bibliothèque Nationale of Paris alone; almost certainly many more copies of the text slipped unnoticed into collections of miscellaneous treatises and sermons extant in other libraries.[41]

This brief but popular text is unusual in several ways. For one thing, it interprets a pericope of the Song of Songs which was not central or important to most medieval exegetes. The *Eulogium* seems to be the first, and may well be the only, medieval Latin commentary to be inspired by these particular verses. Secondly, the text which it expounds is not from the Vulgate. It can be substantially traced to Jerome's emendations of Origen's *Hexapla*, the version studied by Vaccari, which was widely available through a series of quotations in Jerome's *Adversus Jovinianum*.[42] Yet the *Eulogium* shows some small but significant variations on even this text, notably, the change in Song of Songs 4:8 of the preposition *from* (Vulgate *de*, Jerome *a, ab*) to the preposition *to (ad)*. One twelfth-century manuscript writes out the biblical text at the beginning of the treatise in this way:

> Ibo mihi ad montem myrrhae
> et ad colles Libani
> et loquar sponsae meae.
> Tota speciosa es proxima mea
> et macula non est in te.
> Veni a Libano sponsa, veni
> ad Libanum venies.
> Et transibis ad montem Seir
> et Hermon
> a cubilibus leonum
> a montibus leopardorum.
> Alleluia.[43]

> I will get me to the mountain of myrrh
> and to the hills of Libanon
> and I will speak to my spouse.
> You are all lovely, my close one,
> and there is no spot in you.
> Come from Libanon, spouse, come
> to Libanon come

and cross over to Mount Seir
and Hermon
from the lions' dens
from the leopards' mountains
Alleluia.

The change of the pronouns emphasizes movement both away from and towards: *from* Libanon *to* Libanon; *from* the animals' dens *to* Mount Seir and Hermon. This double movement is at the heart of the interpretation.

Apart from the opening words ("A bridegroom is speaking here, one who has a bride, and promises to visit her"[44]) the commentary moves entirely on the tropological level:

> But, you ask, who is this bridegroom, who is his bride? The bridegroom is God, the bride is the soul. The bridegroom is at home when he fills the mind with inward joy, he goes away when he takes away the sweetness of contemplation. But by what similitude is the soul said to be the bride of God? She is the bride because she is betrothed by the gifts of grace. She is the bride because she is joined to him by a chaste love. She is the bride, since by the breath of the Holy Spirit she is made fertile with the offspring of the virtues.[45]

The gifts of grace by which the soul is pledged to God are especially adapted for each type of human nature: Some are given the strength to do good works; others weakness to keep from doing evil; others simplicity to avoid pride.[46] The acceptance of the gifts of the Holy Spirit is the first stage of the journey of the soul away from the carnality of the animals' dens, towards the spiritual peaks of Mount Seir and Hermon.

The *Eulogium* is structured around an allegorical understanding of key words which is based on a long tradition of philological interpretation of Hebrew words and place-names. For example, myrrh signifies mortification of the flesh, and Libanus (Hebrew "whitening") signifies fleshly purification; therefore, the journey of the soul is through the penitential mountain of myrrh to the purification of the heart at Libano. We have seen this method employed in Honorius Augustodunensis's interpretation of the same passage; like Honorius, the *Eulogium* is drawing on a well-known set of onomastical allegory texts.[47] But the *Eulogium* gives far more elaborate and developed moral applications of the name allegories. The invitation *from* Libanon *to* Libanon, for instance, opens a discussion of the progressive stages of purification: the soul is invited "from the Libanon made white to the Libanon not made white yet which is white . . . from the heart made clean to the cleanser of hearts, not made clean, but clean."[48]

The mystical union hinted at by this text is never stated explicitly; instead, the *process* is made prominent. The mountain of Seir, which means shaggy, evokes Genesis 25, in which the first-born Esau is overtaken by his brother Jacob. The hairy Esau is the flesh, which God wishes to be conquered with the desire of the spirit, a desire which must be born in each individual soul. Although the Song of Songs only speaks of *Mount* Seir, the *Eulogium* imagines a complex internal geography:

> When the soul takes food only to keep itself alive it is Seir on the mountain. When it seeks food to keep strong, it is Seir on the field. When it begs for the delights of luxury, it is Seir in the valley. . . . One who cuts off the superfluous tramples Seir in the valley; one who minimizes necessities conquers Seir in the field. The soul, however, that yields to nature only those things necessary to stay alive gives a more demanding obedience to Seir on the mountain.[49]

Song of Songs 4:6–8 is thus interpreted as a call to a spiritual progression from incontinence to chastity, from lust to austerity, and "from the many to the one, for the more we draw near to God in fleeing the world, that much more are we gathered into the one."[50] This hoped-for union of the Bridegroom and the Bride on the shining peak of Libanon is, of course, at the heart of the monastic life. Yet the *Eulogium* seems well aware of the snares and the particular manifestations of grace of the world, and never refers to the soul as one of the spiritual elite. Its pragmatic focus on sin and repentance parallels what Caroline Walker Bynum has described as the concern of the Augustinian Canons for behavior as edification and for moral education.[51]

However much it may reveal its origins, the *Eulogium sponsi de sponsa* was, in fact, received equally enthusiastically by both Cistercians and Canons Regular. Almost verbatim citations appear in later writings from both traditions: in a homily of Hugh's contemporary, Gebuinus, chancellor of the Cathedral of Troyes; in a commentary written probably around 1180 by a certain Thomas the Cistercian; and (marked by the rubric "H") in the collection of glosses compiled by the Cistercian Geoffrey of Auxerre, secretary and biographer of Bernard of Clairvaux.[52] The links between these exegetes are understandable, if the origin and authorship of the *Eulogium* are not so easily explained. The Cistercian abbey of Clairvaux was in the vicinity of Troyes, and at least one Canon Regular of the Cathedral of Troyes, Peter Comestor, was also associated with the school at Saint-Victor, in which Hugh was a famous teacher.[53]

It is perhaps no coincidence that twelfth-century Champagne was also the site of a flowering of Jewish commentary on the Song of Songs, especially evident in the work of the eleventh-century Rabbi Shelomo Izhaqui, known as Rashi, and his school. Rashi's famous commentary on the Song of Songs stresses the understanding of God and Israel (parallel to the allegorical, rather than the tropological, readings of Christians), but he seems to have been aware of and even reacting against the tradition of Christian readings of the text, both ecclesiological and moral.[54] Jean Leclercq has suggested that similarities between Rashi and medieval Christian interpreters are best found in their common dependence on the Targum, known to the Christians through Origen.[55] Although the intellectual contacts between Christians and Jews in Champagne in the late eleventh and twelfth centuries may well have influenced the Song of Songs interpretation in both traditions, the passionate love language of the moral readings of the Song is a Christian tradition, a particularly well-adapted response to the christocentric spirituality of the medieval Church.

Identification with Christ, and especially with the suffering body of God incarnate, is the key to this vision of the mystical marriage of the soul. Christian tropological interpretations of the Song of Songs stress that the marriage is consummated only through the overcoming of the earthly human body, but they do so in the most passionate body language. Not only the human body, but also Christ's body, is sometimes graphically represented in this tradition: Bernard speaks of the "dove in the cleft of the rock" (Song of Songs 2:14) as the refuge of the soul not just in the "rock of Christ," as Origen had it, but specifically in Christ's gaping wounds:

> And really where is there safe sure rest for the weak except in the Savior's wounds? . . . They pierced his hands and feet, they gored his side with a lance, and through these fissures I can suck honey from the rock and oil from the hardest stone—that is, to "taste and see that the Lord is good." (Psalm 33:9, Vulgate). . . . The secret of his heart is laid open through the clefts of his body; that mighty mystery of devotion *(sacramentum pietas)* is laid open, laid open

> too the "tender mercies *(viscera misericordiae)* of our God, in which the morning sun from on high has visited us.: (1 Timothy 3:16) Surely his heart *(viscera)* is laid open through his wounds![56]

The fascination with the wounds of Christ as a place of refuge for the soul of humans is developed throughout the later Middle Ages. It appears, for example, as a devotional exhortation in the fourteenth-century *Vita Christi* of Ludolph of Saxony, with specific reference to Song of Songs 2:14.[57] The *Vita Christi* was widely read among the popularizing spiritual teachers of the *devotio moderna*, a movement which began among the Augustinian Canons and reached even into the vernacular piety of the Reformation.[58] Bernard's vision of the soul as a dove nestling in the wounds of Christ the rock thus had an impact on Christian spiritual imagination for several centuries. Tropological readings of the Song of Songs, which began as an exhortation to the spiritual elite of the monastic world, gradually spoke to Christian idealism in a much broader spectrum of teaching about the trials of the soul on earth. This is an excellent example of the power of the genre of· Song of Songs commentary to influence other types of Christian literature, moving in tandem with spiritual concepts developing in the culture at large.

Modern Responses to Medieval "Spiritual Eroticism"

The tropological tradition of Song of Songs interpretation presents the modern reader with a number of seeming paradoxes. Here we find the language of passion and union; indeed, these are the most emotionally charged and even sexually explicit biblical commentaries from the Middle Ages. Yet, the message which the words convey is always one of purity, chastity, and transcendence. The *Eulogium*, for example, speaks of using the body to rise above the body. The vivid, clear, even shockingly fleshly language of these commentaries describes a flesh-denying, spiritual union. Nevertheless, this union is one in which images of body (the human body of sin and the salvific body of Christ) play a crucial role. As Bynum has recently shown, the blood of Christ was widely understood among late medieval spiritual writers as spiritual food, connected to the eucharist, of course, but also to milk from the breast of mother Jesus, or even to the milk of the Virgin Mary which fed God incarnate in human form.

The body of Christ and the human body shared the ability to bleed, feed, die, and give life.[59] It is little wonder, then, that the difficult balance of body and soul in which the tropological tradition of medieval Christian Song of Songs exegesis participates has engaged the attention of modern scholars.

I have discussed in chapter two, in relation to Origen's treatments of the Song of Songs, the reactions of Patricia Cox Miller, William E. Phipps, and Mary Daly to traditional Christian spiritual language of the body.[60] These three very different modern authors have in common an unwillingness, perhaps an inability, to accept the linguistic relationship between body and soul revealed in these ancient texts in other than modern terms. This may be a result of a tendency of modern western culture described by Michel Foucault as a result of the "will to know":

> ... Since the classical age there has been a constant optimization and an increasing valorization of the discourse on sex; and that this carefully analytical discourse was meant to yield multiple effects of displacement, intensification, reorientation, and modification of desire itself.[61]

This "valorization of the discourse on sex" may partially account for the increasingly passionate readings of the Song of Songs in the Christian tradition from Origen to the flowering of tropological exegesis in the twelfth century, a tradition which reflects the increasing western focus on asceticism, spiritual exercise, and mysticism. But Foucault's discussion of increasing *talk* about sex in the context of the modern hypothesis of repression also helps to clarify why twentieth-century interpreters of medieval spiritual discourse become so uncomfortable in the seemingly contradictory presence of pervasive bodily language of spiritual states. As Foucault has noted, it is we, the "other Victorians," who are so eager "to speak of sex in terms of repression," we are the ones who think that to speak about sex is "to speak out against the powers that be."[62] If Foucault's argument is correct, this is a development of modernity, specifically since the "sexual enlightenment" of the sixteenth and seventeenth centuries; in short, it is our problem, not a medieval one. Perhaps it is this development of language about sex in modern western culture that leads Daly, the most vehement critic of the bodily language of Christian spirituality, to an analysis which in general points towards an assesment of the passionate language of the love between God and the soul as "transformed lechery in the name of the sublime," and as "mental manipulation" which "involves deliberate perversion of the natural phenomenon of subliminal perception."[63]

It is fascinating to note again that Daly's critique of patriarchal sublimation shares many assumptions with the assessment of the Song of Songs interpretation of Bernard of Clairvaux given by William Phipps. "If you drive nature out with a pitchfork," Phipps says, quoting Horace, "she will find a way back."[64] Much modern interpretation of medieval love literature has assumed, in the face of searingly passionate language, that in these texts, the body has been driven out. This has sometimes led to remarkable interpretive contortions.

Another example of twentieth-century analysis that has reacted with disbelief at twelfth-century sexual language may illustrate the problem from another angle: I mean the modern attempt to "protect" Heloise, the famous lover of Peter Abelard and exemplary abbess, from her own sensuality. The letters attributed to Heloise portray an abbess who adamantly refused to abandon her sensual nature. In the face of this apparent contradiction, some modern scholarship has not stopped short of erasing Heloise's presence from her own correspondence. The assumption of much scholarship on the Abelard/Heloise correspondence has been that her recorded passion could only be a cautionary tale, told, to borrow Daly's terminology, by a sublimated male.[65]

But, if we allow this language of sensuality its place, what are we to make of the conscious eroticism of these tropological commentaries on the Song of Songs? Certainly, the psychology of authors who chose this language while glorifying and presumably practicing chastity compells the modern reader to find a scheme of interpretation to explain the seeming contradictions. At least one scholar has looked to Jungian archetypes for the key to what was "really" expressed in these works.[66] Jean Leclercq, on the other hand, has pointed to a far simpler solution, claiming that the use of a common language of love to represent different levels of human desire, and the adaptation of human love language to the ineffable love of God, is a "spontaneous symbolism," only to be expected from limited human language.[67]

But none of these explanations is entirely satisfactory. Those who focus on the sublimation of medieval spiritual language of the body work from a particularly twentieth-century point of view, and make more sense in modern than in medieval terms. Daly may be right to point to the role played by Christianity's sublimation of the body in the subjugation of women in western society; certainly, the personification of the flesh as female over against the "male" spirit is a concept of great force, with enduring consequences. Yet, the tropological commentaries on the Song of Songs portray the human *soul* as the female member of the love relationship, and consistently portray this soul, no matter the gender of the body, as the female character of the love story. The question of the gender of the Bride will be more closely scrutinized in the next chapter, where the mariological tradition will be examined; but it is striking that the moral commentaries studied here offer no comment on the presentation of a female character as spiritual "everyman." Obviously, Jungian analysis is equally bounded by its own twentieth-century point of reference. Leclercq's approach to the use of body language for this medieval spiritual drama seems to assume a "spontaneity" which cannot be verified, and which is in any case more descriptive than explanatory. Something in the passion of these medieval texts defies analysis by twentieth-century tools, and leaves us still wondering. In my opinion, rather, the core of the difference between the language of these texts and our perception of this language lies in a different context of the use of symbolism, and in medieval attitudes toward the body itself.

Medieval Christians thought about physicality with a complex of associations which are not immediately recognizable to us. An effort of cultural translation is thus called for in the analysis of these texts. Bynum has broken the ground for a reconstruction of the functions of medieval language of the body from many types of evidence. She shows how such concepts as hunger and abstinence, the incarnation of Christ, the body of the eucharist, and the glorified body of the resurrection were all intimately linked to the spiritual—and bodily—life of Christians on earth. These connections were intensified by a series of struggles over the orthodox manner of their articulation, especially by the rejection of the dualism of the Cathars. But, Bynum says, they were not *caused* by this struggle:

> It is sometimes impossible for us, as it was for contemporaries, to draw a line between Cathar and orthodox asceticisms (both stressed fasting and continence, for example) or between quietist and orthodox mysticism (both, for example, valued desire for God more than "works"). This fact indicates that *all* religiosity of the period was animated in deep ways by the need to take account of (rather than merely to deny) matter, body, and sensual response.

> Indeed, wherever we turn in the later Middle Ages we seem to find the theme of body—and of body in all its aspects, pleasure as well as pain.[68]

This "theme of body" may be an important key to the development of certain western medieval Christian doctrines which never aroused much interest in the eastern Christian tradition: original sin, the "forensic" theory of atonement, the virgin birth of Jesus *in partu*, the real presence (and later transubstantiation) of the historical body of Jesus in the eucharist, and (so to speak) finally, a physical understanding of the glorified body of the resurrection. It is important to note that this last idea, stress on the continuity of the earthly and heavenly bodies, is the opposite of Origen's vision of the body of the resurrection, a formulation which had lost theological credence by the twelfth century.[69] Origen's conception of the marriage of the soul must be understood as based on a very different understanding of physicality; his methods of tropological exegesis of the Song of Songs were adapted over the centuries to a Christian culture which took the reality, and continuity, of the body very seriously indeed.

We have seen that the tropological interpretations of the Song of Songs represent the goal of the Christian life as union with God. Bernard of Clairvaux was very clear about the fact that this ultimate union takes place in the next world rather than this one, a fact which raises again the intimate connection between the tropological and anagogical modes described by Cassian. There is no medieval tradition of exegesis of the Song of Songs in a purely anagogical mode; instead, the resonances of the text with the doctrine of last things were worked out (as described in chapter four) in relation to the drama of Christ and the Church, or (as this chapter has shown) in the ultimate expectation of the mystical union of God and the soul in some reality beyond this earthly plane. It is important to understand, however, that in the medieval conception this spiritual union is also corporeal. Whether addressed to the "perfect" of religious life or to the struggling souls of the *saeculum*, this tradition understood the Song of Songs as the *epithalamium* of a spiritual union which utimately takes place between God and the resurrected Christian—both body and soul.

Notes

1. "L'Histoire du texte," in "Introduction," *Sermones Super Cantica Canticorum 1–35*, OB 1 (1957) p. xv.

2. "De toto illo carmine loqui instituit spemque nobis dedit ex eis quae iam

edidit," *In nat. apost. Petri et Pauli*, serm. III, i, PL 185:183. See Jean Leclercq, "Les sermons sur les Cantiques ont-ils été prononcés?" RB 65 (1955) 71–89, reprinted in *Recueil d'études sur Saint Bernard et ses écrits* vol. 1, 92 (Rome: Edizioni di storia e letteratura, 1962) pp. 193–121; and Leclercq, "Were the Sermons on the Song of Songs Delivered in Chapter?" introduction to Bernard of Clairvaux, *On the Song of Songs II*, trans. Killian Walsh, Cistercian Fathers Series 7 (Kalamazoo, Mich.: Cistercian Publications, 1976) pp. vii–xxx.

3. J. Leclercq, "The Making of a Masterpiece," introduction to Bernard of Clairvaux, *On the Song of Songs IV*, trans. Irene Edmonds, Cistercian Fathers Series 40, (Kalamazoo, Mich.: Cistercian Publications, 1980) pp. ix–xxiv. For the relationship of Bernard to his secretaries, see also Leclercq, "Saint Bernard et ses secrétaires," RB 61 (1951) 208–229, reprinted in *Recueil d'études* vol. 1, pp. 3–25.

4. For the argument that the Song of Songs were interpreted in chapter, see Jean Leclercq, *Monks and Love in Twelfth-Century France* (Oxford: At the Clarendon Press, 1979) p. 38. For the *Brevis commentatio*, see below, note 27.

5. For the history of composition, see the introduction to the first volume of the critical edition of Leclercq, Talbot, and Rochais, OB 1, pp. xvi–xvii.

6. Leclercq, Talbot, and Rochais print both the final version of Sermon 24, and the two shorter partial texts, taken from the South-German and Austrian manuscript transmission of the "Morimond recension," OB 1, pp. 151–162. See also Jean Leclercq, "La Recension de Clairvaux," RB 66 (1956) 63–91, reprinted in *Recueil d'études* vol. 1, pp. 245–274. The task of distinguishing between these recensions was made very difficult by the fact that manuscripts from each tradition had been corrected against each other.

7. See the introduction to OB 1, p. xvi. These sermons speak freely about the campaigns for orthodoxy in which Bernard was involved.

8. A list of Bernard's sources has been compiled by Leclercq, "Aux sources des sermons sur les Cantiques," RB 69 (1959) 237–257, reprinted in *Recueil d'études*, vol. 1, pp. 275–317, in this later printing, see especially p. 281. On Bernard's connection to Origen, see Jean Leclercq, "Saint Bernard et Origène d'après un manuscript de Madrid," RB 59 (1949) 183–195, reprinted in *Recueil d'études* vol. 2, pp. 373–385.

9.

> Vobis, fratres, alia quam aliis de saeculo, aut certe aliter dicenda sunt. Illis siquidem lac potum dat, et non escam, qui Apostoli formam tenet in docendo. Nam spiritualibus solidiora apponenda esse itidem ipse suo docet exemplo: "Loquimur," inquens, "non in doctis humanae sapientiae verbis, sed in doctrina spiritus, spiritualibus spiritualia comparantes;" (1 Corinthians 2:12) item: "Sapientiam loquimur inter perfectos," (1 Corinthians 2:6) quales vos nimirum esse confido, nisi frustra forte ex longo studiis estis caelestibus occupati, exercitati sensibus, et in lege Dei meditati die ac nocte.

Sermo I.i.1, OB 1, p. 3; here and in notes 10–24, my translations, with consultation of translation of Killian Walsh, Bernard of Clairvaux, *On the Song of Songs*

I,II, Cistercian Fathers Series 4, 7 (Kalamazoo, Mich.: Cistercian Publications, 1976).

10.

> Hodie legimus in libro experientiae. Covertimini ad vos ipsos, et attendat unusquisque conscientiam suam super his quae dicenda sunt. Explorare velim si cui umquam vestrum ex sententia dicere datum sit; "Osculetur me osculo oris sui." Non est enim cuiusvis hominum ex affectu hoc dicere; sed si quis ex ore Christi spirituale osculum vel semel accepit, hunc proprium experimentum profecto sollicitat, et repetit libens.

Sermo III.i.1, OB 1, p. 14.

11. "sed ad pedes severissimi Domini mecum pavida iaceat [. . .] prosternere et tu in terram, amplectere pedes, placa osculis, riga lacrimis, quibus tamen non illum laves, sed te." Sermo III.i.2, OB 1, pp. 14–15.

12.

> Longus saltus et arduus est de pede ad os, sed nec accessus conveniens. Quid enim? Recenti adhuc respersus pulvere, ora sacra continges? Heri de luto tractus, hodie vultui gloriae praesentaris? Per manum tibi transitus sit. Illa prius te tergat, illa te erigat. Quomodo erigat? Dando unde praesumas. Quid istud? Decor continentiae et dignae paenitentiae fructus, quae sunt opera pietatis.

Sermo III.ii.4, OB 1, p. 16.

13. Sermo II.iii.5, OB 1, p. 17.

14. For an analysis of Bernard's extremely rich prose style, see Christine Mohrmann, "Observations sur la langue et le style de Saint Bernard," introduction to OB 2, pp. ix–xxxiii. Mohrmann observes: "D'une manière générale, c'est la tension spirituelle plus ou moins grande qui constitue, pour ainsi dire, l'élément régulateur du style de saint Bernard. La fréquence des éléments du style figuré,—parallélismes, antithèses, jeux de mots et de sons, images, métaphorés—augmente à proportion d'une tension intérieure qui résulte, selon les cas, de l'enthousiasme religieux, de la colère, de la douleur, de la tendresses ou d'autres mouvements de l'âme," p. xxv.

15. Sermo XLIII, OB 2, pp. 41–44; "Habete illum semper non retro in humeris, sed ante prae oculis, ne portantes et non odorantes, et onus premat, et odor non erigat." iii.5, p. 44.

16. "At satis distinctum est credo, quid Dei et quid nostrum in nostro sit corde; nec superflue, ut arbitror, sed ut sciant inimici gratiae, absque gratia nec ad cogitandum bonum sufficere cor humanum" Sermo XXXII.iii.7, OB 1, p. 230. The comparison of Abelard to Pelagius is made in Bernard's letter 190 to Innocent III, where he says: "si hoc sapit, cum Pelagio desipit." *Epistolae* vol. 2, OB 8, p. 37.

17.

> Non sapiens, non sanctus, non propheta videre illum sicuti est potest aut potuit in corpore hoc mortali; poterit autem in immortali, qui dignus habebitur. Itaque videtur et hic, sed sicut videtur ipsi, et non sicuti est.

Sermo XXXI.i.2, OB 2, p. 220.

18. Compare to the beginning of Origen's *Commentary*, p. 61.

19.

> Vide autem tu, ne quid nos in hac Verbi animaeque commixtione corporeum seu imaginarium sentire existimes. Id loquimur quod Apostolus dicit, quoniam "qui adhaeret Deo, unus spiritus est." Excessum purae mentis in Deum, sive Dei pium descensum in animam, nostris, quibus possumus, exprimimus verbis, spiritualibus spirituali comparantes.

Sermo XXXI.ii.6, OB 1, p. 233.

20.

> et speciali praerogativa intimis illum affectibus atque ipsis medullis cordis caelitus illapsum suscipiat, habeatque praesto quem desiderat, non figuratum, sed infusum, non apparentem, sed afficientem; nec dubium quin eo iucundiorem, quo intus, non foris.

Sermo XXXI.iii.6, OB 1, p. 223.

21. For Abelard, see note 16 above.

22. "hoc pro litterae textu. Iam vero spiritualem sensum qui in ea latet, sub alio sermonis principio exspectate." Sermo XXXII.iv.10, OB. 1, p. 233.

23.

> Et primo adverte quam eleganter amorem spiritus a carnis discernat affectu, dum dilectum exprimere magis ipsa affectione quam nomine volens, non simpliciter: "quem diligo," sed: "O," inquit, "quem diligit anima mea," spiritualem designans dilectionem.

Sermo XXXIII.i.1.2, OB 1, p. 234.

24. "etenim illa meridies tota est dies, et ipsa nesciens vesperam." Sermo XXXIII.i., OB 1, p. 236.

25.

> non tamen ad meridianum perveniet lumen, nec in illa sui plenitudine videbitur modo, in qua videndus est postea, ab his dumtaxat quos hac visione ipse dignabitur. O vere meridies, plenitudo fervoris et lucis, solis statio, umbrarum exterminatio, desiccatio paludum, faetorum depulsio! O perenne solstitium, quando iam non inclinabitur dies!

Sermo XXXIII.iv.6, OB 1, p. 237.

26. "Serpit hodie putida tabes per omne corpus Ecclesiae." Sermo XXXIII.vii.15, OB 1, p. 244.

27. The text is printed in PL 184:407–436, among the *Opera Aliena et Supposita* of Bernard. It is attributed to William of Saint-Thierry by Stegmüller (3030), but see Ohly, pp. 157–158, and J. Leclercq, "Le Commentaire bref du Cantique attribué à Saint Bernard," in "Études sur Saint Bernard et le texte de ses écrits," ASOC 9 (1953) 105–124, and J. Hourlier, "Guillaume de Saint-Thierry et la *Brevis commentatio in Cantica*," ASOC 12 (1956) 105–114 for the scholarly debates over the question of authorship. It is especially noteworthy that

the pericope of the Song of Songs on which this text comments is congruent with William's first division of the text, see note 34 below.

28. "Tres sunt status amoris Dei in anima christiana. Primus, sensualis vel animalis; secundus, rationalis; tertius, spiritualis vel intellectualis." PL 184:407C. "Secundum hos tres status in Cantico canticorum modo adolescentulae, modo sodales, modo sponsus et sponsa loquuntur suo unusquisque modo." PL 184:411A.

29. "Nam secundum tres status amoris, tria sunt etiam oscula amantis. Primum, propitiatorium vel reconciliatorium; secundum, promeritorium; tertium, contemplatorium. Primum ad pedes, secundum ad manum, tertium ad os." PL 184:411C.

30. Discussion of Trinity from PL 184:412A–413C. On 1:2, "Tria sunt unguenta: compunctionis, ex recordatione peccatorum; devotionis, ex recordatione beneficiorum; pietatis, ex recordatione miserorum." PL 184:415A. For analysis, see Hourlier, pp. 107–109.

31. PL 184:418B–419C.

32. Geoffrey's text is edited in two volumes by Ferruccio Gastaldelli, TT 19, 20 (1974), see above, chapter two, note 73. Gilbert of Hoyland is printed in PL 184:11–252; John of Ford, ed. E. Mikkers and H. Costello, CCCM 17–18 (1970). See also Ohly, pp. 171–183.

33. This is suggested by William's *Vita Bernardi*, PL 185:259–260; see also Hourlier, pp. 113–114. William's *Expositio* is edited by J. M. Déchanet, SC 82 (1962), and translated into English by Mother Columba Hart, William of Saint Thierry, *Exposition on the Song of Songs*, Cistercian Fathers Series 6 (Kalamazoo, Mich.: Cistercian Publications, 1970).

34. According to J. M. Déchanet's introduction to the citical edition, p. 15, the intended division was First Song = 1:1–2:7, Second Song = 2:8–3:5, Third Song = 3:6–8:4, Fourth Song = 8:5–14.

35.

> Non autem profundiora illa mysteria, quae in eo continentur, attentamus, de Christo et Ecclesia; sed cohibentes nos intra nos, et in nobismetipsis nosmetipsos metientes, de Sponso ac Sponsa, de Christo et christiana anima, sensum tantummodo moralem aliquem, in quo omnibus audere licet, pro sensus nostri paupertate perstringimus, laboris nostri non alium requirentes fructum, quam similem materiae, id est amorem ipsum.

Preface, 5, ed. Déchanet, p. 76.

36. See Déchanet's introduction, SC 82, pp. 42–49.

37.

> Interim in pressuris hujus vitae, in adjutorium laboris, ad solatium dilationis, bonae menti sua paradisus, et bonae conscientiae lectulus ordinatur floridus; et in eo non osculum illud aeternum, et perfecta conjunctio, sed osculi ipsius et perfectionis affectata quaedam imitatio, et conjunctionis ac similitudinis illius aliqua similitudo. Nam per Spiritum Sanctum spiritui hominis, et sensui amoris

illuminati, passim, raptim, aliquando illuc attingenti, dulcescit illud quidquid est, et rapit amantem, amatum, potius quam cogitatum, gustatum, quam intellectum; sicque ad tempus, ad horam, afficit amantem, figit tendentem; ut jam non in spe, sed quasi in re, ipsam sperandarum substantiam rerum de verbo vitae quodam experientis fidei argumento, et videre oculis, et tenere ac contrectare manibus sibi videatur.

Song One, Stanza Eight, 99, ed. Déchanet, p. 226.

38. Herde, pp. 1041–1067. Also Friedrich Only, "Geist und Formen der Hoheliedauslegung im 12. Jahrhundert," ZIDA 85 (1954) 181–197.

39. Printed among the works of Hugh of Saint Victor in PL 176:987–994 as *De amore sponsi ad sponsam*. The text also appears in the cycle of Assumption homilies attributed by PL 198 to Peter Comestor, although without apparent manuscript warrant, see E. Ann Matter, "*Eulogium sponsi de sponsa* : Canons, Monks, and the Song of Songs," *The Thomist* 49 (1985) 562–563. Many manuscripts are untitled; I use here the most common title in the manuscript tradition.

40. The *Eulogium* is attributed to Hugh by the *Indiculum omnium scriptorum Magistri Hugonis de sancto Victore que scripsit*, found in one manuscript, Oxford, Merton College 49. This canonical list of Hugh's writings is taken from an "official" compilation made by Gilduin of Saint Victor after 1141, the year of Hugh's death. The *Eulogium* manuscripts are mostly unattributed, although some do give Hugh as the author. See Matter, " *Eulogium*," pp. 560–564.

41. For the manuscripts, see Matter, " *Eulogium*," pp. 560–563. I am grateful to Mlle. Tesnière of the Salle des manuscrits, Bibliothèque Nationale, Paris, for her generous advice and assistance with this collection.

42. Jerome, *Adversus Jovinianum* is PL 23:264. Vaccari's citation of manuscripts of Jerome's hexeplaric version from the ninth and twelfth centuries is important evidence that the text could have instead been drawn from a non-Vulgate Bible.

43. Taken from Paris, B. N. lat. 2479 (c. 12, a codex from the collection of the Count of Thou), f. 74v, where it appears as a rubric. Note the liturgical ending. Most copies of the *Eulogium* begin without quoting the verses.

44. "Sponsus quidam hic loquitur, qui sponsam habet, et spondet se visitaturum eam." PL 176:987B.

45.

Sed quaeris quisnam sit iste talis sponsus, et quae sponsa eius? Sponsus est Deus; sponsa est anima. Tunc autem sponsus domi est, quando per internum gaudium mentem replet; tunc recedit, quando dulcedinem contemplationis subtrahit. Sed qua similitudine anima sponsa Dei dicitur? Ideo sponsa quia donis gratiarum subarrhata. Ideo sponsa, quia casto amore illi sociata. Ideo sponsa, quia per aspirationem Spiritus sancti prole virtutum fecundanda.

PL 176:987C

46.

> Arrha est forti fortitudo sua, qua roboratur, ut ad bonum opus convalescat. Arrha est debili debilitas sua, qua frangitur, ne malum perficiat. Arrha est insipienti simplicitas sua, qua humiliatur, ne superbiat.

PL 176:988B.

47. Chapter three, note 81 above. Like Honorius, the *Eulogium* draws most obviously from the *Allegoriae in sacram scripturam* attributed to Hrabanus Maurus, PL 112:849–1008.

48. "Veni de Libano decandidato ad Libanum non decandidatum, sed candidum. Veni de corde mundato ad mundatorem cordium, non mundatum, sed mundum." PL 176:990B.

49.

> Quando ad vivendum tantum caro sustentamentum accipit, Seir in monte est. Quando vero ad robur nutrimentum quaerit, Seir in campo est. Quando autem ad lasciviendum delicias poscit, Seir in valle est. . . . Qui superflua resecat, Seir in valle conculcat. Qui vero de necessariis aliquid minuit, Seir in campo vincit. Qui autem ad sustentamentum tantum naturae necessaria tribuit, quasi Seir in monte exactiori obsequium reddit.

PL 176:991A–B.

50. "hoc est de multis ad unum progredimur (quia quanto magis mundum fugiendo Deo appropinquare incipimus) tanto magis in unum congregamur. Quod nobis, etc. Amen." PL 176:994A.

51. Caroline Walker Bynum, "The Spirituality of the Canons Regular in the Twelfth Century," in *Jesus as Mother: Studies in the Spirituality of the High Middle Ages* (Berkeley: University of California Press, 1982) pp. 22–58. For Hugh of Saint-Victor in this tradition, see also M. D. Chenu, "La théologie symbolique," in *La Théologie aux douzième siècle* (Paris: J. Vrin, 1976) pp. 191–209.

52. The homilies of Gebuinus are only in manuscript, the earliest of which, Paris, B. N. lat. 14937, is thought by Leclercq to be "une collection authentique," see "Gébouin de Troyes et S. Bernard," RSPT 41 (1957) 632–640, reprinted in *Recueil d'études* 1, pp. 83–93, and Matter, "*Eulogium*," pp. 568–570. The quotation of the *Eulogium* in the lengthy commentary of Thomas the Cistercian is found in PL 206:423, see also B. Griesser, "Thomas Cisterciensis als Verfasser eines Kommentars zum Hohenlied," *Cistercienser-Chronik* 51 (1939) 168–74, 219–224, 263–269, and Matter, "*Eulogium*," pp. 570–573. Geoffrey of Auxerre cites the passage after an interpretation of the *Vulgate* reading of 4:6–8, ed. Gastaldelli vol.1, pp. 230–231.

53. On this connection, see A. Landgraf, "Recherches sur Pierre le Mangeur," RTAM 3 (1931) 292–306, 341–373; and R. M. Martin, "Notes sur l'oeuvre littéraire de Pierre le Mangeur," RTAM 3 (1931) 54–66.

54. R. Chazon, *Medieval Jewry in Northern France: A Political and Social History*

(Baltimore: Johns Hopkins University Press, 1973); A. Grabois, "The 'Hebraica veritas' and Jewish-Christian Intellectual Relations in the Twelfth Century," *Speculum* 50 (1975) 613–634; H. Hailperin, *Rashi and the Christian Scholars* (Pittsburgh: University of Pittsburgh Press, 1963).

55. Leclercq, *Monks and Love*, pp. 110–114. For Origen's connections to Jewish exegesis, see above, chapter two, note 2.

56.

> Et revera ubi tuta firmaque infirmis requies, nisi in vulneribus Salvatoris? . . . Foderunt manus eius et pedes, latusque lancea foraverunt, et per has rimas licet mihi surgere mel de petra, oleumque de saxo durissimo, id est gustare et videre quoniam suavis est Dominus. (Psalm 33:9—Vulgate) . . . Patet arcanum cordis per foramina corporis, patet magnum illud pietatis sacramentum, patent "viscera misericordiae Dei nostri, in quibus visitavit nos oriens ex alto." (1 Timothy 3:16) Quidni viscera per vulnera pateant?

Sermo LXI.ii.3–4, OB, vol. 2., pp. 150–151. My English translation, with consultation of the translation at Irene Edmonds, Bernard of Clairvaux, *On the Song of Songs III*, Cistercian Fathers Series 31 (Kalamazoo, Mich.: Cistercian Publications, 1979) pp. 142–144. For Origen's interpretation of this verse, which understands Christ as the rock, but with no reference to the wounds of the passion, see *Commentary* Book III (IV), ed. Baehrens, pp. 228–232.

57. Ludolph relates the five wounds of Christ to the five senses of fallen man, *Vita Christi* II, 64, 676B, see Sister Mary Immaculate Bodenstedt, *The Vita Christi of Ludolphus the Carthusian*, Catholic University Studies in Medieval and Renaissance Latin Language and Literature XVI (Washington, D.C.: The Catholic University of America Press, 1944) pp. 138–139.

58. Bodenstedt, pp. 53–92, "The Influence of the *Vita Christi*." See also Charles Abbott Conway, Jr., *The Vita Christi of Ludolph of Saxony and Late Medieval Devotion Centered on the Incarnation: A Descriptive Analysis*, Analecta Carthusiana 34 (Salzburg: Institut für English Sprache und Literatur, Universität Salzburg, 1976).

59. Caroline Walker Bynum, *Holy Feast, Holy Fast: The Religious Significance of Food to Medieval Women* (Berkeley: University of California Press, 1987), pp. 270– 274, and "The Female Body and Religious Practice in the Later Middle Ages," *Zone* 3: *Fragments For a History of the Human Body*, 1 (New York: Urzone, 1989) 160–219.

60. See above, chapter two, notes 37, 39, 44.

61. Michel Foucault, *La Volonté de savoir* (Paris: Éditions Gallimard, 1976), translated by Robert Hurley as *The History of Sexuality: An Introduction* (New York: Penguin Press, 1978) p. 23. See also pp. 115–117, "Periodization."

62. Foucault, p. 7.

63. Mary Daly, *Pure Lust: Elemental Feminist Philosophy* (Boston: Beacon Press, 1984) pp. 62, 76. I first developed the connection between Daly and the

tropological commentaries on the Song of Songs, in particular the *Eulogium*, in a lecture given at Oberlin College in February, 1986. I am especially grateful to Marcia Colish for suggestions on the refinement of the argument.

64. William E. Phipps, "The Plight of the Song of Songs," JAAR 42 (1974) pp. 90–91.

65. John F. Benton proposed that the correspondence of Abelard and Heloise was totally falsified in "Fraud, Fiction, and Borrowing in the Correspondence of Abelard and Heloise," *Pierre Abélard—Pierre le Vénérable*, Actes et mémoires du colloques internationaux, 546 (Paris: Centre National de la Recherche Scientifique, 1975) pp. 469–506, followed by debate, pp. 507–511. Benton later revised his thesis to make Abelard the author of both the letters attributed to him and those attributed to Heloise, "A Reconsideration of the Authenticity of the Correspondence of Abelard and Heloise," *Petrus Abelardus (1079–1142): Person, Werk und Wirkung*, ed. Rudolf Thomas et al., Trierer Theologische Studien 38 (Trier: Paulinus, 1980) pp. 41–52; in the same volume, see also the articles by David Luscombe and Peter von Moos. Similar questions about the authenticity of the correspondence have been raised more recently by Hubert Silvestre, "L'Idylle d'Abélard et Héloïse: la part du roman," *Académie Royale de Belgique, Bulletin de la classe des lettres et des sciences morales et politiques*, 5e série, 71 (1985) 157–200. But see Linda Georgiana, "Any Corner of Heaven: Heloise's Critique of Monasticism," *Mediaeval Studies* 49 (1987) 221–253 for analysis of the debate which pitches "très sage Heloys" (Robertson) against the "woman of sensuous mind" (Muckle). A connection between this correspondence and the Song of Songs is further suggested by Georgianna's reference (p. 223, note 8) to a Caedmon recording of Claire Bloom and Claude Rains reading from Abelard and Heloise, with selections from the Song of Songs on the flip side. See also Linda S. Kauffman, "The Irremediable: Heloise to Abelard," in *Discourses of Desire: Gender, Genre, and Epistolary Fictions* (Ithaca, N.Y.: Cornell University Press, 1986) pp. 63–89.

66. L. Krinetzki, "Die erotische Psychologie des Hohen Liedes," *Theologische Quartalschrift* 150 (1970) 43–55.

67. Leclercq, *Monks and Love*, pp. 29–27.

68. Bynum, *Holy Feast and Holy Fast*, p. 253.

69. See above, chapter two, note 7.

Chapter Six

The Woman Who is the All: The Virgin Mary and the Song of Songs

The female gender of one of the voices of the Song of Songs, so much more obvious in Latin than in English, elicited little comment from the medieval exegetes who worked in the allegorial and tropological modes. Of course, as both *Ecclesia* and *anima* are feminine nouns in Latin, there was no linguistic difficulty in putting the words of the Bride in the mouth of the Church or of the human soul. But a logical consequence of medieval fascination with the Song of Songs was an association of the Bride with a human, a woman, although a highly idealized figure, the Virgin Mary. This form of personification begins early in the Latin *liturgical* tradition, and gradually becomes a part of Song of Songs commentary. In the history of western Christian interpretation, *use* of the Song of Songs in praise of the Virgin is a precursor, and to some extent a determinant, of a tradition of exegesis in the mariological mode. The confluence of marian liturgies and mariological Song of Songs exegesis is another interesting example of both the continual inner transformation and the outward expansion of the commentary genre.

The Song of Songs in Liturgies of the Virgin

Veneration of the Virgin Mary in western Christianity is closely linked to theological speculation about the humanity and divinity of Jesus Christ. The paradox of divine incarnation is, of course, a central tenet of Christian doctrine. Periods of high christology, especially those linked to eucharistic formulations, tended to be accompanied by liturgies in honor of the Virgin Mary. Three events in the Virgin's life became the focus of major devotions: her special nativity, her bodily assumption into heaven (both testified to by extra-canonical Christian writings), and her ritual purification according to Jewish law after the birth of Jesus (testified to by the Gospel of Luke).[1] Liturgies for the feasts of the Nativity, Assumption, and Purification of the Virgin Mary had developed uses of the Song of Songs by the seventh century. These references to the Song of Songs became especially prominent, and received elaborate comment tending toward commentary, in the theologically expansive Carolingian Church.[2] The Assumption of the Virgin Mary was the feast which especially brought about a transformation of the liturgical use of the Song of Songs to a marian level of interpreting the text.

Perhaps because of a desire to link liturgical practice to the formative figures of Latin Christianity, two of the most influential Carolingian treatises about the Virgin Mary are pseudonymous, bearing attributions to Augustine and Jerome. Jaroslav Pelikan has pointed out that when tracing theological elements of the early Middle Ages, it is often "more difficult than current conventional wisdom among theologians suggests to tell the difference between the 'pious fraud' of pseudonymity and just plain forgery."[3] In any case, and however they may be judged by modern readers, the anonymous homily *De Assumptione Beatae Mariae Virginis*, which circulated as a work of Augustine, and the pseudonymous work of Paschasius Radbertus known as *Cogitis me* ("You Compel Me"), which was transmitted as Epistle 9 of Jerome, were far more widely read than anything either Jerome or Augustine actually wrote about the Virgin Mary. This fact has a certain irony which is compounded by the probability that Augustine would have disapproved of the unapologetic use of the Song of Songs as a canonical reference to the Assumption of the Virgin.[4]

Cogitis me is probably the earlier treatise, and it certainly makes the more important connection between the Song of Songs and the Feast of the Assumption. It is by far the most popular of a number of mariological works written by the ninth-century monk and sometimes abbot of Corbie, Paschasius Radbertus.[5] The text opens with a conscious literary conceit, claiming that it is a letter of Jerome to his friends Paula and Eustochium, nuns in Bethlehem, when it actually was written by Radbertus for his friends and childhood protectors, Theodrada and Irma, nuns of Soissons. Like Jerome's friends, Theodrada and Irma were a mother-daughter pair dedicated to the life of Christian contemplation. Their relationship to Radbertus was extremely close, since Radbertus had been left as a foundling at the monastery, a house dedicated to the Virgin Mary, where Theodrada (a cousin of Charlemagne) was abbess. He received monastic tonsure at this house before moving to Corbie, where Theodrada's brothers, Adalard and Wala, were abbots in the first third of the ninth century.[6]

Posing as a famous figure from biblical or even classical antiquity was a common enough practice among Carolingian literary figures, especially those, like Radbertus, who had some contact with the ways of the court. But the pseudepigrahical attribution of *Cogitis me* to Jerome had more serious consequences than those, for example, of Charlemagne posing as David or Alcuin playing Horace, for the text passed enthusiastically through the Middle Ages with only one ripple of dissent when Hincmar, Bishop of Reims, had a luxury copy written for his cathedral chapter shortly after the death of Radbertus.[7] To medieval eyes, *Cogitis me* was received as Jerome's elegant testimony to the Feast of the Assumption.

Cogitis me is, moreover, an exemplary document for discerning the influence of particular liturgies on Carolingian theology, and on the changing genre of Song of Songs interpretation. This is particularly so because Radbertus's text stays quite close to one important liturgical source, the Antiphoner of Compiègne, a manuscript from the monastery of Saint-Corneille associated by tradition with Charles the Bald.[8] Quotations from the Song of Songs in the *Cogitis me* can usually also be found in this liturgical tradition, in a series of antiphons and responses to the Common of Virgins, to the Nativity of the Virgin Mary, and, especially, to the Assumption. These liturgical uses brought with them the earliest associations of the Song of Songs with the Virgin Mary, a *devotional* tradition with roots at least as far back as Ambrose.[9]

The liturgy has always provided an arena for the ritual adaptation of sacred texts. In the monastic tradition, the liturgy was not limited to the Mass, but included the continual round of monastic offices, each of which drew antiphonary material from the Bible. This daily liturgical discipline provided a social and intellectual context in which adaptation of the Song of Songs for marian feasts flourished. A striking example of this process can be seen in a composite version of Song of Songs 6:9 and 6:3 which in the Antiphoner of Compiègne appears as an antiphon for the Vespers of the Feast of the Assumption of Mary:

quae est ista quae ascendit
  quasi aurora consurgens
pulchra ut luna electa ut sol
  terribilis ut castrorum acies ordinata[10]

Who is this who ascends
  like the rising dawn
beautiful as the moon, chosen as the sun
  terrible as a battle line drawn up from the camps?

This is not a known Vetus Latina text.[11] In fact, it is extremely close to the Vulgate texts from which it is drawn, varying in only one small but important word: "ascendit" for "progreditur." The change from "goes forth" to "ascends" emphasizes the connection of the verses to the Feast of the Assumption. Radbertus must have been quite familiar with this liturgy, for he quotes this peculiar, "marianized" composite both in the deliberately pseudepigraphical *Cogitis me* and in the first of his Assumption sermons, a text which is accidently pseudepigraphical, having been incorporated into the series of sermons attributed to Ildefonsus of Toledo.[12] Other quotations from the Song of Songs in *Cogitis me* also show the influence of the liturgical tradition of the Antiphoner of Compiègne by particular combinations of verses, or minor textual variants.[13] Scrutiny of these passages suggests how the liturgical tradition led Radbertus to speak of the Virgin Mary as the Bride of the Song of Songs; but the theological use which Radbertus found for Song of Songs texts in his treatises on the Virgin marks the beginning of a new mode of exegesis.

The complexity of this movement from liturgical use to a mode of exegesis is evident in the way Radbertus quotes a crucial passage for marian exegesis of the Song of Songs 4:12b–13:

> Whence it is sung about her in those same Canticles: "A garden enclosed, a fountain sealed, your shoots a paradise." Truly a garden of delights, in which are planted all kinds of flowers, and the good scents of virtues; and so enclosed that it cannot be violated or corrupted by any trick of deceit. Therefore, a fountain sealed with the seal of the whole Trinity, out of which flows the fountain of life, "in whose light we all see light," (Psalm 35:10, Vulgate) since according to John, "He is the one who sheds light on every man coming into this world." (John 1:9). In the shoot springing forth from her womb is the paradise of the heavenly citizen.[14]

In this passage, Mary and Jesus are described by pastoral images of the Song of Songs which become metaphors of salvation: she is a garden, a fountain, out of which springs Christ, the Logos, the paradise of the blessed. Although the imagery is highly laudatory of the Virgin Mary, it nevertheless makes clear that her major virtue lies in being the spotless source of the incarnate God. The function of the Song of Songs here resonates clearly with the commentary genre as it had developed to the ninth century. The tropological or moral understanding of the Song of Songs greatly informs this treatise, in the sense that the Virgin becomes a spiritual model offered to the religious women for whom the treatise was written, perhaps in a conscious echo of Jerome's Epistle 22 to Eustochium.[15] Cassian's allegorical mode is also evident here, mediated through an understanding of Mary as the Church, the "garden enclosed" of many earlier Latin commentaries on the Song of Songs. This subtle mixture of allegory in the service of theology, an approach which could be properly called "mariological" as well as "marian," is the spirit in which Radbertus quotes the "hortus conclusus" passage here. The same attitude is also found in Radbertus's defense of the virginity of Mary *in partu*, and in his commentary on the epithalamial Vulgate Psalm 44, "My heart proffers a good word."[16]

Although Radbertus had set the stage for a mariological reading of the Song of Songs, it was not until the twelfth century that this mode of exposition was fully realized. Liturgies of the Virgin Mary are also very close to the first systematic mariological exposition of the Song of Songs, the *Sigillum Beatae Mariae* of Honorius Augustodunensis. In fact, the liturgy can be said to have sparked this text, since the *Sigillum* begins with a demand "discipuli ad magistrum" why Luke 10:38 (the story of Mary and Martha) and the Song of Songs are read in the Assumption liturgy "about holy Mary, since in no way do they appear clearly to pertain to her."[17] The *Sigillum* is made up of short commentaries on this Gospel and the Epistle of the Assumption (Ecclesiastes 24:1ff.), followed by a complete, line-by-line, exposition of the antiphonal text for the feast, the Song of Songs, understood as depicting the love between God and the Virgin Mary.

Valerie Flint has suggested that the *Sigillum* was written early in Honorius's career, perhaps about 1100, in England, perhaps Worcester.[18] It is a composite work, woven together from a number of sources. The first section, on the Gospel, is a reworking of a homily attributed to Anselm, actually written by Ralph d'Escures, abbot of Saint-Martin of Séez in Normandy.[19] The Ecclesiastes interpretation is adapted from another pseudo-Anselmian sermon, changing the reference from Christ and the Church to the Virgin Mary.[20] This change of reference also characterizes the major part of the treatise, the mariological commentary on the Song of Songs, an interpretation of some ingenuity and great complexity of sources.

Honorius begins this exposition of the Song of Songs with an analogy between Mary and the Church which works on several levels:

> The glorious Virgin Mary manifests the type of the Church, which is shown to be both virgin and mother. Indeed, she [the Church] is proclaimed mother since she is fecundated by the Holy Spirit; through her every day children of God are born in baptism. She is, moreover, called virgin because, inviolably serving the integrity of faith, she is not corrupted by heretical perverseness. So Mary was a mother bringing forth Christ, remaining a virgin after the parturition. Therefore all things which are written about the Church may be sufficiently appropriately read even about her [Mary]. Thus it says: "Let him kiss me from the kiss of his mouth." (Song of Songs 1:1a) This very one whom kings and prophets were not worthy to see or hear, the Virgin was not only worthy to carry in her womb, but even, when born, to frequently give him kisses, receiving many from his sacred mouth. "For your breasts are better than wine." (Song of Songs 1:1b) He who pastures the angels in the bosom of the Father, here sucks at the breast of the virgin mother.[21]

The allegorical fluidity of this passage is remarkable. Subject and object, signified and signifier, slip back and forth even as the mode of interpretation shifts in mid-sentence. As far as the Song of Songs is concerned, Honorius seems to presume that the allegorical interpretation includes the mariological, since "all things which are written about the Church may be sufficiently appropriately (*satis congrue*) read even about her," that is, Mary. There is also a hint of the kiss of mystical union, several decades before Bernard of Clairvaux's third sermon on the Song of Songs, in the rapture with which the Virgin's kisses on the mouth of Christ are described. Finally, an apocalyptic vision of Christ, the shepherd of the angelic flock in the bosom of the Father, is seen in the child nursing at the breast of the virgin mother. As we have seen, these modes of understanding appear in a more highly developed form in Honorius's long Song of Songs commentary, but they are already present in this text from the beginning of his career, adapted to the Virgin Mary.

The *Sigillum* is thus important evidence of the transition from marian use to mariological interpretation of the Song of Songs. Indeed, this is a biblical, rather than a liturgical, commentary. The text of the Song of Songs is the Vulgate (including "progreditur" instead of "ascendit" at 6:9),[22] and the exposition proceeds from verse to verse, each chapter expounding one chapter of the Song of Songs. Yet the *Sigillum* is related to what seems to be a homiletical tradition, perhaps falling between the activities of the choir and the chapter, and testifying to a tradition of spoken reflection on the Song of Songs on feasts of the Virgin.

The homiletical tone of this explanation is evident also in a series of rubrics which begin near the end of the second chapter of the *Sigillum*. The rubrics identify changes of voice in the text, while suggesting a line of interpretation: "The prayer of the Virgin for converts," "The praise of the Son for the Mother," "The praise of the Father for the Virgin," "The words of the Virgin hoping for Christ to come into her," "On the solicitude of the Virgin for the Church of the Jews."[23] This last rubric is one of several which speak of the intercession of the Virgin Mary for the conversion of the Jews. In general, these titles stress the intercessory powers of the Virgin, and suggest a devotional context in which the miracles of the Virgin were a part of a growing cult.[24]

The *Sigillum Beatae Mariae* bears witness to a type of devotion to the Virgin that flourished especially among the Benedictines of Western England. Honorius tells five miracles of the Virgin in this text, four of them (the Jewish boy, Theophilus, Mary the harlot, the salvific belt) near the beginning and another (the miraculous revelation to a holy hermit of the date of the Virgin's Nativity) at the end.[25] Flint has shown that several of these miracles can be traced to the Worcester Passionale, a compilation of mariological texts which also included the *Cogitis me*. Not surprisingly, Honorius alludes to the *Cogitis me* immediately after the story of the hermit.[26] Traces of Paschasius Radbertus are found throughout the commentary, even, perhaps, in a reference to the "hortus conclusus" of 4:12 as the virginity of Mary at the moment of the birth of Christ.[27] The religious life looms large in the *Sigillum*, here again, Mary is represented as the "primum exemplum virginitatis." Her virginity is, moreover, the source of the truly miraculous birth which Christ "reserved" for himself:

> God makes human beings in four ways: from the earth, as Adam; from man alone, as Eve; from man and woman, as us; from woman alone, Christ, since he reserved the privilege for himself.[28]

The *Sigillum*, written at the very beginning of the twelfth century, shows equal influence of the ancient marian liturgical tradition and the growing cult of the Virgin. This century is, of course, the period in which is found the greatest increase in outright devotion to the Virgin, with both liturgical and literary responses. Even in the twelfth century, marian understanding of the Song of Songs was still linked to the liturgy; an even stronger connection was forged between the Song of Songs and the celebration of the Feast of the Assumption by the twelfth-century standardization of verses from the Song of Songs in the monastic office of the day and its octave.[29] A number of twelfth-century sermons for the Assumption reinforce the general marian understanding of the Song of Songs while expanding on the liturgical use of one verse, as does the *Sermo de Assumptione Beatae Virginis* of Hugh of Saint-Victor, written for a certain Gerlandus, abbot of a monastery dedicated to the Virgin Mary.[30]

Commentary on liturgical uses of the Song of Songs is especially interesting in its consistent application of dialogue to the text. Of course, the voices of the Song of Songs always speak either in monologue or dialogue, and we have already noted a tradition of rubrics in Latin Bibles which tended to emphasize this feature of the text. But the antiphonal nature of liturgy, where biblical verses respond to one another, creates an atmosphere of aural awareness of the Song of Songs which is lost to modern readers. When Paschasius Radbertus and Hugh of Saint-Victor wrote homilies on the Assumption, it can be said without exaggeration that they had verses from the Song of Songs ringing in their ears. Honorius's *Sigillum* also obviously began from a liturgical, spoken knowledge of the Song of Songs, and underlined a dialogical mood through its structure—questions and answers between students and a master. This spoken, responsory nature of the earliest marian interpretation of the Song of Songs fades as twelfth-century authors begin consciously to model their works on the commentary genre, becoming more oriented towards mariology than marian devotion. But this is a gradual process.

The Virgin Mary in Song of Songs Commentary

It is with the exegesis of Rupert of Deutz that mariological exposition of the Song of Songs takes the form classic to the commentary genre. Rupert was born near Liège around the year 1075, and spent much of his career in zealous support of monastic reform, especially in the Benedictine houses in the German Empire. He was certainly the paramount Latin Christian writer between Anselm of Canterbury and Bernard of Clairvaux. John Van Engen has called him "the most prolific of all twelfth-century authors," and has shown that he was greatly influenced by the systematic approach to the Bible characteristic of the "masters of the Sacred Page."[31] Rupert's exegesis is squarely and consciously in the midst of the development of theology as a school discipline. He wrote many biblical commentaries, beginning with the two books whose connection was discussed in chapter four, the Apocalypse and the Song of Songs. Rupert's second exegetical work *Commentaria in Canticum Canticorum* (*de Incarnatione Domini*) dates from around 1125.[32] This text is extremely innovative in that it uses Cassian's modes to move the explication of the text beyond the bounds of Cassian's system.

Rupert's title proclaims his theological purpose, a reading of the Song of Songs as a love poem on the mystery of the incarnation of Christ. But here the Song is consistently understood to be in honor of the *vehicle* of this mysterious incarnation, the Virgin Mary. Rupert interprets the entire text of the Song of Songs with reference to the Virgin. Although abstracted from liturgical use, the commentary in some ways continues the dialogical nature of earlier marian exposition on the Song of Songs; much of it is written in the second person, addressing Mary directly, or even in the first person, allowing her to speak for herself in the words of the poems. This treatise, the shortest of Rupert's exegetical works, is much longer than the marian interpretations of the Song of Songs we have considered thus far. This is a fully developed monastic commentary, heavily dependent on several treatises in the allegorical mode: the ninth-century Song of Songs *catena* of Angelomus of Luxeuil, the Song of Songs commentary of Gregory the Great, and also Jerome's *Interpretatio hebraicorum nominum.*[33] We have already seen easy shifts of understanding of the Song of Songs from the Church to the Virgin, but none that developed the new understanding at this theological level. Rupert consistently used sources from the prevailing ecclesiological tradition of the Song of Songs to elaborate a full theology of the Virgin Mary which he found in the text.

In spite of the precedent set by treatises based on the liturgies of the Virgin, both Rupert and his contemporaries seemed very aware of the novelty of this particular interpretation as a biblical commentary, for, as Van Engen says, "it was one thing to write a treatise honoring the Blessed Virgin which drew upon selected verses of the Song hallowed by liturgical usage; it was quite another to interpret the entire Song with reference to Mary."[34] The testimony of a letter of Rupert extant in a twelfth-century schoolbook suggests that this innovation in the Song of Songs commentary genre was actually the center of some controversy. The dispute seems to have revolved around the question of whether it was proper to assume that things understood *generaliter* about the Church are meant to refer *specialiter* to the Virgin Mary. Rupert's reply rejects the use of the scholastic terms "genus" and species" in dealing with this question, and defends his interpretation with reference to the precedent of *Cogitis me*. The letter ends with the explanation that Rupert had only hoped to "add a little something" (*aliquid supererogare*) to the work of the Fathers, since the treasures of Scripture properly belong to all who have the will (*voluntas*) and the skills (*facultas*) to look for them. In this case, the "little something" added is a devotional work, gathering testimony of many voices in honor of Mary, "the only beloved of Christ" (*unicae dilectae Christi Mariae*).[35]

In the dedicatory epistle to Thietmar of Verden, Rupert presents his mariological commentary as a devotional meditation on the Divine Word, Christ, who lives in the human heart and who was incarnated on earth. He describes this meditation as dictated "as much as possible in contemplation of the face of our lady, Mary holy and ever-virgin," perhaps in meditation on a devotional image, and offers the work as a bell *(tintinabulum)* to an old friend whose "ringing" preaching of the Gospel Rupert still remembers.[36]

The prologue, which dedicates the work to Abbot Cuno of Siegburg, describes it as a spiritual battle like that of Jacob with the angel, a proper wrestling match with the mysteries God has placed in Scripture. In the development of this battle metaphor, Mary appears as both the courtly lady and the armorer:

> Therefore, O Lady, Godbearer, true and uncorrupt mother of the Word eternally God and man, Jesus Christ; armed not with my but with your merits, I wish to wrestle with this same man, that is, with the Word of God, and to wrench out a work on the Song of Songs which it would not be unseemly to call *De incarnatione Domini*, to the praise and glory of that Lord, and to the praise and glory of your blessedness.[37]

Some years earlier, Rupert explains, he had been inspired by the Virgin to attempt a verse work on the Song, a project he found himself unable to carry through. It is worth noting that Peter Heliae did eventually accomplish Rupert's youthful goal in a long unpublished verse commentary on the Song of Songs dating from around 1148.[38] But Rupert's meditation on the Song of Songs, however passionate and direct, is still in focus and structure an unmistakable prose commentary. The prologue relates the Song of Songs to seven biblical songs (which are not those of Origen),[39] and then offers a structural division of the Song of Songs into four (rather unequal) parts punctuated by the repeated refrain:

> adiuro vos filiae Hierusalem
> per capreas cervosque camporum
> ne suscietis neque evigilare faciatis
> dilectam quoadusque ipsa velit
>
> I adjure you, daughters of Jerusalem
> by the goats and the stags of the field
> neither arouse nor cause to awaken
> my beloved until she wishes.

This commentary thus conceives the Song of Songs to be divided at 2:7, 3:5, and 8:4 by an injunction to let the beloved sleep.

Furthermore, Rupert says he will base his interpretation on a foundation of historical or actual deeds:

> For, indeed, the mystical exposition will be more firm, nor will it be allowed to fluctuate, if it is held to be built on the history of certain times or rationally demonstrable things.[40]

With respect to the division of the text, this rhetorical structure seems to be Rupert's original, if not terribly influential, insight. Its relationship to the treatise, however, is partial. The commentary is actually divided into seven books, only the first two of which are marked by the rhetorical exclamation beginning "I adjure you, daughters of Jerusalem." Books three to seven take the text roughly a chapter at a time, but across the chapter divisions; the third "adiuro vos" (8:4) comes without special notice in the middle of the last book.[41]

With respect to Rupert's concern to base the *expositio mystica* in history or "real deeds," the commentary presents a challenge equal to its structure. The opening verse, "Let him kiss me with the kiss of his mouth," is immediately placed in the mouth of the Virgin Mary, whose state of spiritual rapture is described by two biblical verses: "what eyes have not seen and ears have not heard and the heart of man has not reached" (1 Corinthians 2:9), and "Behold the handmaid of the Lord, do unto me according to your word" (Luke 1:38).[42] Here it seems to be the *historical* sense that speaks of the Virgin Mary, or rather, that is the spiritually elevated moment of her speaking these words. Likewise, the "little foxes" of 2:15 refer to Herod, whom Jesus called "that fox" (Luke 13:32); again, the words are placed in Mary's mouth.[43] The rhetorical shift here is from "spoken about" to "speaking," a movement that is directly tied to content, since both of these passages also relate directly to the birth of Jesus.

Other places, in contrast, seem to have a sense of universal history, relating Mary both to Eve before her and to the Church which she helped to found. For example, the interpretation of 1:11, "my nard gave forth its fragrance," relates Eve's "stink of pride" to Mary's sweet-smelling nard of humility.[44] Far more complex is the interpretation of 4:12–15, where the "garden enclosed" is described in lush detail. The verse is immediately likened to the paradise planted by God:

> That one is the ancient paradise, the earthly paradise; this one is the new paradise, the celestial paradise. And the planter of each is the one and the same Lord God. In that one he placed the man he had formed (cf. Genesis 2:15), in this one he formed the man who with him in the beginning was God (cf. John 1:1). "From [that] soil he brought forth all trees that are beautiful to the sight, and sweet to the taste, and the tree of life in the middle of paradise." (Genesis 2:9) He blessed this soil, this his earth, and he brought forth from it the seeds of all graces and the models (*exemplaria*) of all virtues. And that tree of life is Christ, God and man, the lord of the celestial paradise.[45]

The repetition of the words *hortus conclusus* in the text of the Song of Songs indicates to Rupert that the verses speak of Mary, who was *conclusa*, "closed," both when she conceived, and at the moment of the birth of Jesus.[46]

The interpretation of the garden continues with a series of juxtapositions to the four cosmological corners of the earth: the four parts of paradise, "the four sacraments necessary for salvation" (Christ's incarnation, passion, resurrection, ascension), the four evangelists (man, ox, lion, eagle), the four rivers (Nile, Ganges, Tigris, Euphrates).[47] Each of these sets of four, on a different order of reality, stands in a special relationship to the Virgin, who is represented by the garden divided into four parts. The structure is established in reference to the salvation history which was so elaborately developed in the second Song of Songs commentary of Honorius.

Analysis of any part of Rupert's commentary on the Song of Songs "*de incarnatione Domini*" brings us up against many traditional elements of the Song of Songs commentary genre. Rupert interprets the text, although in relation to the Virgin Mary, by means of Cassian's allegorical and tropological modes. Mary is totally identified with the female speaker of the Song of Songs, and then she is interpreted according to the standard modes of Song of Songs exegesis. According to the allegorical mode, Mary becomes here not only the symbol of the Church, but the embodiment of it. On the tropological level, she is also the model of monastic virtues: virginity, humility, and obedience.[48]

These dual roles were conceived and forged in a period of great contemplative emphasis on the Virgin Mary, by a man who freely admitted to using the Virgin as a focus for contemplation on the incarnation of Christ. In some ways, then, Rupert's treatise can be seen to participate in developing trends of the cult of the Virgin.[49] Even more, considered from the point of view of Song of Songs commentary, Rupert's work is evidence of the great complexity which the commentary genre had achieved by the twelfth century. This flexible multivalence in the service of marian doctrine may have had a direct impact on Honorius (in whose long commentary are found many of the same themes), and a more dispersed influence on other commentators, including those who did specifically choose a consciously mariological mode of interpretation, rather than just marian content. The importance of Rupert's example is seen, for example, in the late twelfth-century commentary of Alan of Lille.

Like Honorius, Alan is a twelfth-century figure who defies simple categorization. He was thoroughly a man of the schools, having studied at Paris and perhaps at Chartres; yet he died a Cistercian, in fact, a monk of Cîteaux.[50] An early work, the *De planctu Naturae*, in which Lady Nature (*Natura*) laments the disaster humanity has made of creation, became a set school text and was regularly studied into the age of printing. This treatise served as an introduction to a more refined and difficult allegory of *Natura*, the *Anticlaudianus*. Alan's youthful fame was based on these books and a number of other school texts.[51]

Yet Alan experienced a sort of conversion when he went to teach in Montpellier, and encountered the spiritual battle which pitted the Cathars and Waldensians against the Cistercian Order. In this tumultous spiritual environment, he began to write catechetical works, eventually commenting on the Our Father, various creeds, and the Song of Songs.[52] These are also teaching texts, but focused on "practical" rather than "speculative" theology, and tied to the *cloister* schools. G. R. Evans has written about Alan:

> No doubt if he had been born a little later, he would have become one of the Friars Preachers. The Dominican Order in the thirteenth century would have been able to make use of his talents as a scholar and a teacher in a way that no single Order or school could do in the twelfth.[53]

But, of course, Alan was not born a bit later. He was an example of a counter-movement in twelfth-century Christian history, a movement from the schools to the monasteries. He is by no means alone in this twelfth-century pattern, which can also be seen in the lives of Honorius Augustodunensis and Peter Abelard. Evidently, the monastic life of prayer and study still held appeal to late twelfth-century intellectuals, and was able to absorb Alan's talents as a teacher and preacher. In this environment, especially considering his opposition to the Cathars, it is little wonder that Alan turned to exegesis of the Song of Songs. In doing so, he participated in a literary tradition which by this time had developed a highly complex articulation of bodily language for the love between God and the orthodox Church, the individual soul, and the type of both, the Virgin Mary.

Alan may have commented on the Bible in a systematic way, in either a cloister or a cathedral school. A set of unpublished glosses on the songs of the Old and New Testaments makes use of the rhetorical framework of the *accessus ad auctores* found in Honorius: *titu-*

lus, materia, intentio, modus agendi.[54] This scholastic compilation may have been recorded by Alan's pupils, or it may have been Alan's own work book, one of the sources from which he made exegetical lectures. *In Cantica Canticorum ad laudem Deiparae Virginis Mariae elucidatio*, the only one of his biblical commentaries to survive, was probably one of those lectures. Significantly, it was written down only at the special request of the prior of Cluny, and is extant in copies from important monastic houses: Klosterneuburg, Fleury, and St. Marien.[55] This text, which probably dates from Alan's years at Cîteaux, thus provides an unusual glimpse into his *monastic* teaching plan, and the role played in it by the Song of Songs.

Alan's *Elucidatio* on the Song of Songs makes references to both the spiritual elite and the life of contemplation, in specifying the difference between the Bridegroom's "manifest" teaching through the windows and the "more obscure " teaching through the lattices of Song of Songs 2:9.[56] The Church in the world is also a major concern of the treatise, often leading to a type of exegetical preaching, as in this open condemnation of the "little foxes" of Song of Songs 2:15:

> "Catch for us the little foxes, who destroy the vineyards." By "foxes," which are tricky animals living in caves in the earth, the heretics are understood; by "vineyards," the Churches are understood. The heretics demolish these same vineyards by any means they can. Inasmuch as they decry Christ and his mother, they work to weaken [var. sicken] the faith of the Church. Therefore, these can be the words of the faithful to Christ and to the Virgin: "catch for us," that is, pull down to our service, "the foxes," that is, the heretics, "little," on account of imbecility; since as much as they struggle against the Church, so much will they be sickened. "Who destroy the vineyards," that is, they draw away from ecclesiastical faith.[57]

This passage demonstrates the extreme rhetorical clarity of Alan's style, a style especially adapted for teaching. The commentary is systematic, straightforward, and, as the relation of the "little foxes" to heretics suggests, somewhat traditional in its interpretations. Even the addition of the Virgin Mary to the interpretation is always in tandem with Christ and/or the Church. Alan's calm, didactic voice contrasts rather sharply with the breathless devotional tone of Rupert's commentary, yet it is clear that the two treatises are closely connected at the level of content.

Alan, for example, repeats Rupert's argument about the way in which the Song of Songs refers to the Virgin Mary:

> Thus, although the song of love, that is, the wedding hymn of Solomon, rather specially and spiritually refers to the Church, nevertheless, it relates most specially and spiritually to the Virgin, as we will explain (insofar as we can) by divine command. Therefore, the glorious Virgin, hoping for the presence of the spouse, desiring the glorious conception announced by the angel, striving for the divine Incarnation, says: "Let him kiss me with the kiss of his mouth."[58]

In his interpretation of 1:14, "behold you are fair/your eyes of doves," Alan is yet more explicit about the way the Virgin functions in the multiple levels of meaning of the Song of Songs, "as the divine Scriptures should be understood not according to the letter, but according to the spirit, and spiritual mystery should be seen in them."[59] In one sense, the Virgin's part in the narrative of the Song of Songs is on the allegorical level, it has to do with this world, with the incarnation of Christ on earth. Yet, the anagogical sense is also evoked with the phrase "behold you are fair," understood as "having to do with the age to come" (*ad futurum saeculum pertinet*), since the Virgin represents human perfection.

Alan sets his interpretation within both the accepted commentary tradition and the developing framework of marian devotion. For instance, Song of Songs 1:16, "the beams of our house are of cedar," is understood as both the body of Christ (which is the Church), and the body of Mary. With an open quotation from the Pseudo-Augustinian sermons, Alan makes an explicit connection to the Assumption:

> For just as we believe that the body of Christ was not dissipated by decay, as it is written "You will not give your Holy one to see corruption," (Psalm 15:10, Vulgate), thus it is probable that the body of Mary is alien to the corruption of decay: Thus Augustine says in the sermon *De Assumptione Virginis*: "We believe not only the flesh which Christ assumed, but even the flesh from which he assumed flesh, to have been assumed into heaven."[60]

In the exposition of Song of Songs 4:8, "come from Lebanon / come, you will be crowned," Alan combines the traditional place-name allegories with yet another manifestation of late twelfth-century marian devotion, the celebration of the Coronation of the Virgin:

> From these mountains, then, the glorious Virgin is crowned: when the princes of this world are converted to the faith, and received into eternal beatitude, and they withdraw into the company and the praise of the Virgin. From the peaks of these mountains she is crowned, when by the princes subject to the catholic faith she is praised and glorified in Christ.[61]

This passage indicates that the concept of the Coronation of the Virgin, a devotion which grew rapidly in the late twelfth century, is closely linked to the eschatological expectation of the glorified Church, "when the princes of this world are converted to the faith, and received into eternal beatitude." This association is made explicit by a number of manuscript illuminations in which the crowned Church (see Plates 4, 7) and the crowned Virgin are distinguishable only through accompanying motifs.[62] Alan's imagery is extremely flexible; at some points, the Virgin and the Church seem to have become symbolically merged:

> For the Virgin Mary is similar to the Church of God in many ways. Just as the Church of God is the mother of Christ in its members through grace; thus the Virgin is the mother of Christ, of its head through human nature. And just as the Church is without spot or wrinkle, even so is the glorious Virgin.[63]

As Riedlinger notes, this comes close to the doctrine of the Immaculate Conception of Mary, a concept which did not become dogma until the nineteenth century.[64]

The *Elucidatio* of Alan of Lille shows the full complexity of mariological Song of Songs commentary. The Mary of this treatise is rather like one of the allegorical personifications of Alan's *De planctu Naturae* and *Anticlaudianus*, far abstracted from any human woman. Alan even stresses Mary's elevation by portraying a very different biblical figure, Mary Magdalene, as acting out some narrative parallels between the Gospels and the Song of Songs. So it is *Mary Magdalene* who mourns, "widowed for her spiritual man, that is, Christ"; the *Magdalene*'s search for Christ at the tomb is recollected from the Song of Songs 3:1 "on my bed through the nights/I sought him whom my soul loves"; it is to the garden in which *this* Mary sought him that Christ descends in Song of Songs 6:1.[65] As for the Virgin Mary, her appearance in the Song of Songs has much the same function as Alan's *Natura*: to urge the human gaze upwards, "from history to the mystical sense." She is the model and the inspiration for the mystical life.[66]

Critical Reflections on the Development of Marian Exegesis

This discussion of medieval readings of the Song of Songs in relation to the Virgin Mary suggests that the tradition is not just "marian," relating to Mary, or even "mariological," having to do with doctrinal definitions regarding Mary, but also specifically linked to worship. The liturgical background of this mode of Song of Songs exegesis brings a level of specific devotional participation into the commentary tradition, participation in the growing cult of the Virgin. Marian commentary on the Song of Songs is a special case of the transformation of a primary genre into a secondary genre, of what Bakhtin has described as the ability of secondary genres to:

> absorb and digest various primary (simple) genres that have taken form in unmediated speech communication. These primary genres are altered and assume a special character when they enter into complex ones. They lose their immediate relation to actual reality and to the real utterances of others.[67]

Of course, liturgy is in itself a formalized type of speech genre. Though not so flexible as other forms of spoken discourse, it is nevertheless an oral, performative, form of communication and, hence, in spite of repeated medieval efforts at standardization, open to myriad adaptations. When a verse from the Song of Songs was sung as an antiphon for the Assumption of the Virgin, it was transformed from God's voice speaking to humans (the "direct communication" of biblical revelation) to human voices speaking to heaven (to the Virgin Mary and to God) in praise and petition. I have suggested in this chapter that the direct address of liturgical language greatly influenced the voice of early marian commentaries on the Song of Songs. Yet, as this conception of the Song of Songs was "digested" by the commentary tradition, the immediacy of liturgical communication was changed into a far more mediated literary form. The antiphons of the Virgin still rang in the ears of Rupert and Alan, but their sound was muted; they had become simply another source for mariological commentary.

The interpretations considered in this chapter, therefore, are the most striking example of Song of Songs commentary as a secondary or "complex" genre. Here, the image of the Virgin Mary has no one fixed form, but changes shape from liturgy to commentary, from verse to verse. Mary is seen as at once the Church and the soul, the Bride, mother, and child of God. She is seen in the historical, allegorical, tropological, and anagogical levels of understanding the Song of Songs. Ann Astell has described marian interpretation of the Song of Songs as "historicized allegory."[68] As I noted at the end of chapter five, there is no tradition of Song of Songs commentary specifically in the anagogical mode, but the Virgin Mary, as type of both the Church and the soul, incorporates this level of understanding rather explicitly. Mariological exegesis of the Song of Songs, in fact, incorporates the entire tradition of Song of Songs commentary throughout the Latin Middle Ages, absorbing every level of understanding which it had inherited. These works are not necessarily the most structurally or rhetorically complicated interpretations of the Song of Songs (Rupert and Alan, for example, do not come close to the elaborate structure of Honorius's second exposition), but they are conceptually and typologically more complex, resonating with a whole other world of Christian spirituality, devotion to the Virgin.

Perhaps mariological commentaries on the Song of Songs also signal the waning, even the exhaustion, of the commentary tradition, as they look out to concerns which go beyond the limits of a monastic literary genre. By the twelfth century, a complex allegorical understanding of the Song of Songs had spread into numerous traditions of popular devotion to the Virgin, traditions visible over subsequent centuries and even into our own. Devotion to the Virgin Mary is still an important, some would say a growing, aspect of western Christianity. The "Marian Year" proclaimed by Pope John Paul II from the Feast of the Assumption, 1987 to the same feast of 1988 reflects the enormous amount of belief in and veneration of the Virgin in twentieth-century Christianity, a religious phenomenon which is only beginning to be analyzed from the perspective of the history of Christianity.[69] The Song of Songs commentary genre came into confluence only briefly with this vibrant tradition of marian devotion. There are, actually, relatively few marian commentaries on the Song of Songs, mostly from one period—the twelfth century. These did not so much change the development of marian devotion as testify to one stage of it, one predominantly liturgical voice and its devotional and theological ramifications.

It should also be noted that even the earliest uses of verses from the Song of Songs in liturgies of the Virgin are evidence of a function of the Song of Songs throughout the Middle Ages on a different literary level from that of the commentary tradition, namely, as proof-texts or biblical tropes. This use was by no means totally divorced from the genre of Song of Songs commentary begun by Origen; in fact, it was often informed by the patterns and expectations which consistently structured the genre in time. But this use does indicate a different "horizon of expectations" against which the Song of Songs was also read, and which exerted greater influence on this form of commentary than on the traditional ecclesiological and tropological readings.[70] The difficult relationship between broad reference and commentary is a sign of the continual outward expansion of the genre. It is also the most striking characteristic of the topic of the next chapter, the influence of Song of Songs commentary on the vernacular literature of the later Middle Ages, both devotional and secular.

Notes

1. The best-known Latin text about the nativity of the Virgin Mary is the so-called *Pseudo-Matthew*, dating no later than the early eighth century, see the codicological study of Jan Gijsel, *Die unmittelbare Textüberlieferung des sogenanntes Pseudo-Matthäus*, Verhandelingen v.d. Koninklijke Academie voor Wetenschappen, Letteren en Schone Kunsten von België, Klasse der Letteren vol. 96 (Brussel: Paleis der Academiën, 1981), and the review by Guy Philippart, "Le Pseudo-Matthieu au risque de la critique textuelle," *Scriptorium* 38 (1984) 121–131. Versions of the text also found in Constantinus Tischendorf, *Evangelia Apocrypha* (Leipzig: H. Mendelssohn, 1876) pp. 50–105, and M. R. James, *Latin Infancy Gospels* (Cambridge: At the Clarendon Press 1927). For the tradition of texts on the "dormitio" and "transitus" of the Virgin Mary, see M. Jugie, *La Mort et l'Assomption de la sainte Vierge* (Vatican City, 1944), and M. R. James, *Apocryphal New Testament* (Oxford: At the Clarendon Press 1924) pp. 211–213 for the death scene of the Virgin on her couch, surrounded by the disciples. The Purification is found in Luke 2:22–23. An extremely influential sermon for this event is *In Ypapanti sanctae Mariae* (*In Purification sanctae Mariae*) by the late eighth-century Italian author Ambrosius Autpertus, ed. Robert Weber, CCCM 27B (1979) pp. 983–1002.

2. For the liturgy, see Joannes Beumer, "Die marianische Deutung des Hohen Liedes in der Frühscholastik," *Zeitschrift für Katholische Theologie* 76 (1954) 411–439. The Carolingian development has been further studied by Leo Scheffczyk, *Das Mariengeheimnis in Frömmigkeit und Lehre der Karolingerzeit* (Leipzig: St. Benno-Verlag, 1959).

3. Jaroslav Pelikan, "The Odyssey of Dionysian Spirituality," introduction to *Pseudo-Dionysius: The Complete Works*, trans. Colm Luibheid (New York: Paulist Press, 1987) p. 11.

4. See the study of Giuseppe Quadrio, *Il Trattato "De Assumptione Beatae Mariae Virginis" dello Pseudo-Agostino e il suo influsso nella Teologia Assunzionistica Latina* (Rome; Apud Aedes Universitatis Greogrianal 1951), and A. M. la Bonnardière, "Le Cantique des Cantiques dans l'oeuvre de saint Augustin," *Revue des études augustiniennes* 1 (1955) 225–237.

5. As noted by Pelikan, p. 12. The text is edited by Albert Ripberger, *Paschasii Radberti Epistula Beati Hieronymi ad Paulam et Eustochium de Assumptione Sanctae Mariae Virginis* CCCM 55C (1985) pp. 97–162, reprinted from SpF 9 (1962). Other mariological treatises of Radbertus are *De partu Virginis*, ed. E. Ann Matter, CCCM 55C (1985) pp. 5–89; a series of sermons on the Assumption attributed to Ildefonsus of Toledo, PL 96:239–259, new edition by Robert Maloy forthcoming in CCCM; and *De nativitate sanctae Mariae*, PL 30:297–305.

6. According to the testimony of Engelmodus of Soissons, *Ad Radbertum abbatem*, MGH PLAC vol.2, 62–66. See also Radbertus's lives of Adalard and Wala, ed. G. H. Pertz, MGH *Scriptorum* vol.2, pp. 524–569.

7. For the Carolingian pseudepigraphical tradition, see Alcuin's poem 13, MGH PLAC vol.1, p. 237, and Radbertus's life of Wala, the *Epitaphium Arsenii*, an example of the continuation of this custom after the reign of Charlemagne. For Hincmar's dilemma about the *Cogitis me*, see C. Lambot, "L'Homélie du Pseudo-Jérôme sur l'assomption et l'évangile de la nativité de Marie d'après une lettre inédite d'Hincmar," RB 46 (1934) 265–282, and H. Barré, "Le Lettre du Pseudo-Jérôme sur l'assomption est-elle antérieure à Paschase Radbert?" RB 68 (1958) 203–224.

8. This manuscript, Paris, B. N. lat. 17436, is usually dated between 860 and 877, but may have been completed as late as 880 according to Bruno Stäblein, "Antiphonar," *Die Musik im Geschichte und Gegenwart* vol.1, pp. 545–549. The printed edition is by R. J. Hesbert, *Antiphonale Missarum Sextuplex* (Brussels: Vromant, 1935).

9. For Ambrose's relation of the Song of Songs to the Virgin Mary, and thus to all consecrated virgins, see the discussion of Ohly, pp. 32–41.

10. *Corpus Antiphonalium Officii* vol. III, *Invitatoria et Antiphonae*, ed. R. J. Hesbert, *Rerum Ecclesiasticarum Documenta*, Series Maior, Fontes IX (Rome: Herder, 1967) #4425.

11. Neither Vaccari, p. 28 nor Sabatier, p. 385, lists this reading.

12. This version of the verse is quoted in *Cogitis me*, ed. Ripberger, p. 129, and in the Pseudo-Ildefonsine sermo 1, PL 96:241D. For the Pseudo-Ildefonsine sermon cycle, see Robert Maloy, "The Sermonary of St Ildephonsus of Toledo: A Study of the Scholarship and Manuscripts. I. The Problem and the Scholarship in the Printed-Book Period. II. The Manuscript Period," *Classical Folia* 25 (1971) 137–199, 243–301.

13. For example, the composite of parts of Song of Songs 1:14, 2:1, 2:13, 3:6, 5:12, 6:12, and 8:5 which appears as a *Responsorium* for the feasts of the Assumption, the Nativity of the Virgin, and the Common of Virgins, *Corpus Antiphonalium Officii* vol. IV, *Responsoria, Versus, Hymni et Varia*, ed. R. J. Hesbert, *Rerum Ecclesiasticarum Documenta*, Series Maior, Fontes X (Rome: Herder, 1970) 7878; and in *Cogitis me*, ed. Ripberger, p. 149.

14.

Vnde canitur in eisdem Canticis de ea: "Hortus conclusus, fons signatus, emissiones tuae paradisus." Vere hortus deliciarum, in quo consita sunt uni-

> versa florum genera, et odoramenta virtutum, sicque conclusus, ut nesciat uiolari neque corrumpi ullis insidiarum fraudibus. Fons itaque signatus sigillo totius trinitatis, ex quo fons uitae manat, "in cuius lumine omnes uidemus lumen," (Psalm 35:10, Vulgate) quia iuxta Iohannem, "ipse est qui illuminat omnem hominem uenientem in hunc mundum." Cuius profecto emissio uteri, supernorum ciuium est paradisus.

Cogitis me, ed. Ripberger, pp. 135–136.

15. Jerome, Epistle 22, ed. I. Hilberg, CSEL 54, 1 (1912) pp. 143–211. See also chapter two, note 56 above.

16. Radbertus, *De partu Virginis*, 1, 320, ed. Matter, p. 57; *Expositio in Psalmum XLIV*, PL 120:1006D. Both of these treatises were also dedicated to Irma and Theodrada of Soissons.

17. "Rogamus igitur te omnes uno ore iterum novum laborem subire, et nobis causa charitatis aperire cur Evangelium: 'Intravit Jesus in quoddam castellum' (Luke 10:38), et Cantica Canticorum de sancta Maria legantur, cum nihil penitus ad eam pertinere videantur." PL 172: 495D. The text continues to 518D.

18. Valerie Flint, "The Chronology of the Works of Honorius Augustodunensis," RB 82 (1972) 220–221; "The Commentaries of Honorius Augustodunensis on the Song of Songs," RB 84 (1974) 197–200.

19. Flint, "The Chronology," p. 220 note 4, citing the study of André Wilmart, "Les Homélies attribuées à S. Anselme," AHDLMA 2 (1972) 16–27. The sermon is printed in Migne as Anselm's sermon 9, PL 158:644–649. This Ralph went to England for political reasons having to do with the Investiture Controversy; he became Bishop of Rochester in 1108, and Archbishop of Canterbury in 1114.

20. Sermon 1 in the collection, PL 158:585; Wilmart, "Les Homélies," pp. 6–7; Flint, "The Commentaries," pp. 200–201.

21

> Gloriosa virgo Maria typum Ecclesiae gerit, quae virgo et mater exstitit, etiam mater praedicatur, quia Spiritu sancto fecundata, per eam quotidie filii Deo in baptismate generantur. Virgo autem dicitur, quia integritatem fidei servans inviolabiliter, ab haeretica pravitate non corrumpitur. Ita Maria mater fuit Christum gignendo, virgo post partum clausa permanendo. Ideo cuncta quae de Ecclesia scribuntur, de ipsa etiam satis congrue leguntur. Dictitur ergo: "Osculetur me de osculo oris sui." Quem reges et prophetae non meruerunt videre vel audire, hunc Virgo non solum meruit in utero portare, sed etiam nato crebra oscula dare; plurima a sancto ejus ore percipere.
>
> "Quia meliora sunt ubera tua vino." Qui pascit angelos in sinu Patris, hic suxit ubera Virginis matris.

PL 172:499D–500A.

22. PL 172:512A–B.

23. "Oratio Virginis pro conversis," PL 172:503D; "Laus Filii de Matre," PL 172:505 D; "Laus Patris de Virgine," PL 172:507C; "Sequuntur verba

Virginis, Christum in se venire optantis," PL 172:508B; "Sequitur sollicitudo Virginis pro Ecclesia de Judaeis," PL 172:516A. See John C. Gorman, *William of Newburgh's Explanatio Sacri Epithalamii in Martrem Sponsi*, SpF 6 (1960) pp. 39–40 for a discussion of these homiletical rubrics. It would be interesting to know their connection to the tradition of textual rubrications studied by de Bruyne, see chapter three, note 34.

24. See also PL 172:512C, and 515C. For miracles of the Virgin Mary, see Benedicta Ward, *Miracles and the Medieval Mind: Theory, Record and Event, 100–1215* (Philadelphia: University of Pennsylvania Press, 1982) especially pp. 132–165.

25. PL 172–500A–C; PL 172:517C. See also Flint, "The Commentaries," p. 201.

26. Compare *Sigillum*, PL 172:517D to *Cogitis me*, 89, ed. Ripberger, pp. 149–150. Both the Feast of the Assumption and the Feast of the Nativity of the Virgin are explicitly mentioned in this section. Flint cites an even closer borrowing (at 501D) from an anonymous sermon on the Purification of the Virgin found in the Worcester Passionale, "The Commentaries," p. 202 note 5.

27. "quae erat in partu conclusus scilicet signaculo sancti Spiritus. 'Hortus conclusus' iterum, quia post portum [partum?] non est reclusum virginitatis signaculum." PL 172:507D. This is reminiscent of the argument of Radbertus's treatise *De partu Virginis*.

28.

> Quatuor modis facit Deus homines, de terra ut Adam; de solo viro ut Evam; de viro et femina ut nos, de sola femina Christum, quod sibi reservavit privilegium.

Pl 172:17B.

29. Beumer, pp. 414–415.

30. PL 177:1209–1222. See Riedlinger, p. 214, note 1.

31. John Van Engen, *Rupert of Deutz* (Berkeley: University of California Press, 1983) 3. See especially "Black Monks and the Study of Theology," pp. 96–105.

32. The text is edited by Hrabanus Haacke, CCCM 26 (1974). The title "de incarnatione Domini" is found in the oldest manuscript: Brussels, Bibliothèque Royale cod. 10608 (c. 13) and several fourteenth- and fifteenth-century manuscripts, cf. Haacke, pp. xv–xxi. Besides the Apocalypse and the Song of Songs, Rupert also wrote on the Gospels of John and Matthew, the twelve Minor Prophets, the Pentateuch, the Former Prophets. The list is in chronological order, see Van Engen, pp. xvii–xix.

33. That Rupert follows the commentary of Angelomus rather closely is evident from the *Index Scriptorum* of Haacke's edition, p. 187 (189–90 for the influence of Gregory and Jerome). For Angelomus on the Song of Songs, PL 115:551–628, see above, chapter four, note 68.

34. Van Engen, p. 293.

35. Because of the way in which it has been preserved, the recipient of this letter remains unidentified. See L. Csoka, "Ein unbekannter Brief des Abtes Rupert von Deutz," *Studien und Mitteilungen zur Geschichte des Benediktiner-Ordens* 84 (1973) 383–393, and Van Engen, pp. 341–342.

36. "Accipe, pater mi, tintinabulum hoc et, si bene resonat, admitte tibi et affige tunicae pontificali, memor parui amici tui, quotiens cum sacro tinnitu sanctae praedicationis ingrederis et egrederis sanctuarium in conspectu Domini, non moriturus sed uicturus, cum 'enarraueris opera Domini'. (Ecclesiastes 17:8)" *Epistula ad Thietmarum*, ed. Haacke, p. 4. Van Engen suggests that this refers to an image of the virgin on which Rupert meditated "in contemplatione faciei," p. 293, note 108.

37.

> Igitur, o domina Dei genitrix, uera et incorrupta mater Verbi aeterni Dei et hominis Iesu Christi, non meis, sed tuis armatus meritis cum isto uiro, scilicet cum Verbo Dei, cupio luctari, ut de Canticis canticorum opus extorqueam, quod non dedeceat uocari de Incarnatione Domini, ad laudem et gloriam eiusdem Domini, ad laudem et honorem tuae beatitudinis.

Ed. Haacke, pp. 5–6.

38. Peter Heliae, *Canticum metrice*, Stegmüller 6615. Rupert's desire to write such a poem is mentioned in his prologue, ed Haacke, pp. 6–7.

39. Ed. Haacke, pp. 7–8, compare to Origen, ed. Baehrens, GCS 23 (1925) pp. 81–83, and Angelomus, PL 115:557.

40.

> Tunc enim expositio mystica firmius stat, neque fluitare permittitur, si super historiam certi temporis uel rei demonstrabilis rationabiliter superaedificata continetur.

Ed. Haacke, p. 8.

41. Book VII, ed. Haacke p. 160. The treatise is divided as follows: Book I = Song of Songs 1:1–2:6; Book II = 2:7–3:4; Book III = 3:5–4:11; Book IV = 4:12–5:1; Book V = 5:2–6:1; Book VI = 6:2–7:10; Book VII = 7:11–8:14.

42. Book I, 1–9, ed. Haacke, p. 10.

43. Book II, 349, ed. Haacke, p. 52.

44. "Olim in Eua malo superbiae fetore offensus et ob hoc ab humano genere auersus fuerat, nunc autem delectatus bono odore, nardo humilitatis meae, sic ad genus humanum conuersus est." Book I, ed. Haacke, p. 30.

45.

> Ille est paradisus antiquus, paradisus terrenus; iste est paradisus nouus, paradisus caelestis. Vtriusque plantator est unus idemque Dominus Deus. In illo "posuit hominem quem formauerat" (cf. Genesis 2:15); in isto formauit hominem, qui "apud ipsum in principio Deus erat." (cf. John 1:1) De ista humo produxit "omne lignum pulchrum uisu, et ad uescendum suaue. Lignum etiam

uitae in medio paradisi." (Genesis 2:9) Istam humum, istam terram suam benedixit, et ex ea cunctarum germina gratiarum et cunctarum exemplaria uirtutum produxit. Ipsum quoque lignum uitae Christum, Deum et hominem, dominum paradisi caelestis.

Book IV, ed. Haacke, p. 86.

46. Book IV, 88–93, ed. Haacke, p. 87. Rupert shows here that he is aware of liturgical and homiletical traditions about the virginity of the Virgin *in partu*.

47. Book IV, 227,ed. Haacke, pp. 91–92.

48. M. Peinador, "Maria y la iglesia en la historia de la salvación según Ruperto de Deutz," *Ephemerides Mariologicae* 18 (1968) 337–381; Van Engen, pp. 295–297. This interweaving of the allegorical and the tropological is especially clear in Book VII, where a "historical" sense of Mary is tied to the text only at the beginning and the end.

49. Van Engen notes the parallel between Rupert's portrait of Mary and the apse mosaic of Santa Maria in Trastevere, Rome, p. 295, but this mosaic has also been related to the illustrations of Honorius's long commentary, see above, chapter 3, note 68. Gorman describes Rupert's position on what came to be the great mariological dogmatic statements of the nineteenth and twentieth centuries (the Immaculate Conception and the Assumption), pp. 31, 45.

50. For Alan's life, see Marie-Thérèse d'Alverny, *Alain de Lille, Textes inédits* (Paris: J. Vrin, 1965) pp. 11–29, and G. R. Evans, *Alan of Lille: The Frontiers of Theology in the Later Twelfth Century* (Cambridge: Cambridge University Press, 1983) pp. 1–19.

51. *De planctu Naturae*, ed. N. M. Häring, *Studi Medievali* 19 (1978) 797–879, *Anticlaudianus*, ed. R. Bossaut (Paris: J. Vrin, 1955). On the allegory of these works, see Christel Meier, "Zwei Modelle von Allegorie im 12. Jahrhundert: Das allegorische Verfahren Hildegards von Bingen und Alans von Lille," in *Formen und Funktionen des Allegorie*, ed. Walter Haug (Stuttgart: Metzler, 1979) pp. 70–89. See also d'Alverny, pp. 32–37, for these texts and for Alan's school texts from his years in Paris and Chartres. I would like to thank Jeanne E. Krochalis for her thoughtful suggestions about the interpretation of Alan.

52. See Evans, pp. 17–18; N. M. Häring, "A Commentary on the Our Father by Alan of Lille," AC 31 (1975) 149–177; "A Commentary on the Apostle's Creed by Alan of Lille," AC 30 (1974) 1–46; "A Commentary on the Creed of the Mass by Alan of Lille," AC 30 (1974) 281–303; "A Poem by Alan of Lille on the Pseudo-Athanasian Creed," *Revue d'histoire des textes* 4 (1974) 226–238 Alan's *In Cantica Canticorum ad laudem Deiparae Virginis Mariae elucidatio* is printed in PL 210:51–110, see also d'Alverny, pp. 75–79.

53. Evans, pp. 11–12.

54. d'Alverny, p. 76 assigns this gloss to Alan of Lille, although it is listed as a work of "Alanus Magister" by Stegmüller, vol. 2 (1950), #946. See above, chapter three, notes 49 and 50, for the *accessus ad auctores* in Honorius.

55. d'Alverny, p. 73 for a discussion of the phrase "ad preces prioris Cluniacensis edita." The text is printed in PL 210:51–110 from the 1654 Antwerp

edition of C. de Visch. For manuscripts, including Klosterneuburg 18, Orléans 53 (Fleury), and Trier, Stätsbibliothek 182 (St. Marien), see Stegmüller vol. 2 1950) #948.

56. See PL 210:69B for the discussion of the difference between the "manifesta doctrina" of the windows and the "obscurior doctrina" of the lattices in Song of Songs 2:9, and PL 210:77C for a discussion of contemplation and mystical union.

57.

> "Capite nobis vulpes parvulas, quae demoliuntur vineas." Per vulpes quae sunt fraudulenta animalia et in speluncis terrae habitantia, intelliguntur haeretici; per vineas, Ecclesiae intelliguntur. Has itaque vineas haeretici quantumcunque possunt demoliuntur. In hoc enim quod Christo et ejus matri derogant, fidem Ecclesiae demoliri [var. infirmare] laborant. Possunt ergo esse verba fidelium ad Christum et ad Virginem: "capite nobis," id est destruite ad nostram utilitatem, "vulpes," id est haereticos, "parvulas," propter imbecillitatem; quia, licet contra Ecclesiam nitantur, tamen infirmantur. "Quae demoliuntur vineas," id est fidei ecclesiasticae detrahunt.

PL 210:71B.

58.

> Unde cum canticum amoris, scilicet epithalamium Salomonis, specialiter et spiritualiter ad Ecclesiam referatur, tamen specialissime et spiritualissime ad gloriosam Virginem reducitur quod divino nutu (prout poterimus) explicabimus. Gloriose igitur Virgo sponsi optans praesentiam, desiderans gloriosam conceptionem ab angelo nuntiatam, affectans divinam Incarnationem, ait sic: "Osculetur me osculo oris sui."

PL 210:53B. See also Honorius's *Sigillum*, note 23 above.

59. "quia Scripturas divinas non jam secundum litteram, sed secundum spiritum intelligat, et aspiciat in eis spiritualia mysteria." PL 210:63B.

60.

> Sicut enim credimus corpus Christi putredine non esse resolutum; unde legitur: "Non dabis Sanctum tuum videre corruptionem" (Psalm 15:10, Vulgate) ita probabile est a corruptione putredinis esse alienum corpus Mariae: Unde Aug. in sermone *De Assumptione Virginis*: Non solum carnem quam Christus assumpsit, sed etiam carnem de qua assumpsit credimus esse assumptam in coelum.

PL 210:64A. See Quadrio, pp. 243–245 for a discussion of this quotation and its role in the developing doctrine of Mary's assumption into heaven.

61.

> De his ergo montibus coronatur Virgo gloriosa: quando principes saeculi convertuntur ad fidem, et recipiuntur in aeternam beatitudinem, et cedunt in Virginis societatem et laudem. De vertice horum montium coronatur, quando

> principibus subjectis catholicae fidei, illa ab his honoratur et glorificatur in Christo.

PL 210:80D–81A. For the development of the theme of Mary's royal status in the Latin middles ages, see Scheffczyk, pp. 477–496.

62. Compare, for example, two initial miniatures from the thirteenth-century Parisian "Bari Atelier" reproduced by R. Branner, *Manuscript Painting in Paris* (Berkeley: University of California Press, 1977): the crowned Church, plate 293 (from Frankfurt, Museum für Kunstgewerbe, Linel L. M. 17, f.305), and the crowned Virgin with child, plate 385 (from le Mans, B. M. 262, volume II, f.239v). On the artistic and liturgical developments of the cult of the Coronation, see Philippe Verdier, *Le Couronnement de la Vierge* (Paris: J. Vrin, 1980).

63.

> Virgo enim Maria similis est Ecclesiae Dei in pluribus. Sicut enim Ecclesia Dei mater est Christi in membris per gratiam; sic Virgo mater est Christi, capitis per humanam naturam. Et sicut Ecclesia est sine macula et ruga, ita et Virgo gloriosa.

PL 210:60A, on Song of Songs 1:8.

64. Riedlinger, pp. 223–226.

65. PL 210:70A, 72B, 91B.

66. "ab historia ad mysticum sensum," PL 210:102C. Alan's comment on 2:5, "Support me with flowers/surround me with apples" (PL 210:66C–D) is especially eloquent on this point. The Virgin does, in fact, appear in *Anticlaudianus* IX.

67. M. M. Bakhtin, "The Problem of Speech Genres," trans. Vern W. McGee, in *Speech Genres and Other Late Essays*, ed. Caryl Emerson and Michael Holquist (Austin: University of Texas Press, 1986) p. 62: see discussion in chapter one, especially notes 11, 15.

68. Ann W. Astell, "The Exemplary Bride: *Ecclesia* and Mary," chapter 2 of *The Song of Songs in the Middle Ages* (Ithaca, N.Y.: Cornell University Press, forthcoming). Astell points out the emphasis in marian commentaries on a strong identification between the reader and the Bride.

69. For modern devotion to the Virgin Mary in a historical setting, see Rosemary Radford Ruether, *Mary—The Feminine Face of the Church* (Philadelphia: Westminister Press, 1977); E. Ann Matter, "The Virgin Mary: A Goddess?" in *The Book of the Goddess, Past and Present*, ed. Carl Olson (New York: Crossroads Publishing Company, 1985).pp. 80–96; and, from a different point of view, Victor and Edith Turner, *Image and Pilgrimage in Christian Culture: Anthropological Perspective* (New York: Columbia University Press, 1978) pp. 203–230.

70. The term of Hans Robert Jauss, "Genres and Medieval Literature," in *Toward an Aesthetic of Reception*, trans. Timothy Bahti (Minneapolis: University of Minnesota Press, 1982), see above, chapter one, note 22.

Chapter Seven

The Genre as Trope: The Song of Songs in Vernacular Literature

In showing how commentary on the Song of Songs developed as a medieval genre, this book has frequently looked backward, to historical precedent and literary tradition. This final chapter will instead suggest some ways in which the genre moved outward from its monastic setting to influence other, frequently secular, trends of European literature. This will involve a shift of focus away from Latin literature on overtly Christian subjects to vernacular literature which gradually served more secular purposes. As the genre underwent a series of "internal transformations," it gradually became something else, involving an eventual break from the "horizon of expectations" of the literary world which crafted the tradition of commentary on the Song of Songs.[1]

But the break is neither precipitous nor absolute. As the mariological tradition of interpretation has shown, the Song of Songs played a multifaceted role in medieval Christianity. In general, Latin monastic authors used the genre freely, dipping into it for images which served as tropes, poetic or rhetorical figures which carry meaning according to an established code. In this case, the code of the Song of Songs was so well established by the commentary tradition that the quotation of a single verse could be immediately understood to speak, for example, of the relationship between a bishop and his church, or a nun and her heavenly Bridegroom; or it could be used as a proof-text for the virginity of Mary, or of the sanctity of the monastic life.[2] All of these examples have a basis in the commentary genre, as well as the ability to move beyond their literary origins in actual rhetorical function.

At least three types of vernacular literature show close connections to Latin exegesis of the Song of Songs while making different kinds of breaks with the tradition. Interpretations based on the recognized ideas of the genre can be seen in: 1) vernacular commentaries on the Song of Songs, 2) vernacular devotional writings, and 3) a broad variety of poetry in vernacular languages. All three types have formal and spiritual links to the commentary tradition. In fact, it is only in some forms of medieval vernacular poetry that quotations from the Song of Songs lose a sense of divine revelation and modulate into an understanding of the text as a human love story. There is no strict chronological development in this modulation, even though vernacular commentaries used the Song of Songs a century earlier than did witty love poetry in the vernacular. All three forms of reference to the Song of Songs are found throughout the vernacular literary tradition.

Vernacular Commentaries on the Song of Songs

The Song of Songs genre first passed into vernacular languages in a very conservative form, the translation of an already existing commentary. The earliest vernacular version of the genre, Williram of Eberberg's double reworking of Haimo, comes from a monastic environment, and continues a mode of interpretation centering on Christ and the Church. This mid-eleventh-century treatise combines a transposition of Haimo in Latin Leonine hexameters with a prose paraphrase in early Middle High German. Most manuscripts are set up in three parallel columns, the Vulgate text in the middle, Latin poetry on the left, and German prose on the right.[3]

Williram clearly intended to use the Song of Songs in support of the Cluniac Reforms. In the preface, he sounds a note of concern for the purity of the Church, praising Lanfranc and calling for the repentance of the institution as a collection of Christian souls. In this, he is like other exegetes of his century (for example, Robert of Tombelaine and John of Mantua), eager to show the Song of Songs as a mystical love story, in which both soul and Church must overcome sin to be worthy of the heavenly Bridegroom.[4] Mostly, however, Williram's German commentary is similar to Haimo's Latin one, at least it continues the same interpretation. This vernacular version of Haimo was widely available to the late medieval and early modern German reading audience; the last known manuscript was written in 1523 and is almost contemporary with the first printed edition.[5] The extent to which Williram was integrated into the German literary tradition can be seen by the liberties taken with his complex text: in the first printing and in one twelfth-century manuscript, the German paraphrase is translated back into Latin, while a fifteenth-century copy is exclusively in German, but a German brought up to date by the scribe.[6] Williram's greatest literary achievement was to make the most popular text of the commentary genre easily available to readers outside the Latin monastic world.

A more original, although also profoundly traditional, vernacular commentary on the Song of Songs is the anonymous twelfth-century German work known as the *St. Trudperter Hohelied*.[7] This text addresses a community of religious women, using the Song of Songs to spur its readers ever higher in *minnichlichen gotes erkennusse*, "loving knowledge of God." The work is extremely intimate (both the prologue and the commentary begin with *Wir*, "We,") and seems as much aimed at an elite monastic audience as the great Cistercian commentaries on the Song of Songs.[8] It may be, like Epistle 22 of Jerome, and the *Cogitis me* of Paschasius Radbertus, written by a male spiritual counselor for cloistered women, although its immediate, inclusive tone raises the possibility that the author may have been a member of the community for which it was written. The *St. Trudperter Hohelied* makes ample use of Williram's earlier German version of Song of Songs exegesis, but, especially in the prologue, also shows the influence of Latin Song of Songs commentaries, including those of Bernard of Clairvaux and Honorius Augustodunensis.[9]

The interpretation of this commentary is essentially, but not simply, mariological. Like the mariological commentary considered in the last chapter, the *St. Trudperter Hohelied* gravitates thematically towards the tropological mode, using Mary as a model of the pious soul, her life a lesson in contemplative prayer. For example, the interpretation of Song of Songs 2:10 counsels the recipients to "stand up" from their "sweet sleep" of contemplative prayer to meet the Bridegroom.[10] The nuns are also urged to strive for Mary's peculiar multivocality: "when you have gained reconciliation through your beauty, then you shall be known as a daughter of God, and a mother of Christ, and a bride of the Holy Spirit."[11] Even the interpretation of Song of Songs 2:14, "a garden enclosed," after a brief discussion relating the text to the Virgin, continues with an elaborate description of the holy life of those in whom God, the heavenly gardener, dwells.[12] This work describes such a profound connection to God, and reaches such an emotional pitch, that it has been called the beginning of the tradition of German mysticism.[13] Surviving manuscripts of the *St. Trudperter Hohelied* suggest that it was read by a wide variety of both male and female monastics; one section of the commentary was even more widely diffused, being incorporated into various collections of German homilies from the fourteenth century.[14]

A vernacular tradition of spiritual instruction through commentaries on the Song of Songs was not limited to German-speaking lands, or to the Middle Ages. In fact, sixteenth-century Spain was an important Christian environment for these traditional teachings in new languages. Fray Luis de Leon, a descendent of converted Jews, was the author of *El Cantar de Cantares*; this work begins with a restructuring of the Song of Songs as a spiritual drama, and continues with a moral interpretation. It has been called a "philological Christian humanist interpretation," but possible connections to the Kabbalistic tradition have also been noticed.[15] A more famous contemporary, the Carmelite mystic Teresa of Avila, turned to the commentary genre in *Conceptos del Amor de Dios Sobre unas Palabras de los Cantares*, on the parts of the Song of Songs used in the Carmelite Office, which describes the kiss of God's mouth in terms as passionate as those of Bernard of Clairvaux, speaking of herself as a worm, unworthy of God's embrace, and afflicted by a particular difficulty she ascribes to her sex in understanding Scripture, particularly the Song of Songs.[16] These early-modern Spanish commentaries on the Song of Songs show that a rather traditional form of the genre still had power in the devotional world of Mendicant and Carmelite spirituality.

Vernacular commentaries on the Song of Songs certainly drew on the Latin commentary genre, using both explicit texts and, even more strikingly, the assumption of well-established modes of interpretation. The commentaries of Williram, Fray Luis, Teresa of Avila, and the *St. Trudperter Hohelied* take interpretative stances developed by the Latin exegetical tradition, moving in the allegorical, tropological, or mariological modes. Yet they are all written in a devotional mood which was one part, but not the whole, of the Latin Song of Songs commentary genre. Vernacular commentary is still an *inner* transformation of the genre, one that has a certain sympathetic vibration with the trend toward moral exegesis in Latin expositions. Even the most complex expressions of multivocality developed in Latin commentaries (the association of the Virgin Mary with the Song of Songs, for example) are found in vernacular texts. But, however traditional their roots, these vernacular commentaries, by virtue of their more accessible language, had a special power to influence the volatile world of medieval Christian lay piety.

The Song of Songs in Vernacular Devotional Literature

Although the influence of Latin commentaries on the Song of Songs is most evident in vernacular texts which continue the form of line-by-line exposition, the interpretative assumptions of the commentary genre, and the accompanying vision of reality, can also be seen in vernacular treatises which use selected verses from the Song of Songs to give counsel about the devotional life. There is enormous variety in medieval devotional treatises in the vernacular: variety of form, language, audience, and intention. Yet, as a few examples will show, such texts present an understanding of the Song of Songs filtered through the well-known genre of commentary, and assuming the traditional interpretations of the genre. Sometimes the Latin tradition is visible only through a double filter, as vernacular literature begins to exert its own influence and Latin exegesis, having left its mark, fades into a literary background. This "second generation" relationship to the Latin commentary genre describes the use of the Song of Songs in the visionary text of the thirteenth-century Beguine, Mechtilde of Magdeburg.

Either the *St. Trudperter Hohelied* or another early German Song of Songs commentary in the tropological mode may have been available to Mechtilde. Or, perhaps, aspects of the tradition were well known to her through vernacular preaching. In any case, although Mechtilde claimed she knew no Latin, verses from the Song of Songs used according to the traditional spiritual interpretations appear frequently in her devotional work *The Flowing Light of the Godhead*.[17] Here the love between God and the soul is expressed throughout in nuptual imagery, in many places with explicit reference to the Song of Songs. The general theme of *Minne*, love, is expressed early in the work, when the soul exclaims "For I am sick with love for him. "[18] The spiritual kiss of God is the climax of the spiritual union, when Mechtilde describes herself as so "thoroughly kissed" by the mouth of God that she is raised above all the choirs of angels.[19] The rapture of the soul is described with a quotation of Song of Songs 4:7, "You are all fair, my friend, and there is no spot in you."[20]

In contrast, a much closer relationship to the Latin commentary genre is shown by the anonymous French *roman, La Queste del Saint Graal*, a text with clear connections to the Cistercian literary world, which in some ways echoes Bernard of Clairvaux.[21] When quotations from the

Song of Songs appear in this text, they tend to be explicated with overt reference to the tradition of Latin exegesis. The best example is the telling of the dream of Sir Boors. After a banquet prepared for him in a tower by the mysterious "disinherited woman," Boors dreams of two birds; one, "white as a swan," demands that Boors serve him, to which the black bird responds "you must serve me tomorrow, and do not despise me that I am black. Know that my blackness is worth more than the whiteness of the other." Some days later, Boors tells his dream to a man "dressed in the robe of religion." This man explains to Boors that the white bird signifies a young woman who loves him, the black bird signifies his great sin in refusing her love. Still later, in an abbey where he had just received communion, Boors again tells his experiences and dreams "word for word" to a saintly abbot. The abbot gives quite another interpretation of the dream of the birds:

> The black bird which you saw should be understood as the Holy Church who says: "I am black but I am beautiful: know that my blackness is worth more than the whiteness of the other. For the white bird which resembled a swan you should understand the enemy, and I will tell you how. A swan is white on the outside and black inside. It is [a figure of] the hypocrite, who is yellow and pale and seems to one who sees the outside the servant of Jesus Christ, while inside it is so black and so horrible with filth and with sin that it badly fools the world. [Thus] the enemy appeared to you in the guise of a man of religion.[22]

The reference to the Song of Songs commentary genre (in this case, the allegorical mode of interpretation) in *La Queste del Saint Graal* is extremely conscious, so much so that the author includes a warning about erroneous, carnal interpretation.

An author who actually participated in the Latin commentary genre as well as in the tradition of vernacular devotional treatises is the fourteenth-century English hermit Richard Rolle. Rolle began his career in the world of clerical study at Oxford before retiring to a life of solitary contemplation. In his *Latin* commentary on the opening verses of the Song of Songs, he begins:

> With a soul sighing for the delights of eternal
> places, a clear voice intones in the terrestrial orb:
> "Let him kiss me with the kiss of his mouth!"
> A certain beloved asks a kiss from the lover.[23]

This theme is strongly expressed in Rolle's Middle English devotional writings, for example, in *Incendium Amoris*, which quotes Song of Songs 8:6, "love is strong as death, jealousy is as cruel as hell," to urge rejection of the world.[24] Rolle's epistle known as *Ego Dormio*, an impassioned meditation involving hymns and prayer addressed to a nun of Yedingham, uses the Song of Songs to portray the passion of Christ as the focus of the religious life.

The title of this epistle is taken from its *incipit*, a Latin quotation of Song of Songs 5:2 that is immediately translated into English:

> *Ego dormio et corm meum vigilat.* They that desire love, listen, and hear of love. In the song of life it is written: "I sleep, and my heart wakes."[25]

Rolle's description of the Song of Songs as "the song of life" sets a theme which is essential to his purpose in this treatise, the teaching of spiritual union with God. Rolle exhorts the nun of Yedingham: "For he will live with you, if you will love him: He asks you no more than your love."[26]

"Love" is not so easily understood, however. The text takes off from the quotation of Song of Songs 5:2 to develop an elaborate spiritual map of three grades of love, through which a human being may attain union with God. The discussion of each degree begins with a definition, develops as counsels, and ends with a hymn. The first degree of love is a holy life marked by keeping the ten commandments, keeping from the seven deadly sins, and doing nothing to arouse the wrath of God.[27] The second degree is to forsake all people and things of the world to follow Christ in poverty.[28] The third and final degree of love is a state one cannot achieve by human effort, for it must be given by the grace of God. In this third state of love, the soul is so lifted up to God that all earthly sorrows fade, all life turns to joy and all prayers to melody:

> Then is Jesus all your desire, all your delight, all your joy, all your solace, all your comfort; all I know is that your song should always be of him, your rest should always be in him. Then may you say:
>
> I sleep and my heart wakes
> Who shall tell my beloved
> I long continually for his love?[29]

The treatise ends with the third hymn, "Cantus amoris," a passionate love poem to Jesus. The incorporation of hymns and prayers emphasizes the grounding of this treatise in late medieval piety.

The Song of Songs makes only two obvious entrances in Rolle's *Ego*

Dormio, at the beginning and near the end; but the spiritual teachings of commentaries in the tropological mode are evident throughout. The words "I sleep, but my heart keeps watch," Song of Songs 5:2, as the beginning of the spiritual ascent of the soul to God, frame the explanation of the three levels of the spiritual search. As in Bernard of Clairvaux's *Sermo* 3, the final stage is mystical rapture, not expressed here through the kiss of Song of Songs 1:1, but by another verse, Song of Songs 2:5, "for I languish with love." The treatise thus depends on the "horizon of expectations" of Latin commentary on the Song of Songs without actually participating in the commentary genre.

Two texts which have an even more complicated relationship to Latin commentary on the Song of Songs again come from sixteenth-century Spain. The *Subida del Monte Carmelo* and *Noche Oscura* of the Carmelite colleague of Teresa of Avila, John of the Cross, are both guides to stages of spiritual awareness and contemplative union with God.[30] These treatises meld the three types of vernacular use of Song of Songs interpretation I suggested at the beginning of this chapter, for they give devotional teachings on a moral level, structured on a verse-by-verse explication of, not the Song of Songs itself, but a poem (somewhere between a hymn and a ballad) which John wrote on the vignette of the awakened lover beginning at Song of Songs 5:2. Both *Noche Oscura* and *Subida de Monte Carmelo* comment on the same poem; in the former text, the poem is titled "Songs of the Soul," in the latter, it follows this rubic:

> Songs. In which the soul sings the happy fortune (*la dichosa ventura*) it had passing through the dark night of the faith, in its nakedness and purgation, to the union with the beloved.[31]

The poem describes the *dichosa ventura* of escaping unseen into the dark in pursuit of the one for whom the speaker's heart is burning. It begins with a quiet solemnity, and builds up to a wave of sensual images from the Song of Songs:

> O night which guided,
> O night lovelier than the dawn;
> O night which joined
> Lover (*Amado*) with Beloved (*Amada*)
> *Amada* transformed into *Amado!*[32]

The last three verses evoke other passages of the Song of Songs, speaking of lovers sleeping on flowery breasts and feeding among the lilies, activities reserved for the highest level of closeness to, that is, union with, God.

These treatises on the spiritual life by John of the Cross take one step back from the commentary tradition, basing themselves on a poetic adaptation of several verses rather than directly on the text itself. But the use of the Song of Songs here is still based on the ancient traditions of commentary, out of which discrete verses were plucked to act as tropes. It is the code of Song of Songs tropological exegesis, in fact, that supplies the meaning for the verses on which the elaborations are based.

Spiritual use of the Song of Songs in vernacular piety, removed from the exegetical tradition yet clearly dependent on it, continues well into the modern period, becoming, unlikely as it may seem at first thought, a favorite basis for spiritual writing by New England Puritans.[33] Protestant devotion, in fact, often demonstrates a knowledge and acceptance of the genre, especially the context of liturgy. In hymns and other music intended for worship and personal piety, the horizon of expectations of the commentary genre can be traced into the eighteenth century. Famous examples of the power of these ideas are found in Johann Sebastian Bach's Cantata *Wachet auf, ruft uns die Stimme* (BWV 140).

The cantata as a whole is based on a chorale of Philipp Nicolai adapted from the parable of the wise and foolish virgins in Matthew 25. The Gospel text provides its own interpretation, that the parable speaks of the coming of the Kingdom of Heaven. Tempering this eschatological mood, however, is the long tradition of moral explication evident in the cantata's use of several verses from the Song of Songs. The first recitative (#2) puts together three images from the Song of Songs: "daughter of Sion" (3:1), "into your mother's house" (3:4), and a description of the Bridegroom as "a young stag, bounding over the hills" (2:8–9, 8:14). The second recitative (#5) paraphrases more fully: "I will engrave you upon my heart and on my arm just like a seal" (8:6), and "on my left hand thou shalt rest, my right hand shall embrace thee" (8:3). These references to the Song of Songs work together with the words of the Gospel as an invitation to the soul to awake and meet the heavenly Bridegroom in spiritual union, a familiar theme in Latin tropological commentaries. The second duet between Christ and the soul (#6) revolves around the repeated words "Mein Freund ist mein, und ich bin sein," almost a direct quotation of Song of Songs 2:16 and 6:2, verses in which the heavenly lover and the human beloved declare their mutual belonging.[34]

This cantata is by no means the only use of medieval imagery of the

Song of Songs in German Lutheran piety, but only an example to show the power of the inherited imagery. In such Protestant liturgical settings, even though the Song of Songs commentary genre has been totally absorbed by another literary and devotional form, echoes of the received interpretations of the Song of Songs are nevertheless hauntingly clear.

The Song of Songs as Trope: Latin and Vernacular Poetry

The third form of vernacular literature in which the influence of Latin commentary on the Song of Songs is evident is perhaps the most complicated, and will require a two-part discussion. Poetry in vernacular languages which either is based on the Song of Songs or uses verses with reference to traditional Christian interpretation draws not just on the genre of Latin commentary, but also on a literary world of Latin poetry which had independently established its own sophisticated uses of Song of Songs exegesis. My analysis will first take up poetic adaptations of the Song of Songs in Latin, then turn to the more diverse ways in which familiar themes from the genre are present in vernacular poetry.

The Song of Songs in Latin Poetry

Latin poetry based on images of the Song of Songs began to develop in tandem with the genre of commentary as early as the ninth century, showing dependence on the allegorical and tropological modes of exegesis. The powerful bishop Hincmar of Reims began a shift from commentary to poetic reflection in a strange work, the *In ferculum Salomonis*. This is a *carmina figurata*, meant to take the shape of Solomon's litter (Song of Songs 3:9–10) while commenting on the text of these verses as a description of the splendor of the Church. The form of the poem was only recently understood by modern scholars, while a better-known prose version (or rather, *Explanatio* of the poem), dedicated to Charles the Bald, is printed in the *Patrologia Latina*. Hincmar's explication is deeply traditional and characteristically Carolingian, basically a paraphrase of the Venerable Bede.[35]

Tropological interpretation of the recurring motif of seeking the beloved, a theme found in Song of Songs 3:1 and 5:2 which we have already noted in vernacular devotional treatises, is the inspirational text for a number of Latin devotional poems which describe the travails of the soul's search for union with Christ. Perhaps the earliest is the lovely eleventh-century Latin poem ascribed to Peter Damian:

> Who is this who knocks at the door,
> breaking the sleep of night?
> He calls me: "O fairest of virgins,
> sister, spouse, most splendid jewel!
> rise quickly to open, sweetest one.
>
> I am the son of the highest king,
> the first and the most new,
> I came here from heaven into this darkness
> to set free the souls of captives,
> suffering death, and many injuries."
>
> Presently I left my bed,
> I hurried to the bolt
> that the whole house might lie open to my love,
> and my mind might most fully see
> whom it longs greatly to see.
>
> But he had already gone away,
> he had left the door.
> What could I, wretched one (*miserrima*), do?
> Weeping, I followed that youth,
> whose hands molded men.
>
> The watchmen of the City found me,
> they plundered me,
> they took and gave away my cloak,
> they sang to me a new song
> with which I will be led into the palace of the King.[36]

Raby comments laconically on this text: "The theme seems to be the visit of Jesus to the devout soul"; to one familiar with the tradition of Song of Songs interpretation, it stands out as a striking example of the turn to spiritualizing exegesis by the eleventh-century monastic reformers, rendered in poetic form. In fact, Peter Damian elsewhere shows his extreme familiarity with the Song of Songs commentary genre: in a sermon for the feastday (the heavenly birthday) of virgin saints (*In natali virginum*), a section on the Song of Songs of his *Collectanea in Vetus Testamentum*, where the tropological explication of Song of Songs 5:2 is given; and in a letter to Empress Agnes, which uses the lines of Song of Songs 6:2, "return, return, Sulamite," as a refrain.[37]

A Latin poem which moves farther from the tradition through a blurring of the categories of sacred and profane literature is the well-known *Iam dulcis amica venito*, in theme and imagery full of the Song of Songs. Peter Dronke has described the manuscript variants which transformed the poem from a court entertainment to a devotional *conductus* for liturgical or para-liturgical (that is, devotional outside of established ritual) use. Dronke has suggested that the secular purpose may have even predated the sacred form of this "remarkable fusion of classical and Solomonic language."[38]

Latin liturgical sources often seem to have set the expectations for poetic use of the Song of Songs; as chapter six has shown, the Song of Songs is especially visible in feasts of the Virgin Mary. A twelfth-century sequence for feasts of the Virgin praises Mary by evoking a marian reading of spiritual union implicit in selected fragments of the Song of Songs: "a cluster of cypress, a bundle of myrrh," "at noontime, the bridegroom calls you," "Arise, arise, my neighbor, / The winter flees, and the vineyard flowers."[39] Another Latin poem, which Raby calls "A Mystic Pastourelle," also emphasizes a mariological interpretation, taking the form of a dramatic exchange between Christ and Mary; here, all of the dialogue is either based on or taken whole cloth from the Song of Songs.[40]

These examples from Latin poetry suggest that the commentary genre directly inspired and informed poetic uses of the Song of Songs that follow the tropological interpretation of the love between God and the soul. Latin poetry that assumes a marian reading of the Song of Songs, on the other hand, seems to be, like the marian tradition of commentary, directly linked to liturgies of the Virgin.

The Song of Songs in Vernacular Poetry

A connection between a marian understanding of the Song of Songs and marian liturgies is also evident in one of the earliest vernacular poems to draw on the commentary tradition, the anonymous eleventh-century para-liturgical French lyric *Quant li solleiz converset en leon*. This poem speaks of the sun entering the astrological sign of Leo as the mark of the approaching Feast of the Assumption, celebrated on August 15. It joins the courtly (almost formulaic) scene of a young woman weeping for reunion with her lover to the longing of the Virgin Mary to join her heavenly Bridegroom. Song of Songs 5:8, "daughters of Jerusalem, announce to my beloved that I languish with love," is used in this poem to emphasize the Virgin's desire to be with God.[41]

The other modes of biblical interpretation developed by the commentary genre are also apparent in vernacular poetry from medieval France. A series of medieval French poetic adaptations of the Song of Songs participate in a high literary tradition and seem to hover between the poetry of the court and the cloister. Three French poetic versions of the Song of Songs are extant, part of a vigorous tradition of twelfth-century French verse renditions of the Bible. One is a set of short paraphases of several verses of the Song of Songs (5:10, 4:11, 5:7), in the voice of the Church. This work recalls and is obviously modeled on the commentaries in the allegorical mode discussed in chapter four.[42] The other two, which will be briefly examined here, are cast very much in the tradition of courtly literature.

An untitled twelfth-century version from the north of France, found in a manuscript of Le Mans, continuously explicates Song of Songs 1:1–5:14 in a poetic style used by courtly epic, octosyllabic rhymed couplets.[43] Marginal references to the Vulgate show that the poem was based on the Latin Bible. A prologue describes the Song of Songs as a poem of love between Christ and the Church or Christ and the soul; several verses show the influence of Origen, as for example the closing warning that it be kept from "the hand of a child."[44] For all that it follows traditional interpretations, the Le Mans poetic version gives an excellent example of the Song of Songs commentary genre transformed into a rather secular form and function. For example, it is dedicated to a lady, and presented as a *roman* in which the interlocutors address one another as "Damoiselle," "amie," and "Bels sire."[45]

The world of the court is also echoed in the third medieval French paraphrase of the Song of Songs, which dates from the thirteenth century. As it explicates the first three chapters of the Song of Songs, this poem makes an allusion to the *Roman de la Rose*, which it characterizes as "less honest" than its own discussion of love.[46]

A rather odd medieval vernacular adaptation of the Song of Songs in the form of courtly poetry is *Das Hohe Lied* of Brun of Schonebeck, an educated layman of Magdeburg. This is a long poem (12,719 verses long) written in the year 1276.[47] One section of Brun's work portrays Solomon as an epic hero in the high medieval style: like Brun, a member of the constabulary, and a wise, handsome, rich, and beloved King.[48]

Another passage gives a mariological interpretation, recently shown to derive from Honorius Augustoduniensis, which, like much mariological exegesis, is expanded to also relate the Bride to the soul.[49] *Das Hohe Lied* is a multifaceted and complicated work, with overtones of eschatology and many allusions to folk religion and popular devotion. It is an excellent example of both the broad range of influence of the commentary genre and the transformation of the tradition of Song of Songs interpretation into poetry addressing an essentially lay segment of medieval Christian society.

The poetry which I have discussed to this point can all be easily grounded, with respect to imagery and thematic development, in the genre of medieval Latin commentary on the Song of Songs. This observation does not require elaborate scrutiny, since the poems themselves give up many clues about the ultimate sources of the themes and images which they celebrate. It is, however, important to realize that these evocations of received understanding of the Song of Songs are not commentaries on the text. Instead, they mark the transformation of the genre into new genre, serving very different literary purposes. Dronke comes very near the core of this transformation when he describes a kind of "poetic liberation" in uses of the Song of Songs in medieval lyric:

> One kind of poetic liberation followed from the dream-logic that the Song of Songs bestowed; the other principle kind of poetic liberation, linked with this first, followed from the multivalence of the love-language itself, the imagery that hovers between sensuality and mysticism, or indeed bridges them.[50]

The medieval Latin genre of interpretation of the Song of Songs extended the inherent "dream-logic" of the poems into a complex realm of signification which functioned on many textual levels. As we have seen, the exegetical process of turning images into narrative was brought by monastic authors to focus on some major concerns of medieval Christianity: the purity of the church, the sanctity of the monastic life, the example of the Virgin Mary, the spiritual quest for union with God. By the time of the flowering of medieval vernacular literature, the poetic imagery of the Song of Songs could not be entirely separated from this complex web of signification.

But, in my estimation, the commentary genre expanded even more radically into medieval vernacular literature, influencing poetry which is not primarily (and sometimes not even marginally) oriented towards singing the love between Christ and the Church, Christ and the soul, or God and the Virgin Mary. A final legacy of the commentary genre is the rich complexity of meaning which could be evoked by even the simplest quotation of the Song of Songs.

For example, the proclamation "my beloved is mine and I am his" (Song of Songs 2:16, cf. 6:2) obviously evokes purely human passions, passions which announce themselves without guile in the famous minnesinger poem beginning "du bist mîn, ich bin dîn."[51] The Song of Songs can still be glimpsed in this poem, but the reference is evidently made here with a totally secular, even carnal, purpose in mind. Is this poem, then, just a song of human love, or does it too reveal a connection to the most sacred song sung by Solomon? Is it, perhaps, meant as a joke, a goliardic pun on centuries of spiritualized readings of the human love language of the Song of Songs? It seems to me that even this use of a verse from the Song of Songs, however remote from the spirit of medieval exegesis, can be said to function as a trope, a reference which still has the power to recall the genre with a subtle, perhaps even a subversive, allusion to the realm of spiritual love.

Such subtle use of medieval Latin literary conventions in overtly secular vernacular writings has been acknowledged and studied by several modern critics. Paul Zumthor, for one, has described the passage of ultimately biblically-based medieval tropes into the world of vernacular literature.[52] Concentrating particularly on literary codes, Giovanni Pozzi has shown many examples of verses from the Song of Songs among the stock literary phrases readily available, and often pulled out, to describe the beauty of the courtly lady in Provencal, French, and Italian poetry. While acknowledging their biblical origin, Pozzi describes the extreme conventionality of these secularized verses from the Song of Songs, which make up a significant part of his "dossier of the canon of beauty."[53]

Examples of the use of the Song of Songs as trope in medieval vernacular poetry could be multiplied, but a few examples will suffice to reinforce my point. The carnal and spiritual meanings of flowers in such poems as Guillaume de Machaut's *Blanche com lys, plus que rose vermeille* have their poetic origin in the Song of Songs and its tradition of interpretation.[54] Use of the genre as trope is found not just in love poetry, but also in political diatribes by secular poets which could be described as "hate poetry," such as the lamentable hunting metaphor by which the fifteenth-century German poet Han Folz uses the little foxes of Song of Songs 2:15 to open a one-sided polemical "dialogue" between the Church and the Synagogue.[55]

I will leave further elaboration and refinement of the transformations of the Latin Song of Songs commentary genre into tropes of vernacular literature to scholars who specialize in medieval vernacular languages. My purpose in venturing out of Latin monastic literature, the primary *locus* of the genre and the focus of this book, has been to show how vigorous, far-reaching, and multifaceted a literary influence was exerted by medieval Latin commentary on the Song of Songs. Although traditional readings developed by the commentary genre may be far from a modern understanding of the Song of Songs, the legacy of these readings in European literature can be traced far beyond the monastic world in which allegorical, tropological, and mariological readings of the text were formulated.

Notes

1. For the theory of "internal transformation" of a genre, see Maria Corti, *An Introduction to Literary Semiotics*, trans. Margherita Bogat and Allen Mandelbaum (Bloomington and London: Indiana University Press, 1978) pp. 124–131, and above, chapter one, note 12; chapter four, note 85. For the literary "horizon of expectations" of a genre, see Hans Robert Jauss, "Theory of Genres and Medieval Literature," in *Toward an Aesthetic of Reception*, trans. Timothy Bahti (Minneapolis: University of Minnesota Press, 1982) pp. 79, 88, see chapter one, note 22, chapter six, note 70.

2. See Rosemarie Herde for a discussion of these themes. I am grateful to Ulrike Wiethaus for the suggestion that this process went on in Latin literature as much as in vernacular languages.

3. *The "Expositio in Cantica Canticorum" of Williram Abbot of Ebersberg, 1048–1085*, ed. E. H. Bartelmez (Philadelphia: American Philosophical Society, 1967) p. xi and frontispiece. See also M. L. Dittrich, "Die literarische Form von Willirams Expositio in Cantica Canticorum," ZIDA 84 (1953) 180–197; Ohly, pp. 98–100; Riedlinger, pp. 97–100.

4. Bartlemez, p. 1; Riedlinger, p. 100. For Robert of Tombelaine and John of Mantua, see chapter four above.

5. Bamberg, Stätliche Bibliothek MS. A 73 (1523, by Fr. Ambrosius Brunner), Bartelmez, p. xv, figure 5, p. 571; *Willirami Abbatis in Cantica Salomonis Mystica Explanatio per Menradum Maltherum in luce restituta* (Hanover, 1528), Bartelmez, p. xi, n.4.

6. Wolfenbüttel, Herzog-August Bibliothek MS. Gud. Lat. 131 (c.12) has

the German rendered in Latin, Bartelmez Appendix I, pp. 547–552. The all-German copy is in Maihingen, Fürstlich Oettingen-Wallerstein'sche Fideikommissbibliothek, Bartelmez Appendix III, pp. 557–570.

7. The text is named for the monastery of Sankt-Trudpert near Freising, provenance of one fourteenth-century manuscript, Vienna Ö.N.B. 2719 (Theol. 593). Another copy is Klosterneuburg 767, cf. H. Maschek, "Eine unbeachtete Handscrift des sog. St. Trudperte Hohenliedes," ZfDA 75 (1938) 27–28. A new critical edition by Friedrich Ohly is soon to be published. I have used the edition of Hermann Menhardt, *Das St. Trudperter Hohe Lied, Kritische Ausgabe*, Rheinische Beiträge und Hülfsbücher zur germanischen Philologie und Volkskunde 21, 22 (Halle: Max Niemayer Verlag, 1934). See also the discussion of Riedlinger, pp. 226–233.

8. *Incipit* of prologue: "Wir wellen kösen uon deme oberösten liebe," ed. Menhardt, p. 123. *Incipit* of commentary: "Wir haben virnomin von deme heilige geiste," p. 128. In contrast, the Latin mid-twelfth-century commentary of Wolbero of St. Pantaleon, also addressed to nuns, begins: "Dilectissimis sororibus in Insula Rheni Deo et beatae Mariae militantibus, Wolbero peccator," PL 195:1005. The theme of *Minne* is sounded immediately in the *St. Trudperter Hohelied* by the repeated phrase "minne in!" in the prologue, p. 124; see also the reference to "minnichlichen gotes erkenneusse," section 145, p. 286.

9. F. Ohly, "Der Prolog des St. Trudperter Hohenliedes," ZfDA 84 (1953) 198–232. The discussion of the seven gifts of the Holy Spirit in relation to seven patriarchs, ed. Menhardt, p. 125, is reminiscent of the Second Prologue of the long commentary of Honorius Augustodunensis, PL 172:353D–358C, and chapter three above. See also Albert Lietzmann, "Zum St. Trudperter Hohenlied," *Beiträge zur Geschichte der deutschen Sprache und Literatur* 61 (1937) 378–401.

10. The interpretation of Song of Songs 2:10 at section 32, ed. Menhardt, p. 158, exhorts: "stânt ûf von deme sůzzen slâfe der contemplationis orationis lectionis. [î] le dîn unde chum vur dur [nutz] dîner[r] brůdere, daz ist diu heilige cristenheit die d[û] uirwesin solt," lines 13–17.

11. "dâ wurde dû gordenôt ein t[oh]ter gotis unde ein muter christes unde ein brûth des hailigen gaistes," section 52, lines 11–13, ed. Menhardt, p. 180.

12. "Dû bist ein besolzzener garte mîn suester. . . . Das chît uon unserre frowun. . . . Noch sint ouch garten, da wonet inne got. daz ist gaistlich leben unde ioch ieclich gaistlich menneskin," section 57, ed. Menhardt, pp. 185–186.

13. Riedlinger, pp. 226–227.

14. Besides the manuscripts from Sankt-Trudpert and Klosterneuberg (note 7 above) the text is found in copies from Stift Mattighofen in Upper Austria (Klagenfurt: Bischöfliche Bibliothek, XXX d 6) (c. 15), in a copy from the Franciscans of Munich (dated 1510), and in fragments preserved in Nürnberg and Munich, see Menhardt, pp. 1–42, 58–91. The excerpt known as the *Traktat vom Palmbaum* was adapted from several sections of the St. Trudperter Hohenlied (Menhardt's source *C, pp. 28–29, 117–119). It was transmitted as an inde-

pendent text, and also became part of the so-called "St. Georgener Predigers," Menhardt, pp. 43–58.

15. Fray Luis de Leon, *Cantar de Cantares*, ed. Jorge Guillen (Salamanca: Ediciones Sigueme, 1980). I wish to thank Israel Burshatin for bringing this text to my attention. The connection to Kabbalistic thought is suggested by Harold Bloom, in his introduction to *Modern Critical Interpretations: The Song of Songs* (New York: Chelsea House Publishers, 1988) pp. 3–4.

16. Edited by Silverio de Santa Teresa, *Obras de Sta. Teresa de Jesus*, vol. IV, *Biblioteca Mistica Carmelitana* 4 (Burgos: El Monte Carmelo, 1917) pp. 213–351. Teresa speaks of her difficulty in understanding Scripture, especially the Song of Songs, in the Prologue and the first chapter, pp. 213–221. See also Pope, pp. 186–188.

17. The original Low German text is lost, but a Middle High German version has been edited by Gall Morel, *Offenbarungen der Schwester Mechtild von Magdeburg oder Das fliessende Licht der Gottheit* (Regensburg, 1869/ Darmstadt: Wissenschaftliche Buchgesallschaft, 1963) I am indebted to the ongoing study of Mechtilde by Ulrike Wiethaus. For important bibliography, see Caroline Walker Bynum, *Jesus as Mother* (Berkeley: University of California Press, 1982), and Elizabeth Avilda Petroff, *Medieval Women's Visionary Literature* (New York and Oxford: Oxford University Press, 1986) pp. 207–221. Petroff reprints part of the translation of Lucy Menzies, *The Revelations of Mechtilde of Magdeburg, or The Flowing Light of the Godhead* (London: Longman's Green and Co., 1953).

18. 1,3: "Und das ich minnesiech nach ime bin," ed. Morel, p. 7.

19. 2,23: "Er durkússet si met sinem goetlichen munde," ed. Morel, p. 45; 3,1: "In dem Kusse wart si do ufgeruket in die hoehsti hoehi vber aller engel kore," p. 56.

20. 3,10: "du bist alles schoene, min fruendine und kein flekke ist an dir," ed. Morel, p. 81.

21. The text is edited by A. Pauphilet, *La Quest del Saint Graal* (Paris: H. Champion, 1923), second ed. 1984; its relation to Cistercian piety is described by E. Gilson, "La mystique de la grâce dans *La Queste del saint Graal*," *Romania* 51 (1925) 321–347, especially 325, 347.

22.

> Par le noir oisel qui vos vint veoir doit len entendre Sainte Eglyse, qui dist: "Je suis noire mes je suis bele: saichez que mielz valt ma nerté que autrui blancheur ne fet." Par le blanc oisel qui avoit semblance de cisne doit len entendre l'anemi, et si vos dirai comment. Li cisnes est blans par defors et noirs par dedenz, ce est li ypocrites, qui est jaunes et pales, et semble bien, a ce qui defors en apert, que ce soit des serjanz Jhesucrist; mes il est par dedenz si noirs et si horribles d'ordures et de pechiez qu'il engigne trop malement le monde. [. . . Quant li anemis t'aparut in semblance d'ome de religion.

Ed. Pauphilet, pp. 185–186; p. 171 for the dream of the birds, p. 179 for the false interpretation, and p. 286, note 185. See also p. 15, lines 21–24 for an interesting use of Song of Songs 3:6; p. 263, lines 17–18 for the allegory of liles and roses, Song of Songs 2:1.

23. "Suspirantis anime deleciis eternorum, vox in orbem terrarum clare intonat: 'Osculetur me osculo oris sui!' Dilecta utique a dilecto petit osculum." O. Madon, "Le Commentaire de Richard Rolle sur le Cantique des Cantiques," *Mélanges de science réligieuse* 7 (1950) 313, text 311–325.

24. Richard Rolle, *Incendium amoris*, ed. Hope Emily Allen (New York: The Modern Language Association of America, 1927), especially chapter 10.

25. "*Ego dormio et cor meum vigilat*. Þai þat lyste lufe, herken, and here of luf. In þe sang of lyf it is written: 'I slepe, and my hert wakes.' quoted from *English Writings of Richard Rolle*, ed. Hope Emily Allen (Oxford: At the Clarendon Press, 1931) pp. 61–72; quotation p. 61. In this translation and those of notes 26 and 29 I am grateful for the advice of Richard Dury.

26. "For he will with þe dwell, if þou will lufe him: he askes þe na more bot þi lufe." *Ego Dormio*, p. 61.

27. *Ego Dormio*, pp. 63–64, beginning: "Þe fyrst degre of lufe es, when a man haldes þe ten commandementes, and kepes hym from þe seven dedely synnes, and es stabyl in þe trowth of hali kyrke; and when a man wil nought for any erthly thing wreth God, bot trewly standes in his servyce, and lastes þarin til his lyves ende," and ending with the first hymn, which begins: "Alle perisches and passes þat we with eghe see."

28. "Þe toþer degre of lufe, þat es, to forsake al þe worlde, þi fader and þe moder, and al þe kyn, and folow Criste in poverte," p. 64. The second stage continues until p. 69, ending with "Meditacio de passione Christi."

29. "Þan es Jesu al þi desyre, al þi delyte, al þi joy, al þi solace, al þi comforth; al I wate þat on hym ever be þi sang, in hym all þi rest. Þen may þow say:

> I slepe and my hert wakes.
> Wha sall tyll my lemman say
> For hys lufe me langes ay? "

Ego Dormio, pp. 69–70, "Cantus Amoris," pp. 70–72.

30. Both are edited by Silverio de Santa Teresa in *Obras de san Juan de la Cruz*, vol. 2, Biblioteca Mistica Carmelitana 11 (Burgos: El Monte Carmelo, 1929). Hereafter, "the Carmelite edition."

31.

> Canciones. En que canta el alma la dichosa ventura que tuvo en pasar por la oscura noche de la fé, en desnudez y purgacion suya a la union del Amado.

Carmelite edition, p. 4.
In the *Argumento*, Juan de la Cruz says:

> Toda la doctrina que entiendo tratar en esta *Subida del Monte Carmelo*, está incluída en las siguientes canciones, y en ellas se contiene el modo de subir hasta la cumbre del monte, que es el alto estado de la perfección que aquí llamamos unión del alma con Dios."

Carmelite edition, p. 3.
See also *Noche Oscura*, pp. 362–363.

32. Verse five:

¡Oh noche que guiaste,
Oh noche amable más que el alborada;
Oh noche que juntaste
Amado con amada,
Amada en el Amado transformada!

Carmelite edition, pp. 4,362.

33. American Puritan fascination with the Song of Songs is demonstrated very well by Prudence L. Steiner, "A Garden of Spices in New England: John Cotton's and Edward Taylor's Use of the Song of Songs," *Allegory, Myth, and Symbol*, ed. Morton W. Bloomfield, Harvard English Studies 9 (Cambridge, Mass.: Harvard University Press, 1981) pp. 227–243, although not with reference to Christian allegorical exegesis. See also Pope, pp. 240 ff. for other English and American Protestant allegorical interpretations.

34. J. S. Bach, *Wachet auf, ruft uns die Stimme*, BWV 140. A student edition which also gives a description of the cantata as a whole has been by Gerhard Herz (New York: W. W. Norton & Company, 1972).

35. Hincmar of Reims, *Explanatio in ferculum Salomonis*, PL 125:817–834. For the key to the *carmina figurata*, see Burkhard Taeger, *Zahlensymbolik bei Hraban, bei Hincmar, und im "Heliand,"* Münchener Texte und Untersuchungen zur deutschen Literatur des Mittelalters (München: Beck, 1970) pp. 144–147. See also Ohly, pp. 87–91. I am guided by an unpublished essay on this text by Burton Van Name Edwards.

36.

Quis est hic qui pulsat ad ostium
noctis rumpens somnium?
me vocat: "O virginum pulcherrima,
soror, coniux, gemma splendidissima!
cito surgens aperi, dulcissima.

Ego sum summi regis filius,
primus et novissimus;
qui de caelis in has veni tenebras,
liberare captivorum animas:
passus mortem et multas iniurias."

Mox ego dereliqui lectulum,
cucurri ad pessulum:
ut dilecto tota domus pateat,
et mens mea plenissime videat
quem videre maxime desiderat.

At ille iam inde transierat,
ostium reliquerat.
quid ergo, miserrima, quid facerem?
lacrimando sum secuta iuvenem,
manus cuius plasmaverunt hominem.

Vigiles urbis invenerunt me,
expoliaverunt me,
abstulerunt et dederunt pallium,
cantaverunt mihi novum canticum
quo in regis inducar palatium.

Ed. F. J. E. Raby, *The Oxford Book of Latin Medieval Verse* (Oxford: At the Clarendon Press, 1959) #115, p. 158. My translation. See Raby's note, p. 476, for the problems of attribution. The poem also appears in the *Expositio de Cantica Canticorum* of Bruno of Segni, PL 164: 1233–1288.

37. Raby, p. 476. See also *Collectanea in Vetus Testamentum, Testimonia de Canticis Canticorum*, cap. XV, PL 145:1148–1149; for the letter, see Peter Dronke, *Medieval Latin and the Rise of the European Love-Lyric* (Oxford: At the Clarendon Press, 1968), vol. 1, p. 199, note 2.

38. A version is printed in Raby, #122, pp. 172–173, notes, pp. 476–477. See also the discussions of Dronke, *Medieval Latin*, vol. 1, pp. 271–277, and "The Song of Songs and Medieval Love-Lyric," in *The Bible and Medieval Culture*, ed. W. Lourdaux and D. Verhelst (Leuven: Leuven University Press, 1979) pp. 237–262, ending with a printing of the secular and religious versions. I would like to thank Eileen Kearney for calling this article to my attention.

39.

verse 10: Ille tuus unicus,
Ille tibi dilectissimus,
Cypri botrus,
myrrhae fasciculus.

verse 12: Veni, veni, filia,
Intra nostra cubilia;
Surge, surge, propera,
Fugit hiems, floret vinea.

Anonymous sequence, *Analecta Hymnica*, ed. C. Blume and H. M. Bannister, vol. 54 (1915) # 224, pp. 356–357.

40. Raby, pp. 310–312.

41. Ed. J. Acher, "Essai sur le poème Quant li solleiz converset en Leon." *Zeitschrift für französische Sprache und Literatur* 38 (1911) 47–94. See the extensive discussions of this poem by Dronke, "The Song of Songs and Medieval Love Lyric," pp. 252–257, and Ohly, pp. 278–280.

42. The paraphrase is found on the final folio of Paris, B. N. lat. 2297, a liturgical collection. It is edited by G. Paris, "Petit poème dévot du commence-

ment du XIIe siècle," *Jahrbuch für romanische und englische Literatur* VI (1866) 362–369, and W. Foerster and E. Koschwitz, *Altfranzösisches Uebungsbuch* (Leipzig: O. R. Reisland, 1911) pp. 163–168. Verses 19–21 quote from Song of Songs 5:10; 25–30 from 4:11; 30–39 from 2:11; 43–51 from 5:7; 58–61 from 1:5.

43. Le Mans, B.M. 173, ff. 33v–110r, ed. C. E. Pickford, *The Song of Songs: A Twelfth-Century French Version* (Oxford: Published for the University of Hull by the Oxford University Press, 1974). See also J. Bonnard, *Les Traductions de la Bible en vers francais au Moyen Âge* (Paris: Imprimérie nationale, 1884) pp. 152–62, where the poem is attributed to Landi de Waben. This is accepted by Ohly, *Hohelied- Studien*, pp. 280–302, but questioned by Pickford. The style is discussed by Pickford, p. xviii.

44.

> Mais tant requier que cist romanz
> Unkes ne viegne en main d'enfant,

Verses 3505–3506, p. 97. For Origen, see above, chapter two, note 28.

45. The dedication is at the end, verses 3499–3500, p. 97. See Pickford, p. xxxv for a discussion of courtly themes. This definition of courtly love as a specifically high medieval concept has been challenged by Dronke:

> I am convinced that this received opinion, this belief in a wholly new concept of love, is false. I am convinced that the question, why did this new feeling arise at such a place, at such a time, in such a society, is a misleading one. For I should like to suggest that the feelings and conceptions of *amour courtois* are universally possible, possible in any time or place and on any level of society.

Medieval Latin, vol. 1, p. 2.

46. Found in B. N. lat. 14966, cf. Bonnard, pp. 162–166.

47. Brun's poem is edited by A. Fischer, *Bibliothek des Litterarischen Vereins in Stuttgart* CXCVIII (Tübingen, 1893), cf. introduction, pp. vii–xxiv. See also Fischer's earlier work, *Das Hohe Lied des Brun von Schonebeck* (Germanische abhandlungen), vol. 2, ed. K. Weinhold (Breslau, 1886). Ulrike Wiethaus, who brought this text to my attention, is planning a study of Brun from the perspective of medieval Christian mysticism.

48. verse 62–428; "sprach Solomon der konstabel," verse 267, p. 9.

49. A. Hübner, "Das Hohe Lied des Brun von Schonebeck und seine Quelle," *Festgabe für Ulrich Pretzel sum 65. Geburtstag dargebracht*, ed. W. Simon (Berlin: E. Schmidt, 1963) pp. 43–54.

50. Dronke, "The Song of Songs and Medieval Love-Lyric," pp. 259–260.

51. Ed. C. von Kraus, *Minnesangs Frühling* (Leipzig: S. Hirzel, 1964) p. 1.

52. Paul Zumthor, *Langue et technique poétiques à l'époque romane (Xle–XIIIe siècles)* (Paris: Librairie Klincksieck, 1963) p. 84: "Lorsque de tels topi ont passé en langue Vulgaire, leur localisation reste en général la même qu'en Latin."

53. Giovanni Pozzi, "Codici, stereotipi, topoi e fonti letterarie," in *Intorno al*

"*codice*," Atti del III Convegno della Associazione Italiana di Studi Semiotici (Pavia: La Nuova Italia, 1975), pp. 37–76. See especially the "Dossier del canone delle bellezze," pp. 67–76.

54. Edited by C. Chichmaref, *Guillaume de Machaut, Poésies Lyrics* (Paris: H. Champion, 1909) p. 90.

55. *Die Meisterlieder des Hans Folz*, ed. A. L. Mayer, *Deutsche Texte des Mittelalters* XII (Berlin: Akademie-Verlag, 1908). I was made aware of this text by Katharina von Kellenbach.

Conclusion

It is a long way from third-century Alexandria to early modern Europe. As the Song of Songs moved through these overlapping and contrasting worlds, it was read by each generation as biblical evidence of God's love— for his people, collectively and individually, and for the medieval Christian ideal of the perfection of humanity, the Virgin Mary. The foundations for allegorical, tropological, and mariological exegesis of the Song of Songs were set early in the history of the genre: the first two by Origen, the last by marian liturgies which in the West began about the fourth century. As I have shown, among the developments in these commentaries over time are a series of shifts in emphasis of interpretation which legitimize the definition of Song of Songs exegesis as genre. Readings of the Song of Songs as depicting the love between Christ and the Church dominated the early period, while the moral level of the tropological mode became especially important after the eleventh century, and the understanding of the Bride as the Virgin Mary especially flourished in the twelfth century. The dominant interpretations of earlier periods tended to be absorbed, rather than discarded, by later interpretations, so that, as the commentary genre continually refined itself in relation to both internal and external stimuli, it became ever more complicated.

The related but contrasting movements of extreme traditionalism and continual re-interpretation stressed in this book show the outlines of a significant genre of medieval literature. I have described medieval Christian commentary on the Song of Songs as a genre because its cumulative vision, of the understanding of the love poems attributed to Solomon as reflecting the collective or individual spiritual life of Christians, was a vision of reality for Christian writers of many centuries, establishing the horizon of expectations with which they approached the text. Like all genres, this one was transformed over time, first internally, through refinement and re-establishment of its allegorical presuppositions, and gradually also externally, as the genre moved beyond its literary framework to influence a number of other Christian literary forms.

Each interpretation of the Song of Songs discussed in this book thus enters into a complicity of understanding, as each reading also comes to terms with the beautiful and elusive "Solomonic" poems on its own. What chronological development can be observed in the commentary genre is certainly linked to previous commentaries, but above all results from repeated confrontation with a text which, especially as a book of the Bible, never fails to elicit multivalent response. The ultimate source of the Song of Songs commentary genre is, therefore, not the doctrinal and institutional evolution of medieval Christianity, nor the literary and psychological assumptions of monastic authors, but the enduring fascination of the poems which celebrate the love between Bridegroom and Bride.

At a number of points in this book, I have made suggestions for future study of the consequences of the Song of Songs commentary genre: its connection to exegesis of the Apocalypse, its relation to Latin liturgy, its further development in vernacular literature, its influence on Protestant piety. Of course, close study of individual or related commentaries is also needed. I would add to these suggestions the observation that scholastic theology would doubtless prove an interesting field for an investigation of the reception and development of the genre in the later Middle Ages. I hope that this book will have a part in helping these, and other areas of research, to flourish.

APPENDIX: Latin Commentary on the Song of Songs to 1200

* Indicates treatises on other subjects which contain important interpretations of the Song of Songs
ET = English Translation

THIRD CENTURY

Origen, *Commentarium in Cantica Canticorum* to 2:15
translated by Rufinus of Aquileia
ed. Baehrens, *Origenes Werke* 8, GCS 33 (1923) pp. 61–241
Stegmüller # 6200
Origen, *Homiliae in Cantica Canticorum* to 2:14
translated by Jerome
ed. Baehrens, *Origenes Werke* 8, GCS 33 (1923) pp. 26–60
ed. O. Rousseau, SC 37bis (1966)
Stegmüller # 6199
ET: R. P. Lawson, *Origen. The Song of Songs. Commentary and Homilies*, Ancient Christian Writers Series 26 (New York: Newman Press, 1957)

FOURTH–FIFTH CENTURIES

Ambrose of Milan, *Commentarius in Canticum Canticorum*
PL 15:1947–2060 (collected by William of Saint-Thierry, c.12)
Stegmüller # 3028
*Ambrose of Milan, *De Isaac vel anima*
ed. C. Schenkl, CSEL 32, 1 (1896) pp. 640–700
Stegmüller # 1232

Apponius, *In Canticum Canticorum expositionem*
ed. B. de Vregille and L. Neyrand, CCSL 19 (1986)
Stegmüller # 1421
Summariola in Apponii Cant. lib. vii–xii
(collected by Lucas of Mont Cornillon, c. 12)
ed. J. Faber (Freiburg in Br., 1538)
Maxima Bibliotheca Patrum XIV (Lyon, 1677) pp. 128–139
Stegmüller # 5401
Gregory of Elvira, *Tractatus de epithalamio (In Cantica Canticorum libri quinque)*
ed. J. Fraipont, CCSL 69 (1967) pp. 167–210
Stegmüller # 2629
*Jerome, Epistle 22, *Ad Eustochium*
ed. I. Hilberg, CSEL 54, 1 (1910) pp. 143–211

SIXTH–SEVENTH CENTURIES

Gregory the Great, *Expositio in Canticum Canticorum* to 1:8
ed. P. Verbraken, CCSL 144 (1963) 1–46
ed. R. Bélanger, SC 314 (1984)
Stegmüller # 2639
Isidore of Seville, *In libros veteris ac novi testamenti prooemia De libris Salomonis*, PL 83:164–165
Stegmüller # 5195
Pseudo-Isidore of Seville, unpublished commentary
Incipit: "Ubi per epithalamium carmen coniunctionem Christi et ecclesiae mystice canit"
Stegmüller # 5291, 5307
Justus of Urguel, *In Canticum Salomonis explicatio mystica*
PL 67:961–994
Stegmüller # 5332
Pseudo-Paterius, *Liber de expositione veteris et novi testamenti de diversis libris S. Gregorii M. concinatus*, PL 79:905–916
Stegmüller # 6277

EIGHTH–NINTH CENTURIES

Alcuin, *Compendium in Canticum Canticorum*
PL 100:641–664

(as Isidore of Seville, PL 83:1119–1132)
Stegmüller # 1092, # 5266

Angelomus of Luxeuil, *Enarrationes in Cantica Canticorum*
PL 115:551–628
Stegmüller # 1092

Anonymous, Paris B. N. lat. 2822, unpublished commentary
Incipit: "Vox ecclesiae unionem atque reconciliationem sponsi sui ac domini praestolantis"
cf. J. Leclercq, *Analecta monastica* I (1948) p. 206
Stegmüller # 1672, # 10365

The Venerable Bede, *In Cantica Canticorum*
ed. D. Hurst, CCSL 119B (1985) pp. 166–375
Stegmüller, # 1610

Haimo of Auxerre, *Commentarium in Cantica Canticorum*
PL 117:295–358
(as Cassiodorus, PL 70:1055–1106)
Stegmüller # 1895, 3079

Hincmar of Reims, *Explanatio in Ferculum Salomonis*
PL 125:817–834
Stegmüller # 3562

*Paschasius Radbertus, *Cogitis me* (Pseudo-Jerome Epistle 9 to Paula and Eustochium)
ed. A. Ripberger, SpF 9 (1962) and CCCM 55C (1985) pp. 97–162.

TENTH–ELEVENTH CENTURIES

Anonymous, unpublished commentary
Incipit: "Salomon trinomius fuit"
Cf. Riedlinger, pp. 120–121
Stegmüller # 9533

Anselm of Laon, *Enarratio in Canticum Canticorum*
PL 162:1187–1228
Stegmüller # 1358

Anselm of Laon (?), *Glosulae super Cantica Canticorum Salomonis*
Paris, B. N. lat. 568, ff. 1–64
Cf. Riedlinger, p. 112

Anselm of Laon (?), unpublished commentary

Incipit: "Dicendum est in primis, quod auctor huius operis Spiritu sancto"
Cf. Riedlinger, pp. 121–124
Stegmüller # 10690

Bruno of Segni (or Asti), *Expositio in Cantica Canticorum*
PL 164:1233–1288
Stegmüller # 1854

Glossa ordinaria

a. *Glossa ordinaria, Canticum Canticorum*, PL 113:1125–1168
b. *Biblia latina: cum glossa ordinaria Walafridi Strabonis aliorumque et inter lineari Anselmi Laudunensis* (Strassburg: Adolf Rusch, for Anton Koberger, not after 1480) vol. 3 (unfoliated)
c. *Biblia sacra cum Glossa interlineari, ordinaria et Nycolai Lyrani Postill.* (Venice, 1588) vol. 3, ff. 355–368
d. ed. Leander de S. Martina (Antwerp, 1634) vol. 3, pp. 1827–1894

Stegmüller # 3574

Glosae super Cantica Canticorum, unpublished gloss
Laon, B.M. 98, ff. 117v–140v

John of Mantua, *In Cantica Canticorum*
Iohannis Mantuani in Cantica Canticorum et de Sancta Maria tractatus ad Comitissam Matildam
ed. B. Bischoff and B. Taeger, SpF 19 (1973)

Peter Damian, *Collectanea in Vetus Testamantum. Testimonia de Canticis Canticorum*
PL 145:1141–1154
Stegmüller # 6602, 17

Robert of Tombelaine, *Commentariorum in Cantica Canticorum*
PL 150:1361–1370 (to 1:11)
PL 79:493–548 (1:12 to end, as Gregory the Great)
Stegmüller # 7488

Williram of Ebersberg, *Expositio in Cantica Canticorum*
ed. E. H. Bartelmez (Philadelphia: American Philosophical Society, 1967)
Stegmüller # 8378

TWELFTH CENTURY

Alan of Lille, *In Cantica Canticorum ad laudem Deiparae Virginis Mariae elucidatio*

PL 210:51–110
Stegmüller # 948

Alexander Neckham, *Expositio super Cantica Canticorum et laudem Gloriose et Beate Virginis Matris et mysterio Incarnationis libri IV*
Unpublished commentary
Stegmüller # 1168

*Balduin of Canterbury, *Tractatus octavus*, "De vulnere caritatis" (Song of Songs 4:9)
PL 204:477–484;
Tractatus decimus, "Pone me ut signaculum" (Song of Songs 8:6)
PL 204:511–518;
Tractatus quartus decimus, "Introduxit me in cellam vinarium" (Song of Songs 2:4)
PL 204:539–546

Bernard of Clairvaux, *Brevis Commentatio in Cantica*
PL 184:407–436
Stegmüller # 3030

Bernard of Clairvaux, *Sermones super Cantica Canticorum*
OB 1–2 (1957–1958)
Stegmüller # 1721

ET: Killian Walsh, vols. I–II, Cistercian Fathers Series 4, 7 (Kalamazoo, Mich., 1976)
Irene Edmonds, vol. III–IV, Cistercian Fathers Series 31, 40 (Kalamazoo, Mich., 1979, 1980)

Geoffrey of Auxerre, *Expositio in Cantica Canticorum*
ed. Ferruccio Gastaldelli, TT 19, 20 (1974)
Stegmüller # 2414

*Geoffrey of Saint-Victor, *Sermo in generali capitulo* (on Song of Songs 4:7) ed. Riedlinger, pp. 188–193

*Gerhoch of Reichersberg, *Commentarius aureus in Psalmos et Cantica Ferialia*
PL 193:619–1814, PL 194:9–486
Stegmüller # 2476

Gilbert Foliot, *Expositio in Cantica Canticorum*
PL 202:1147–1304
Stegmüller # 2490

Gilbert of Hoyland, *Sermones in Canticum Salomonis*
PL 184:11–252.
Stegmüller # 2493

ET: Lawrence C. Braceland, 3 vol., Cistercian Fathers Series 14, 20, 26 (Kalamazoo, Mich., 1978, 1979)

Gilbert of Stanford, unpublished commentary
Incipit: "Scriptura sacra morem rapidissimi fluminis tenens . . . Osculetur—Legimus in evangelio, negotiatorem bonas margaritas"
Stegmüller # 2533

Honorius Augustodunensis, *Sigillum Beatae Mariae*
PL 172:495–518
Stegmüller # 3574

Honorius Augustodunensis, *Expositio in Cantica Canticorum*
PL 172:347–496
Stegmüller # 3573

Pseudo-Honorius, *Explicatio in Cantica Canticorum*
PL 172:519–542
Stegmüller # 3575

Hugh of Saint-Victor (?), *Eulogium sponsi de sponsa (De amore)*
PL 176:987–994
Stegmüller # 97, 11307

*Hugh of Saint-Victor, *Sermo de Assumptione Beatae Mariae*
PL 177:1209–1222
Stegmüller # 3818

Irimbert of Admont, *Commentarius allegoricus in selecta quaedam loca Cantici canticorum*
ed. B. Pez, *Thesaurus anecdotorum novissimus* II, 1 (Augsburg, 1721) pp. 367–424
Stegmüller # 5154

John of Ford, *Super extremam partem Cantici Canticorum sermones CXX*
ed. E. Mikkers and H. Costello, CCCM 17–18 (1970)

ET: Wendy M. Beckett, 7 vol., Cistercian Fathers Series, 29, 39, 43, 44, 45, 46, 47 (Kalamazoo, Mich., 1982–1987)
Stegmüller # 4467

Lucas of Mont Cornillon, *Vox optantis Christi adventum (Moralitates in Canticum)*
PL 203:489–592
Stegmüller # 5402, 6964

Peter Heliae, *Canticum metrice*, unpublished commentary
Incipit: "Osculetur me—osculo det sponsus, cessent oracula vatum"
Stegmüller # 6615

Peter Riga, *Aurora*

ed. P. E. Beichner (Notre Dame, Ind., 1965)
Stegmüller # 6825

Philip of Harvengt, *Commentaria in Cantica Canticorum*
PL 203:181–490
Stegmüller # 6963

Richard of Saint-Victor (?), *In Cantica Canticorum explicatio*
PL 196:405–524
Stegmüller # 7330

Rupert of Deutz, *Commentaria in Canticum Canticorum (de incarnatione Domini)*
ed. H. Haacke, CCCM 26 (1974)
Stegmüller # 7561

Rupert of Olmütz, *In Cantica*, unpublished commentary
Incipit: "Osculetur me—solet me—solet evenire et saepius evenit"
Stegmüller # 7548

Stephen Langton, *In Cantica Canticorum*, unpublished commentary
Incipit: "Legitur Salomon habuisse tre nomina . . . Osculetur (me)—Id est: Delectet et certificet"
Cf. Riedlinger, pp. 132–136
Stegmüller # 7808

Thomas the Cistercian (Thomas of Valcellis), *In Cantica canticorum commentarii*
PL 206:17–860
Stegmüller # 8195

William of Newburgh (Guilelmus Parvus), *Explanatio sacri Epithalamii in Matrem Sponsi*
ed. John Gorman, SpF 6 (1960)
Stegmüller # 3009

William of Saint-Thierry, *Expositio super Cantica Canticorum*
ed. J. M. Déchanet, SC 82 (1962)
Stegmüller # 3026

ET: Mother Columba Hart, Cistercian Fathers Series 6 (Kalamazoo, Mich., 1970)

William of Weyarn (or Vivaria), *Carmen ad gratiam dilectae dilecti*, unpublished commentary
Incipit: "Incipit iam vota mea mecum, virgo beata . . .
Osculetur os ore verbum de Patris amore integra concipiam"
Stegmüller # 3050

Wolbero of St. Pantaleon, *Commentaria vetustissima et profundissima super*

Canticum Canticorum Solomonis quod hebraice dicitur Sir Hasirim in IV libros distributa
PL 195:1001–1278
Stegmüller # 8395

Index of Biblical References

Index of Manuscripts

Index of Modern Scholars

General Index

University of Pennsylvania Press
MIDDLE AGES SERIES
Edward Peters, General Editor

Edward Peters, ed. *Christian Society and the Crusades, 1198–1229*. Sources in Translation, including The Capture of Damietta by Oliver of Paderborn. 1971

Edward Peters, ed. *The First Crusade: The Chronicle of Fulcher of Chartres and Other Source Materials*. 1971

Katherine Fischer Drew, trans. *The Burgundian Code: The Book of Constitutions or Law of Gundobad and Additional Enactments*. 1972

G. G. Coulton. *From St. Francis to Dante: Translations from the Chronicle of the Franciscan Salimbene (1221–1288)*. 1972

Alan C. Kors and Edward Peters, eds. *Witchcraft in Europe, 1110–1700: A Documentary History*. 1972

Richard C. Dales. *The Scientific Achievement of the Middle Ages*. 1973

Katherine Fischer Drew, trans. *The Lombard Laws*. 1973

Edward Peters, ed. *Monks, Bishops, and Pagans: Christian Culture in Gaul and Italy, 500–700*. 1975

Jeanne Krochalis and Edward Peters, ed. and trans. *The World of Piers Plowman*. 1975

Julius Goebel, Jr. *Felony and Misdemeanor: A Study in the History of Criminal Law*. 1976

Susan Mosher Stuard, ed. *Women in Medieval Society*. 1976

Clifford Peterson. *Saint Erkenwald*. 1977

Robert Somerville and Kenneth Pennington, eds. *Law, Church, and Society: Essays in Honor of Stephan Kuttner*. 1977

Donald E. Queller. *The Fourth Crusade: The Conquest of Constantinople, 1201–1204*. 1977

Pierre Riché (Jo Ann McNamara, trans.). *Daily Life in the World of Charlemagne*. 1978

Edward Peters, ed. *Heresy and Authority in Medieval Europe*. 1980

Suzanne Fonay Wemple. *Women in Frankish Society: Marriage and the Cloister, 500–900*. 1981

Edward Peters. *The Magician, the Witch, and the Law*. 1982

Barbara H. Rosenwein. *Rhinoceros Bound: Cluny in the Tenth Century*. 1982

Steven D. Sargent, ed. and trans. *On the Threshold of Exact Science: Selected Writings of Anneliese Maier on Late Medieval Natural Philosophy*. 1982

Benedicta Ward. *Miracles and the Medieval Mind: Theory, Record, and Event, 1000–1215*. 1982

Harry Turtledove, trans. *The Chronicle of Theophanes: An English Translation of* anni mundi *6095–6305 (A.D. 602–813)*. 1982

Leonard Cantor, ed. *The English Medieval Landscape*. 1982

Charles T. Davis. *Dante's Italy and Other Essays*. 1984

George T. Dennis, trans. *Maurice's Strategikon: Handbook of Byzantine Military Strategy*. 1984

Thomas F. X. Noble. *The Republic of St. Peter: The Birth of the Papal State, 680–825*. 1984

Kenneth Pennington. *Pope and Bishops: The Papal Monarchy in the Twelfth and Thirteenth Centuries*. 1984

Patrick J. Geary. *Aristocracy in Provence: The Rhône Basin at the Dawn of the Carolingian Age*. 1985

C. Stephen Jaeger. *The Origins of Courtliness: Civilizing Trends and the Formation of Courtly Ideals, 939–1210*. 1985

J. N. Hillgarth, ed. *Christianity and Paganism, 350–750: The Conversion of Western Europe*. 1986

William Chester Jordan. *From Servitude to Freedom: Manumission in the Sénonais in the Thirteenth Century*. 1986

James William Brodman. *Ransoming Captives in Crusader Spain: The Order of Merced on the Christian-Islamic Frontier*. 1986

Frank Tobin. *Meister Eckhart: Thought and Language*. 1986

Daniel Bornstein, trans. *Dino Compagni's Chronicle of Florence*. 1986

James M. Powell. *Anatomy of a Crusade, 1213–1221*. 1986

Jonathan Riley-Smith. *The First Crusade and the Idea of Crusading*. 1986

Susan Mosher Stuard, ed. *Women in Medieval History and Historiography*. 1987

Avril Henry, ed. *The Mirour of Mans Saluacioune*. 1987

María Rosa Menocal. *The Arabic Role in Medieval Literary History*. 1987

Margaret J. Ehrhart. *The Judgment of the Trojan Prince Paris in Medieval Literature*. 1987

Betsy Bowden. *Chaucer Aloud: The Varieties of Textual Interpretation*. 1987

Felipe Fernández-Armesto. *Before Columbus: Exploration and Colonization from the Mediterranean to the Atlantic, 1229–1492*. 1987

Michael Resler, trans. *EREC by Hartmann von Aue*. 1987

A. J. Minnis. *Medieval Theory of Authorship*. 1988

Uta-Renate Blumenthal. *The Investiture Controversy: Church and Monarchy from the Ninth to the Twelfth Century*. 1988

Robert Hollander. *Boccaccio's Last Fiction: "Il Corbaccio."* 1988

Ralph Turner. *Men Raised from the Dust: Administrative Service and Upward Mobility in Angevin England*. 1988

David Anderson. *Before the Knight's Tale: Imitation of Classical Epic in Boccaccio's "Teseida."* 1988

Charlotte A. Newman. *The Anglo-Norman Nobility in the Reign of Henry I: The Second Generation*. 1988

Joseph F. O'Callaghan. *The Cortes of Castile-León, 1188–1350*. 1989

William D. Paden. *The Voice of the Trobairitz: Essays on the Women Troubadours*. 1989

William Chester Jordan. *The French Monarchy and the Jews: From Philip Augustus to the Last Capetians*. 1989

Edward B. Irving, Jr. *Rereading "Beowulf."* 1989

David Burr. *Olivi and Franciscan Poverty: The Origins of the* Usus Pauper *Controversy*. 1989

Willene B. Clark and Meradith T. McMunn, eds. *Beasts and Birds of the Middle Ages: The Bestiary and Its Legacy*. 1989

Richard C. Hoffmann. *Land, Liberties, and Lordship in a Late Medieval Countryside: Agrarian Structures and Change in the Duchy of Wrocław*. 1990

J. M. W. Bean. *From Lord to Patron: Lordship in Late Medieval England*. 1990

Mary F. Wack. *Lovesickness in the Middle Ages: The* Viaticum *and Its Commentaries*. 1990

Robert I. Burns, S. J., ed. *Emperor of Culture: Alfonso X the Learned of Castile and His Thirteenth-Century Renaissance*. 1990

E. Ann Matter. *The Voice of My Beloved: The Song of Songs in Western Medieval Christianity*. 1990

Patricia Terry. *Poems of the Elder Edda*. 1990

Ronald Surtz. *The Guitar of God: Gender, Power, and Authority in the Visionary World of Mother Juana de la Cruz (1481–1534)*. 1990